**NOW YOU CAN UNDERSTAND THE
BOOK OF REVELATION**

PRESENTED TO: _____

ON: _____

MESSAGE: _____

_____

_____

_____

_____

_____

_____

PRESENTED BY: _____

D1160198

"About the Time of the End,
a body of men will be raised up
who will turn their attention to the Prophecies,
and insist upon their literal interpretation,
in the midst of much clamor and opposition."

—*Sir Isaac Newton*

Now you can understand the book of REVELATION

by Jim McKeever

Omega Publications
P.O. Box 4130
Medford, Oregon 97501

NOW YOU CAN UNDERSTAND THE
BOOK OF REVELATION

Copyright © 1980 by James M. McKeever

All rights reserved. No part of this book may be
reproduced or transmitted in any form or by any
means, electronic or mechanical, including photo-
copying, recording, or by any information storage
retrieval system, without written permission from
the Publisher.

Omega Publications
P.O. Box 4130
Medford, Oregon 97501

Printed in the Unites States of America
First printing – August, 1980

Library of Congress Catalog Card Number 80-68245

ISBN 0-931608-07-4 (Hardbound)
ISBN 0-931608-08-2 (Softbound)

*"How thrilled I am to receive your . . .
newsletter with all the up-to-date data on the
world situation, etc. It is really fantastic. Jim,
there are very few people that have had a
ministry in my life and stretched my vision
like you have."*

—**Josh McDowell**, author of
Evidence That Demands a Verdict
Campus Crusade for Christ

This book is dedicated first and foremost to the glory of God and of His Son and our Savior and Master, Jesus Christ.

On the human level, this book is dedicated to my three wonderful children who know and love Jesus Christ as their Savior: Mike, Dawn, and Christa.

TABLE OF CONTENTS

"I read with interest your new book, and found it extremely interesting. You have some unique concepts and I heartily agree in your view of the tribulation. You are doing a splendid job, and I enjoy reading your newsletter."

—Pat Robertson, 700 Club

ACKNOWLEDGEMENTS

I would like to start off by acknowledging that there are many people who have contributed to my personal spiritual growth and insights, some of which are reflected in this book. I can never possibly name them all, but I am particularly indebted to Dr. Bill Bright, Dr. W. A. Criswell, Rick Durfield, Dr. Billy Graham, Jerry Hassel, Corrie Ten Boom, Dr. Carlton Booth and the late Dawson Trotman. I also very much appreciate the insight gained from Barry Thompson.

I would also like to thank those who were responsible for the typing and proofreading of the book: Arlene Myers and Teresa McKeever. Without their diligent work, this book would not have been possible. My son, Mike McKeever, was also an invaluable help in very many ways.

I am especially appreciative of The Lockman Foundation, copyright holders of the *New American Standard Bible,* for their permission to quote extensively from this excellent translation. Unless otherwise indicated, all Bible quotations are taken from this translation.

More than anyone else, however, my wife Jeani is responsible for the existence of this book. Not only did she provide the usual loving functions of a writer's wife, such as giving gentle encouragement and inspiration, but she also served officially as editor, proofreader, contributor of ideas, critic, and best friend. I praise the Lord for her and her valuable contribution to this book. I cannot imagine a more perfect wife and co-laborer. I am grateful to the Lord that He has given me such a wonderful lady for my wife.

At the top of the list I would have to thank the Holy Spirit, who is our only real teacher, who both inspired and guided me as I sought God's wisdom to write this book in a way that would glorify Jesus Christ.

Jim McKeever
P.O. Box 4130
Medford, Oregon 97501

INTRODUCTION

I have always disliked long introductions to books, so I will try to make this as brief as possible. First and foremost, I must clearly state that this book is written to those individuals who know for sure that Jesus Christ is their Savior. It doesn't matter whether they are Catholic, Protestant, or of some other faith, as long as they acknowledge that Jesus Christ is the Son of God and that the way to heaven is through Him. If you are not absolutely certain that you have received Christ as your personal Savior, I ask you to stop now and read Appendix B on page 323, which discusses how to become a Christian. The things we will be discussing in this volume will have very little meaning for you unless you have first made this all-important step of accepting Christ as your Savior and Master.

Satan will do anything he can to keep Christians from reading the book of Revelation. He will try to convince them that:

"It's not important to understand the book of Revelation."

"It's full of weird symbols you can't understand."

"You don't need to understand prophecy; just study those things you need for today."

"The book of Revelation will just confuse you."

This list could go on and on. God knew that Satan would try to keep Christians away from the book of Revelation, and so He included a promised blessing to those who read and *heed* the words contained in Revelation. In fact, this beatitude, which appears in both the first and last chapters of the book of Revelation, is the only beatitude in the Bible that is repeated.

This book concentrates on the "heed" aspect of the book of Revelation. How do you *heed*—incorporate into your daily life—the things found in the book of Revelation? God commanded us to do this, so there must be some things in this prophecy that we need to be practicing daily. The entire last chapter in this book reviews the things found in the book of Revelation that we should be heeding.

In times past, understanding and heeding the book of Revelation was almost optional for a Christian. I believe that today it has become critical and essential to our understanding of what is happening in the world today, where we are going, and what we should be doing.

You certainly cannot heed anything unless you understand it. We hope that this book will be used by the Holy Spirit to help take away some of the mystery from the book of Revelation and to help you understand it. At a very minimum, we know you are going to be blessed if you follow God's admonition to read it.

I would personally appreciate your prayers that this book would glorify God and His Son Jesus Christ, and that God would use this book to alert the body of Christ as to what is coming and what they should do.

May the Lord bless you and enrich your spiritual life as you read this volume.

Jim McKeever

1

AN ENCOUNTER WITH
JESUS
(Revelation 1)

Before we begin looking at what the book of Revelation has to say, I would like to first dispel some common misconceptions about this book of the Bible. Satan would like to convince Christians that they should not read the book of Revelation. He will use any tactic that he can in order to achieve his end.

Satan's most frequent method for causing God's people not to read the book of Revelation is to convince them of something like this:

1.   "You can't understand the book of Revelation."

2.   "It's all in symbols and weird creatures. It was never meant to be understood."

3.   "There are too many varying opinions on it; therefore, you should ignore it."

4.   "It really doesn't matter about the end of the age; all that is important is living right now."

If Satan can use these, or any of his other lies, to prevent a Christian from reading and understanding the book of Revelation, then he has won a major victory.

God, on the other hand, tells us not only to read the book of Revelation, but also that we are to understand it—and not only to understand it, but to *heed* the things written in it. In fact, He promises a special blessing to all those who read (and hear) the words of this prophecy, and who heed them. In a moment we will look at this blessing (really a beatitude) that God has promised to us if we will read the book of Revelation and heed what it says. But let us first review some of the other beatitudes.

MORE BEATITUDES

In the first eleven verses of Matthew 5 we have some beatitudes, such as these:

3 "Blessed are the poor in spirit, for theirs is the kingdom of heaven. . . ."

7 "Blessed are the merciful, for they shall receive mercy. . . ."

In every one of these instances, there is a blessing attached to something that you either *are* or *do*. There are nine of them. Blessed are you—or happy are you—if you are or become something, or if you do something. For example, we are promised that if we are merciful, we will receive mercy.

There are also seven beatitudes scattered through Revelation. With the nine from the Sermon on the Mount, that makes sixteen beatitudes in all. The first one, which we have been discussing, is found in Revelation 1:

3 Blessed is he who reads and those who hear the words of the prophecy, and heed the things which are written in it; for the time is near.

Just as with the beatitudes in Matthew 5, this says that we are going to receive a blessing if we do something. What is the "thing" that we are to do here? We are to read the book of Revelation, to hear it, and to take heed of it. Taking heed of it means we are going to apply it to our lives. It means that the actions and attitudes are going to become an intricate part of us. Heeding the book of Revelation is so important that the Holy Spirit had the blessing (beatitude) repeated at the end of the book:

7 ". . . Blessed is he who heeds the words of the prophecy of the book."

—Revelation 22

Incidentally, I might just give you the rest of the beatitudes that are scattered throughout Revelation:

14:13 ". . . 'Blessed are the dead who die in the Lord from now on!' " "Yes," says the Spirit, "that they may rest from their labors, for their deeds follow with them."

16:15 ". . . Blessed is the one who stays awake and keeps his garments, lest he walk about naked and men see his shame."

19:9 ". . . 'Blessed are those who are invited to the marriage supper of the Lamb.'". . .

20:6 Blessed and holy is the one who has a part in the first resurrection; over these the second death has no power, but they will be priests of God and of Christ and will reign with Him for a thousand years.

22:14 Blessed are those who wash their robes, that they may have the right to the tree of life, and may enter by the gates into the city.

God promises blessings or rewards to those who fill the requirements of the beatitudes. So you can expect a real blessing as you *read and heed* the message of the book of Revelation. We have to understand it in order to heed it. Right? Praise God, we *can* understand its message, or God would not have encouraged us to heed it.

THE OUTLINE OF THE BOOK
(REVELATION 1:19 AND 4:1)

This is also the only book in the Bible which gives its own outline, so you never have to guess about what pattern it will follow. Revelation 1:19 says:

19 Write therefore the things which you have seen, and the things which are, and the things which shall take place after these things.

The three sections that comprise this book are stated clearly:

1. The things that you have already seen (past)

2. The things that are (present)

3.   The things that will take place after these things (future)

The things already seen (part one), John shares in the middle portion of Revelation 1. Let us now turn to Revelation 4:1:

> 1 After these things I looked, and behold, a door standing open in heaven, and the first voice which I had heard, like *the sound* of a trumpet speaking with me, said, "Come up here, and I will show you what must take place after these things."

In this verse the angel says that he will show John the third part of the outline. So in verse 1 of Chapter 4 we see the introduction of part three—that which is to come. Between Revelation 1:19 and 4:1 John writes about "the things that are" (part two).

Thus, the book of Revelation follows its own outline, being divided into these three parts:

1.   The things already seen—Revelation 1:8-18

2.   The things that are—Revelation 2 and 3

3.   The things to come—Revelation 4 through 22

GENERAL INTERPRETATIONS OF THE BOOK

There are several general interpretations of the book of Revelation. However, before discussing these, I believe that it is important to be aware of the date on which John actually wrote the book. The year 96 A.D. is generally accepted by most Biblical scholars as the actual date when it was written. *Halley's Bible Handbook* has this to say about it:

> John had been banished to the Isle of Patmos (1:9). This, according to Apostolic tradition, was in the Persecution of Domitian, about A.D. 95. The next year, A.D. 96, John was released, and permitted to return to Ephesus. The use of the past tense, 'was,' in Patmos, seems to indicate that, while he saw the Visions in Patmos, it was after his release, and return to Ephesus, that he wrote the book, about A.D. 96.
>
> —Zondervan Publishing House, p. 683-684

Now let's look at some of the various interpretations of the book of Revelation. None of these interpretations are without difficulties. Thus, I don't believe that any teacher of the book of Revelation can afford to be dogmatic and make categorical statements, claiming that his interpretation is the only valid one. All that a teacher really can do is to share what the Spirit of God has shown him up to that point in time. I would like to discuss very briefly the four traditional approaches to interpreting the book of Revelation, and to add one to those.

1.   Contemporary interpretation: This interpretation regards the book of Revelation as primarily dealing with the Christians who were contemporaries of John. Proponents of this view say that it is a picture of the conflict between the new Christians and the Roman Empire, and that it is an encouragement for the Christians of that time. This interpretation, which is not too widely held, has many difficulties. They claim that the destruction of the Temple in 70 A.D. fulfills part of this prophecy. What they don't understand is that the book of Revelation was not written until twenty-six years after the destruction of the Temple, in 96 A.D. Thus, the 70 A.D. destruction of the Temple would not qualify for fulfilling this prophecy. Also, as we will see later in this book, many of the plagues predicted in the book of Revelation, and particularly things such as the events of the seventh trumpet, did not occur during the early centuries of Christianity.

2.   Historical interpretation: This interpretation claims that the book of Revelation deals with the entire period of God's dealing with man. Thus, the plagues in Egypt were fulfillment of prophecy in the book of Revelation. Those of this persuasion claim that most of the events prophesied in Revelation have already occurred, such as the destruction and reconstruction of the Temple. This interpretation presents some of the same difficulties outlined above, plus some additional ones because, beginning in Chapter 4, the angel said to John that he would show him things "yet to come." In other words, these would be things that would occur sometime after 96 A.D.

3.   Futurist interpretation: This interpretation places the entire book of Revelation in the future. Advocates of this theory interpret the letters to the seven churches as depicting the church age, and everything from Revelation 4 on as dealing with the events surrounding Christ's return to earth. The only difficulty with this point of view is that it says that the letters to the churches deal with the period of time after 96 A.D. The Holy Spirit said to John that the content of the letters to the churches were the "things that are"—that is, conditions that existed during the time when John received this vision.

4.   *Spiritual interpretation:* This interpretation proposes basically that John had one or more visions, and that we ought to treat them similarly to the way that we treat visions today. This would mean that these visions should be interpreted separately by each generation of Christians, and that the Holy Spirit would make real to them whatever truth He wishes to speak to that generation. There is certainly some truth to this, and there is a valid spiritual interpretation of many of the events recorded in Revelation.

The difficulty that I have with those who hold to this interpretation is that they tend to discard any physical interpretation of the book of Revelation. They would claim that the plagues coming are simply spiritual plagues, and not physical plagues like the children of Israel experienced. The Bible says, "first the natural, and then the spiritual" (1 Corinthians 15:46). If these people would *add* to the physical or natural interpretation the spiritual interpretation, I would certainly be more comfortable with this point of view, because I believe that many of the spiritual insights that they have are very beautiful and valid. Again, where I would tend to disagree with them is in disregarding basically any physical interpretation.

5.   *End-time interpretation:* This is the interpretation that the Lord has led me to believe, and it did not particularly fit any of the above categories, although it comprises parts of many of them. Perhaps a better name for it would have been the "outline interpretation," because it simply follows the outline that the book of Revelation gives for itself. This interpretation would regard Revelation 1:8–18 as the things which were "seen"; this is the vision that John had of Jesus Christ.

Revelation 2 and 3 would be the things which "are." This present tense portion would be a category contemporary with

John's time. These chapters reveal characteristics of the churches in existence during the first century. There are many things that they were experiencing that we can learn from, but the letters are addressed to seven actual churches that existed at that time.

Revelation 4 through 22 would be viewed as things that are going to be occurring as we experience the great Tribulation, as the current church age ends, during the one thousand year reign of Christ, and then the destruction of the existing heaven and earth and the creation of a new heaven and new earth where we will spend eternity.

In summary, the end–time interpretation is a very simple approach. It follows the outline that the book of Revelation gives for itself and views the book as divided into three parts.

Let us now begin by taking a look at part one of this exciting and understandable book—that is, the vision that John had of Jesus Christ.

REVELATION 1:1–3
–THE REVELATION OF JESUS

1 The Revelation of Jesus Christ, which God gave Him to show to His bond-servants, the things which must shortly take place; and He sent and communicated *it* by His angel to His bond-servant John,

2 who bore witness to the word of God and to the testimony of Jesus Christ, *even* to all that he saw.

3 Blessed is he who reads and those who hear the words of the prophecy, and heed the things which are written in it; for the time is near.

–Revelation 1

Let's start with the first two words: the revelation. The Greek word for revelation is *apocalypse,* which simply means the revelation. That word is used 18 times in the New Testament. It means an uncovering or an unveiling of something that was invisible before but is now being made visible. It does have an ordinary use in the Bible, but used here it primarily means revealed in a supernatural way.

Let's take a look at what Paul says in Galatians 1:

> **11   For I would have you know, brethren, that the gospel which was preached by me is not according to man.**
>
> **12   For I neither received it from man, nor was I taught it, but I *received it* through a revelation of Jesus Christ.**

When Paul was on his way to Damascus, the Holy Spirit directly revealed to him things concerning Christ and the gospel. Daniel and many of the Old Testament prophets also had an apocalypse—a revelation from God.

In Revelation 1:1, John says that it is the revelation "of Jesus Christ." There are two ways that you can interpret this. For example, take David Wilkerson's book, *The Vision*. It's about a vision of David Wilkerson—that is, a vision that David Wilkerson had, not an image of David Wilkerson.

It is the same in this case. God gave a revelation to Jesus of things to come, so that He could show it to His bond-servants. It does not say that this is restricted to just the seven churches in Asia Minor. This is to all of the bond-servants of Christ, and all of the bond-servants of God from the Old Testament. (Abraham believed God and it was accounted unto him as righteousness.) So this book is written to all of the people who will gain an entrance to heaven. The revelation of Jesus Christ, of which John speaks, God gave to Jesus to show to His bond-servants.

Bond-Servants

I might just say a word about bond-servants (bond-slaves is really a better term). If you got in debt over your head in New Testament times, the person you owed the money to could require that you come work for him for a certain number of years to pay off the debt. You would become an indentured servant at that point of time. When your indenture was completed, you would be free to go or to remain in the servant category, but you would not be a slave. However, at the time your debt was paid, you could go to your master and say that you would like to stay on and be his slave for the rest of your life.

The technical term for bond–servant is "he who stands against the door." If you asked your master if you could be his bond–slave, you would stand against a door and he would, with a nail or spike, drive a hole through your ear, which was the sign of a slave. From then on, for the rest of your life, you would be a bond–slave to that master. This is described in Deuteronomy 15:

> 12 "If your kinsman, a Hebrew man or woman, is sold to you, then he shall serve you six years, but in the seventh year you shall set him free.
> 13 "And when you set him free, you shall not send him away empty–handed.
> 14 "You shall furnish him liberally from your flock and from your threshing floor and from your wine vat; you shall give to him as the LORD your God has blessed you.
> 15 "And you shall remember that you were a slave in the land of Egypt, and the LORD your God redeemed you; therefore I command you this today.
> 16 "And it shall come about if he says to you, 'I will not go out from you,' because he loves you and your household, since he fares well with you;
> 17 then you shall take an awl and pierce it through his ear into the door, and he shall be your servant forever. And also you shall do likewise to your maidservant.

We are called to be bond–slaves of Jesus Christ. This is voluntary. Nobody is forcing us to do it, but it is permanent. It's interesting—I had always thought just of the benefit that the master would gain through such an arrangement. He would acquire a slave for the rest of his life. But frequently, if a servant was strong, young, energetic and had a lot of drive, he wouldn't choose to become a bond–slave. It was mostly the weaker ones and the elderly who took this position. So from the other standpoint, when a master accepted someone as a bond–slave, he took on an obligation to care for that slave for the rest of his life.

I get so excited about some of the truths in this! Hopefully, we have all said to Christ, "I want to be your bond–servant for the rest of my life." When we come into that bond–slave relationship, He says, "I accept you and I will take care of you for the rest of your life." Isn't that beautiful!

As we have said, the book of Revelation was not written just to specific churches, but to all bond-servants of God through Jesus Christ. If you are a bond-servant of Jesus, then the book of Revelation was written to *you*.

REVELATION 1:4-8
-TO THE CHURCHES FROM:
THE FATHER, THE HOLY SPIRIT, AND CHRIST

4 John to the seven churches that are in Asia: Grace to you and peace, from Him who is and who was and who is to come; and from the seven Spirits who are before His throne;

5 and from Jesus Christ, the faithful witness, the first-born of the dead, and the ruler of the kings of the earth. To Him who loves us, and released us from our sins by His blood,

6 and He has made us *to be* a kingdom, priests to His God and Father; to Him *be* the glory and the dominion forever and ever. Amen.

7 BEHOLD, HE IS COMING WITH THE CLOUDS, and EVERY EYE WILL SEE HIM, EVEN THOSE WHO PIERCED HIM; AND ALL THE TRIBES OF THE EARTH WILL MOURN OVER HIM. Even so. Amen.

8 "I am the Alpha and the Omega," says the Lord God, "who is and who was and who is to come, the Almighty."

-Revelation 1

There is a lot in here. First we see that John is writing to seven specific churches in Asia Minor. We will have some speculation a little later about why specifically these churches, but you could say the reason is that later those are the seven churches to which Christ sent individual messages. Therefore, it would be natural that John would address this document to them. But, as we saw earlier, the book of Revelation wasn't written just to those Christians in Asia Minor; it was written to all bond-servants of Jesus Christ. That includes me and hopefully you.

Now in verse 4 it says ". . . to the seven churches . . . Grace to you and peace . . ." My definition of grace is this: Because of my sins and iniquities, I deserve (in mathematical terms) minus infinity—minus everything, or all of the wrath of God. God's mercy and forgiveness brings me back up to zero, or back to neutral. He washes my sin penalty away through the blood of Christ. God's grace, then, even though I don't deserve it, gives me positive infinity—all of God's riches and blessings! I will rule and reign with Christ and be a joint heir with Him.

John could not give that grace to these churches. It is God's grace that he was hoping for them to have for their benefit, and God's peace. Could John give them peace? No. This is the peace that Christ left us just before He was tortured to death. He said, "Peace I leave with you; my peace I give to you; . . ." (John 14:27). It is peace that is eternal. Even if you were facing a firing squad, you could have that eternal peace.

Since the grace and peace are not coming from John, let's look at Whom they are coming from. The middle of verse 4 says ". . . Grace to you and peace, from Him who is and who was, and who is to come . . ." We will see later why I believe that this is grace and peace from God the Father. For now, assume that it is.

The last phrase in verse 4 of Revelation 1 reads ". . . and from the seven Spirits who are before His throne . . ." I believe this to be before God's throne. The sentence is finished in the first part of verse 5: "and from Jesus Christ, the faithful witness, the first–born of the dead, and the ruler of the kings of the earth. . . ." We have seen that John is hoping for God's grace and peace for the Christians that he is writing to. Since we saw earlier that this book is written to all Christians who are bond–slaves of Christ, it applies to us! John is hoping for grace and peace to us from God the Father, the Holy Spirit (and possibly the angels that the Holy Spirit controls), and from Jesus Christ.

We always have to recognize that every good and perfect gift comes from above (James 1:17). This is the *first thing* that John is passing on to these people. Most of Paul's letters begin by hoping for grace and peace for the recipient. This was a common salutation in letter writing in those days. And yet when two Christians today say "Peace be with you," it takes on such an infinitely bigger dimension. It really means, "May God's peace dwell richly in your heart, regardless of what you are going through." So back in the first century, when two Christians said "God's grace and peace to you," it meant something much deeper and more beautiful than a mere salutation.

He Loves Us and Releases Us

5 . . . To Him who loves us, and released us from our sins by His blood,

6 and He has made us *to be* a kingdom, priests to His God and Father; to Him *be* the glory and the dominion forever and ever. Amen.

—Revelation 1

I can just see John praising the Lord, and rejoicing as he wrote this! Notice the different tenses in the verbs. These are very important. "To Him who loves us." What tense is that? *Present tense.* Whenever a person reads this—whether it be a thousand years ago, a thousand years from now, or today—He *loves* us (present tense). It is a continuous, ongoing love. Praise God!

The second thing is that He *"released* us from our sins by His blood." What tense is that? *Past tense.* It doesn't say that He has "forgiven" us. What is the difference in being forgiven from your sins and being released from your sins? Have you ever heard someone say, "I have been bound by such–and–such a habit"? Bound and released are opposites. Christ said, "I *have released* you from that sin." The power is there; it has been accomplished. All you have to do is reach out and take it! You can say that you *thought* you lived in bondage but you *have been released.* You *are* set free. You don't have to succumb to that sin anymore. You don't have to be in bondage to any sin. He has released you from your sins—past tense. This is not something that He is going to do; it is something that He has already done! Take advantage of it. It is His gift to you!

John is praising Jesus Christ for a third thing here. He first praises Him because He loves us (He did love us, He is loving us, He will love us). He is praising Him because He has already released us from sin. And thirdly, "He has made us to be a kingdom, priests to His God and Father." Again, that is *past tense.* He *has made us to be* priests. As Christians, you and I are priests.

Now if you were at the scene of an automobile accident, or you were walking down a hospital corridor, and somebody called out, "Find us a priest," you could legitimately step up and say "I am a priest"! What authority do you have? The word of God. You *are* a priest. There are many implications to that, and we could spend a lot of time on this subject, but I would like to look at a couple of things about our priesthood that I think are very important.

What was the function of a priest in the Old Testament? Among many other things, it was to offer sacrifices. So our function, as priests to God, is to offer sacrifices. Have you been offering sacrifices? How do you know? What sacrifices have you been offering? I think that some people offer sacrifices accidentally. They are not really realizing that they are doing it. Let's look at a couple of things specifically that we are supposed to offer.

> 4 And coming to Him as to a living stone, rejected by men, but choice and precious in the sight of God,
>
> 5 you also, as living stones, are being built up as a spiritual house for a holy priesthood, to offer up spiritual sacrifices acceptable to God through Jesus Christ.
>
> —1 Peter 2

So our function, as part of the holy priesthood, is to offer up spiritual sacrifices.

Let's see what a couple of these are:

> 15 Through Him then, let us continually offer up a sacrifice of praise to God, that is, the fruit of lips that give thanks to His name.
>
> 16 And do not neglect doing good and sharing; for with such sacrifices God is pleased.
>
> —Hebrews 13

We can see here that as a royal, holy priest of God through Jesus Christ, there are three specific sacrifices that we are to offer. The first is our praise, in the name of Christ. This can be done anywhere; while you are driving down the street by yourself, you can be singing praises to the Lord, or when Christians are meeting together they can be offering up praise unto God. As a priest you are giving that sacrifice to God directly. You are not going through any other intermediary. The next time you are praising God, be conscious of your role as a priest.

Also, doing good and sharing are mentioned as sacrifices that are pleasing to God. God might lead you to share your home, the things that He has shown you, your time, or any of the things that He has given to you. I will leave it to God to speak to you about sharing and doing good. If you ask Him how to sacrifice these things to Him, I am confident that He will show you.

If you look back on just this last week, how have you done in your role as a priest? How much praise have you really sacrificed to God? How many good things have you sacrificed to God? How much sharing? We need to daily be aware that we are priests, and to ask God what sacrifices *He* wants us to make to Him that day, for His glory.

Let's review the three things that John is praising Christ for in Revelation 1:5-6:

1.   He loves us.

2.   He has released us from sin (not just forgiven us).

3.   He has made each of us to be a priest unto God.

When was the last time that you praised God for making you a priest, like John does here? Praise God, I'm a priest! I have the privilege of offering sacrifices to the God who created the universe!

He is Coming with the Clouds

> 7 BEHOLD, HE IS COMING WITH THE CLOUDS, and EVERY EYE WILL SEE HIM, EVEN THOSE WHO PIERCED HIM; AND ALL THE TRIBES OF THE EARTH WILL MOURN OVER HIM. Even so. Amen.
>
> —Revelation 1

This verse says that Christ is coming back with the clouds. This could have two interpretations, and I am just barely going to touch on them. One interpretation is that the clouds could be physical vapor clouds, like we normally think of. On the other hand, the writer of Hebrews says that we are surrounded by "so great a cloud of witnesses" (Hebrews 12:1). The second interpretation of the clouds at Christ's return is that they would be more of this nature; they could be the clouds of the believers returning with Christ. You can take it either way. I don't think that it matters because I don't believe that we will be looking at the clouds; we will all be looking at Jesus Christ, King of glory!

When Christ does return, every eye is going to see Him, even those who crucified Him, although they are dead now. When Christ returns, the dead in Christ will rise first (1 Thessalonians 4:16). The dead people also will see Christ at His second coming—even the unbelieving dead, because those who crucified Him were not believers.

When Christ does come and the end–time events unfold, it is really going to be exciting. His coming in the clouds is one of the things that will occur at the end of the Tribulation. At least Revelation 1:7 is referring to that time, because the dead people are not going to be resurrected and be alive during the Tribulation. Thus, the return of Christ in this verse is talking about a time at the end of the Tribulation.

REVELATION 1:9–18
–THE VISION OF CHRIST

9   I, John, your brother and fellow–partaker in the tribulation and kingdom and perseverance *which are* in Jesus, was on the island called Patmos, because of the word of God and the testimony of Jesus.

10   I was in the Spirit on the Lord's day, and I heard behind me a loud voice like *the sound* of a trumpet,

11   saying, "Write in a book what you see, and send *it* to the seven churches: to Ephesus and to Smyrna and to Pergamum and to Thyatira and to Sardis and to Philadelphia and to Laodicea."

12   and I turned to see the voice that was speaking with me. And having turned I saw seven golden lampstands;

13   and in the middle of the lampstands one like a son of man, clothed in a robe reaching to the feet, and girded across His breast with a golden girdle.

14   And His head and His hair were white like white wool, like snow; and His eyes were like a flame of fire;

15 and His feet *were* like burnished bronze, when it has been caused to glow in a furnace, and His voice *was* like the sound of many waters.

16 And in His right hand He held seven stars; and out of His mouth came a sharp two-edged sword; and His face was like the sun shining in its strength.

17 And when I saw Him, I fell at His feet as a dead man. And He laid His right hand upon me, saying, "Do not be afraid, I am the first and the last,

18 and the living One; and I was dead, and behold, I am alive forevermore, and I have the keys of death and of Hades.

—Revelation 1

Now John has a vision which is very beautiful and rich. In verse 9, he says "I, John, your brother and fellow–partaker in the tribulation . . ." When he says *brother*, that of course means brother Christian, blood brother. Interestingly, he also felt that he was experiencing tribulation.

While we are on the subject of tribulation, I would like to differentiate between tribulation and the great Tribulation. The children of Israel in the Old Testament certainly experienced tribulation in their various wars, the plagues in Egypt, being carried off into captivity, and being conquered by Rome, and so forth. The Christians in the first three centuries A.D. suffered both persecution and tribulation. In recent times, the Christians in Korea, China, Russia and most of the Communist countries have suffered tremendous persecution. Of even more recent vintage, missionaries in Rhodesia have experienced tribulation and some have even been murdered. This should not surprise us, because through the Scriptures we are told that Christians will experience tribulation.

For example, Jesus had this to say to us in John 16:

33 "These things I have spoken to you, that in Me you may have peace. In the world you have tribulation, but take courage; I have overcome the world."

Here He clearly informs us that we are going to have tribulation, but tells us to have courage, for He will give us victory over the world.

The apostle Paul said that we would enter the kingdom of God through tribulations:

21 And after they had preached the gospel to that city and had made many disciples, they returned to Lystra and to Iconium and to Antioch,

22 strengthening the souls of the disciples, encouraging them to continue in the faith, and *saying,* "Through many tribulations we must enter the kingdom of God."

—Acts 14

In Chapter 5 of his letter to the Romans, Paul amplifies on the subject of tribulation:

3 And not only this, but we also exult in our tribulations, knowing that tribulation brings about perseverance;

4 and perseverance, proven character; and proven character, hope;

5 and hope does not disappoint, because the love of God has been poured out within our hearts through the Holy Spirit who was given to us.

Paul further expands on tribulation in a very precious way in Romans 8:

35 Who shall separate us from the love of Christ? Shall tribulation, or distress, or persecution, or famine, or nakedness, or peril, or sword?

36 Just as it is written,

"FOR THY SAKE WE ARE BEING PUT TO DEATH ALL DAY LONG;

WE WERE CONSIDERED AS SHEEP TO BE SLAUGHTERED."

37 But in all these things we overwhelmingly conquer through Him who loved us.

38 For I am convinced that neither death, nor life, nor angels, nor principalities, nor things present, nor things to come, nor powers,

39 nor height, nor depth, nor any other created thing, shall be able to separate us from the love of God, which is in Christ Jesus our Lord.

It is wonderful to know that any terrible thing that might happen to us during any tribulation will not separate us from the love of Christ!

In contrast to the tribulation which some Christians are experiencing today, there is going to be a great Tribulation that Christ predicted in Matthew 24:

20 "But pray that your flight may not be in the winter, or on a Sabbath;
21 for then there will be a great tribulation, such as has not occurred since the beginning of the world until now, nor ever shall. . . ."

Christ said that this great Tribulation was going to be of such magnitude and would comprise such events that nothing like it had occurred "since the beginning of the world until now." He further said that after the great Tribulation, nothing like it would ever occur again. Much of the book of Revelation deals with this great Tribulation. In a sense, John partook of it with us during his visions. Let us now return to our look at Revelation 1.

The Island of Patmos

It is interesting that in Revelation 1:9 John says, "I *was* on the island of Patmos." Since the verb is in the past tense, he evidently was writing this document while no longer on the island of Patmos. There are three possible reasons why he was there. The rest of that verse says he was there because of "the word of God and the testimony of Jesus." This could mean that they exiled him like a political prisoner for his testimony because he was preaching Christ. Another possibility is that he went to Patmos *to* preach Christ—that he was on Patmos because of the testimony of Jesus Christ, and while he was there doing evangelistic outreach work, he received this vision. The third possibility (much like the Spirit leading Paul off to Gaza for a little while) is that at some point in John's life the Lord just said, "I want you to come away for a while"—a month or a year or whatever. He went to Patmos and was spending a prolonged period meditating and seeking the Lord when these things appeared to him. Any one of these points of view would be legitimate.

The island of Patmos is about six miles by ten miles—a fairly small place. It was not a big resort island. I personally think he was probably exiled there for a while. For whatever reason, the Holy Spirit had John there for a time because He wanted to reveal something special to him. When God leads you someplace and you don't understand why, don't fight it; He may have something very special for you there (just ask John).

In the Spirit on the Lord's Day

John was "in the Spirit on the Lord's day," according to Revelation 1:10. All Christians are in the Spirit in a sense, but sometimes the Spirit comes upon us in a special way. Paul mentions in 2 Corinthians 12 that he was caught up into the third heaven where indescribable things were revealed to him. Sometimes the Holy Spirit chooses to totally engulf a person. This was the type of experience that John had on Patmos. I have experienced something similar to that a few times in my life—not with such dramatic results, but the Spirit of God was on me so much that I could hardly breathe. Those of you who have experienced similar things will know what I mean.

The fact that John said it was "on the Lord's day" leads me to believe that this experience occurred in a single day. He also said that he heard a voice behind him. If "the Lord's day" were referring to a several-month period, it would be hard to say that he heard something behind him.

Loud Voice as a Trumpet

While John was in the Spirit praising the Lord, he heard behind him a loud voice which sounded like a trumpet. Probably the brassiness, the power and the carrying force of the voice, as contrasted to somebody saying something softly, could give the feeling of a bugle blast. What that voice said, in that trumpet-like majesty, is recorded in verse 11: *Write a book.* If you heard a voice behind you like that of a trumpet saying "Write a book," you would turn around and look, which is just what John did.

12   And I turned to see the voice that was speaking with me. And having turned I saw seven golden lampstands; . . .

–Revelation 1

That is incredibly significant to me. I will try to show you why in the following scriptures from the book of Exodus:

31   "Then you shall make a lampstand of pure gold. The lampstand *and* its base and its shaft are to be made of hammered work; its cups, its bulbs and its flowers shall be *of one piece* with it.

32   "And six branches shall go out from its sides; three branches of the lampstand from its one side, and three branches of the lampstand from its other side.

33   "Three cups *shall be* shaped like almond *blossoms* in the one branch, a bulb and a flower, and three cups shaped like almond *blossoms* in the other branch, a bulb and a flower—so for six branches going out from the lampstand;

34   and in the lampstand four cups shaped like almond *blossoms*, its bulb and its flowers.

35   "And a bulb shall be under the *first* pair of branches *coming* out of it, and a bulb under the *second* pair of branches *coming* out of it, and a bulb under the *third* pair of branches *coming* out of it, for the six branches coming out of the lampstand.

36   "Their bulbs and their branches *shall be of one piece* with it; all of it shall be one piece of hammered work of pure gold.

37   "Then you shall make its lamps seven *in number;* and they shall mount its lamps so as to shed light on the space in front of it.

38   "And its snuffers and their trays *shall be* of pure gold.

39   "It shall be made from a talent of pure gold . . ."

–Exodus 25

In the tabernacle and in the temple there was a lampstand. It had one vertical branch and three branches on each side of the vertical one, for a total of seven. It was made out of gold. Now that is the Old Testament. To me it represents the nation of Israel. Although there were individual families and tribes, they were still tied together, the tribe of Levi acting as intercessors before God. In looking at the seven golden lights in Revelation, one would expect these multibranched lampstands to be repeated, but they are not. In Revelation 1:12–13, these are seven *individual* golden lampstands—one representing each of the seven churches (Revelation 1:20). If you look at all the churches in existence today, each would (should) have its own lampstand.

To visualize the contrast between the lampstands of the Old and New Testaments, please refer to Figure 1.

I don't know if I can even express in words the things that the Lord showed me about the lampstands, but I'll try. Each body of believers is not tied to a whole mechanism. They are in direct access in their relationship to God.

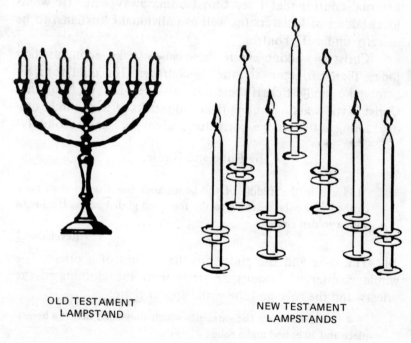

OLD TESTAMENT
LAMPSTAND

NEW TESTAMENT
LAMPSTANDS

Figure 1

The Old Testament lampstand almost looks like a denomination to me. It may be, for legal or tax purposes or for some other reason, that a denomination which controls its churches can be justified. I am not antidenominational. But I am absolutely convinced that spiritually there should be nothing between that candlestick (church) and God. Otherwise, one gets into situations where if a local body (church) wants to do something, they have to first check with the "bishop" who checks with the "cardinal" who checks with the "pope" (for example). I have seen, in the Catholic church and in many of the major American denominations, instances wherein a local body of believers believes sincerely before the Lord that they should do something, but a human "controller" says "No."

I think that this is an abomination. It is great for local churches to be "associated" with one another, and to work together and even pool their resources for a major project. It is external control that I see Christ doing away with. He wants local bodies of believers (as well as individual Christians) to be directly under His control.

Christ is walking about these candlesticks, acting as their judge, their corrector, and their encourager. (He could not walk *among* the candlesticks if there was only one.) Do you think that Christ is still walking among the candlesticks of the churches today, acting as their judge, corrector, and encourager? Absolutely!

The Robe and Girdle

13 and in the middle of the lampstands one like a son of man, clothed in a robe reaching to the feet, and girded across His breast with a golden girdle.

—**Revelation 1**

The robe and the girdle are the clothes of a priest. The whole chapter of Exodus 28 deals with the clothing of the priests, and the robe and the girdle appear there:

4 "And these are the garments which they shall make: a breastpiece and an ephod and a robe . . .

6 "They shall also make the ephod of gold . . ."

As we see in Exodus, the robe and the golden breastpiece are the marks of a priest. In John's description of Christ amidst the lampstands, in His glorified state, He is shown to be our High Priest, wearing clothing exactly like the priests' clothing in the Old Testament. How exciting it is to see God's patterns in the Old Testament repeated in the New Testament! God has not changed! Revelation is *not* a mysterious book full of strange new symbols that we cannot understand!

Divinity

14 And His head and His hair were white like white wool, like snow . . .

—Revelation 1

Some people might say that this verse is depicting the purity of Christ or His holiness. I don't think that is it. I think that it is showing the *divinity* of Christ.

Let's look at a verse in Daniel 7:

9 "I kept looking
   Until thrones were set up,
   And the Ancient of Days took *His* seat;
   His vesture *was* like white snow,
   And the hair of His head like pure wool. . . ."

Those are almost identical to the words used in Revelation 1:14. John was seeing Christ in His divine nature, appearing like God, the Ancient of Days.

The people who saw Christ while He was living on the earth really did not see Christ. They saw all of Christ that could be contained within a human body. If you could strip away the human body, what would Christ look like? I believe we get a glimpse here. He looks both divine, as God, and like a priest, wearing priests' clothing.

If somebody today has a vision and says that he has seen Christ, the first thing that I always ask is what He looked like. If the person says, "Oh, He had long, kind of blondish–brown hair, brown eyes and so forth," I am doubtful that he actually saw Christ.

If someone were to see Christ as He is today, His hair would be white. This is the way Christ is right now. There is no reason for Him to go back and simulate the old robe of flesh when He appears to a person in a vision. He didn't do that with John. This would be one valid test of authenticity for such a vision. If you have had a vision and think that you have seen Christ, this would be a good test to apply, because we can be deceived. Visions can come from sources other than God.

14 . . . and His eyes were like a flame of fire; . . .

—Revelation 1

Christ's eyes are also said to be as a flame of fire, in the description of Him in Revelation 19, when He comes back to wipe out all evil in the battle of Armageddon (Har–Magedon).

The description of Christ's eyes had always mystified my wife, Jeani, until I pointed out to her that in those days the only way to have light was with a flame. It was either a candle, a lamp, or a torch. There was no other means of light at night other than with some type of a flame. When John saw Christ, with eyes emitting light, the only way that he could describe what he saw was "eyes like a flame." I think that if we had the same vision today, we would probably say that His eyes were like searchlights.

In Revelation 2:23, Christ says, ". . . I am He who searches the minds and hearts . . ." Even now, Christ is searching your mind and your heart. Will He be pleased with what He finds there? Psalm 139 says:

> 23 **Search me, O God, and know my heart;**
> **Try me and know my anxious thoughts;**
> 24 **And see if there be any hurtful way in me,**
> **And lead me in the everlasting way.**

I can almost see God with a searchlight shining down into my heart and mind. Search me, O God, reveal to me what is wrong, and cause me to walk in paths of righteousness.

Living Waters

As we read more of John's description of Christ, I must confess that God has not revealed anything to me concerning His feet.

> **15 and His feet *were* like burnished bronze, when it has been caused to glow in a furnace, and His voice *was* like the sound of many waters.**
>
> **–Revelation 1**

When I was praying about His voice, the Spirit said to me that sometimes His voice is very gentle, like the trickling of mountain streams; sometimes it is like the crashing of ocean waves that are grinding rocks into sand. The sound of many waters can be either very gentle or very powerful. I feel that John was somehow hearing a combination of the two. There was a power and yet a gentleness in His voice.

Stars Held in His Right Hand

16 And in His right hand He held seven stars; and out of His mouth came a sharp two-edged sword; and His face was like the sun shining in its strength.

—Revelation 1

We know from verse 20 that these stars were seven angels for the churches. This means that in His hand, Christ is holding messengers (angel meaning "messenger from God"). He is very concerned about what happens to every local body, no matter how big or how small. Christ said:

28 "My sheep hear My voice, and I know them . . .
29 . . . and no one shall snatch them out of my hand.

—John 10

He is concerned for each individual church. He doesn't look at all the Bible churches or all the Baptist churches, but He looks at each church individually. He has an individual angel messenger in His hand for every church. Everything that He is doing builds up these churches.

If you actually envisage a two-edged sword coming out of His mouth, that would be pretty grotesque. Let's use the Bible to see what this really means. In Ephesians, it says the sword of the Spirit is the word of God (Ephesians 6:19). This could imply that when Christ comes back to destroy all the armies of the world, His only weapon will be the words that He will speak. A two-edged sword was probably the worst weapon that was wielded by an individual in those days. Christ's words at the battle of Armageddon will make hydrogen bombs look like firecrackers; it will be an incredibly powerful thing. Actually, I can see His speaking a word simultaneously causing that thing to happen. There would be no time lapse. Nothing can resist His word—no missiles, no armies, no hydrogen bombs . . . not anything.

Revelation 1:16 goes on to say ". . . and His face was like the sun shining in its strength." It does not say a dull sun, but a sun *shining in its strength*. Trying to look at God's face would be like trying to look into the sun. Brilliant! Many times throughout the Old and New Testaments when the glory of the Lord has really been revealed, it caused the one present to fall to his face in reverent worship. I would love to see the glory of the Lord in a way that would cause me to do this.

The Vision of Christ Completed

17   And when I saw Him, I fell at His feet as a dead man. And He laid His right hand upon me, saying, "Do not be afraid; I am the first and the last,

18   and the living One; and I was dead, and behold, I am alive forevermore, and I have the keys of death and of Hades. . . ."
—Revelation 1

John's response was the same as that of the men in the Old Testament. He fell at Christ's feet in worship and awe. Then Christ, in such a beautiful way, laid His hand upon John and said, "Do not be afraid . . ." I can just hear His voice, like a mountain stream. Perfect love casts out fear. If we are totally convinced of Christ's love and protection, we need never be afraid of anything.

We see, in verse 18, that Christ has the keys to death and Hades. In the Old and New Testaments, keys were a symbol of authority. Christ has the ability to lock or to unlock, and He will do as He chooses. When He is tired of death messing around with His people, He is going to lock it up. When He wants Satan in Hades, He will put him in and lock him up. There is no way that Satan will be able to get out, *until Christ releases him*, because Christ has the keys, the authority, and the power.

Summary and Conclusion

Chapter 1 of Revelation ends by giving the outline for the book, in verse 19. John is told to write the things that he has just seen (the encounter with Christ), the things which "are," and following that, the things which will take place later. We read:

> **19** "Write therefore the things which you have seen, and the things which are, and the things which shall take place after these things.
> **20** "As for the mystery of the seven stars which you saw in My right hand, and the seven golden lampstands: the seven stars are the angels of the seven churches, and the seven lampstands are the seven churches. . . ."

—Revelation 1

As we will see, most of the symbolism in the book of Revelation is explained either in the book of Revelation itself or other places in the Bible. Verse 20 solves the mystery of the seven stars and the seven golden lampstands. It plainly tells us what these symbols mean. The book of Revelation *is understandable.* Much of the key to understanding it, we will find in it, if we simply take the time and trouble to read and study it, and to let God speak to us through it.

Now we will look at "the things which are." These are the things which were contemporary to John's time.

2

LETTERS TO THE
SEVEN CHURCHES
(Revelation 2 & 3)

In Chapters 2 and 3 of the book of Revelation, we find the letters that Jesus Christ is writing to the seven churches. All of the letters follow a general form, although there are some exceptions. There are basically four parts to each of the letters.

In the first part of each letter, Christ identifies Himself with a portion of the vision that John has just had. The portion of the vision is usually uniquely geared for the needs of the particular church.

In the second part of each letter, Christ praises the members of that church for the good things that they are doing. This is included in all of the letters except the last one—the letter to Laodicea. Evidently, He could not find anything there worthy of praise.

In the third part of each letter, Christ criticizes the church for what they are doing wrong, or what they could do better. The exception here is the church at Philadelphia. Evidently, they were moving in the Lord's will, and He saw no need for criticism.

The fourth part of each of these letters contains the promises that Christ makes to the overcomers within that church. We should point out that all of the Christians in these churches were not overcomers, and special blessings were promised by Christ to those Christians who were to become, or who already were, overcomers. We will not be dealing with the overcomers and the promises made to them in this book, since it is such a vast subject. In fact, it is the subject of a new book the Lord has laid on my heart. In the interim, if you wish to find out more about the overcomers, you can send for my cassettes entitled "The Overcomers." See the information form at the back of the book concerning this.

REVELATION 2:1-7
–CHRIST'S LETTER TO THE CHURCH AT EPHESUS

Paul wrote a letter to the believers at Ephesus, which we call the book of Ephesians. Here in Revelation 2, Christ writes a letter to the same church at Ephesus. If a Christian had to place more emphasis on one of these letters or the other, which do you think should be emphasized: the letter written by Paul or the letter written by Christ? Most Christians would probably conclude that the letter written by Christ would be the more significant. Yet, in our Bible studies, most of us have been through Paul's letter to the Ephesians many times and rarely, if ever, have truly studied Christ's letter to the Ephesians.

I believe that this is probably true in general. Christians tend to emphasize Paul's letters to the various churches and ignore Christ's letters. Let us breathe a prayer and ask the Lord to forgive us for neglecting Christ's letters to the churches, and ask the Holy Spirit to really speak individually to our hearts as we now embark upon a study of these letters. The first letter in Revelation 2 is to the church at Ephesus.

Since both are part of the word of God, I in no way want to put down Paul's letters to the churches. I simply want to give the emphasis to Christ's letters that I believe they deserve.

1 **"To the angel of the church in Ephesus write:**
The One who holds the seven stars in His right hand, the One who walks among the seven golden lampstands, says this:
2 **'I know your deeds and your toil and perseverance, and that you cannot endure evil men, and you put to the test those who call themselves apostles, and they are not, and you found them** *to be* **false;**

3 and you have perseverance and have endured for My name's sake, and have not grown weary.

4 'But I have *this* against you, that you have left your first love.

5 'Remember therefore from where you have fallen, and repent and do the deeds you did at first; or else I am coming to you, and will remove your lampstand out of its place—unless you repent.

6 'Yet this you do have, that you hate the deeds of the Nicolaitans, which I also hate.

7 'He who has an ear, let him hear what the Spirit says to the churches. To him who overcomes, I will grant to eat of the tree of life, which is in the Paradise of God.' . . ."

—Revelation 2

This is the complete letter. First, we should notice two things. In verse 7 it says, ". . . let him hear what the *Spirit* says . . ." Earlier, it says that Christ is writing this letter. How do these two relate? Who takes the word of God and makes it alive to the hearts of the readers or listeners? . . . The Holy Spirit and Christ are working in conjunction here. People can read the Bible as a history book and it is not the word of God to them. The Holy Spirit has to make it alive in their hearts. Also, notice that it is ". . . what the Spirit says to the *churches* . . . ." Churches here is plural, so we can assume that the Holy Spirit intended for it to be read by more than just the church at Ephesus. It was probably meant for at least these seven churches. I think that we can probably legitimately extend it, and conclude that it is something He wanted churches of all the ages to read.

Let us now look specifically at Christ's letter to the church at Ephesus. Ephesus was the most important sea port in Asia Minor. There was a great deal of ship traffic going through it. We can probably surmise that Aquila and his wife Priscilla were some of the founding elders. In Acts 18:18-21, Paul took Aquila and Priscilla to Ephesus, and then he sailed on. You can also get some background of this group of Christians by reading the book of Ephesians.

In the vision that John had earlier, the seven stars that Christ held in His right hand were the seven angels (messengers) to the seven churches. It said that the seven golden lampstands were the seven churches. In verse 1, we see Christ intimately involved with the churches. It wasn't as though He initiated them and then left them on their own; at this point, He is still intricately involved with the churches, yearning for them to be what they can and should be. I think that we can legitimately say that Christ, even today, is walking among the lampstands of the churches, observing them, judging them, and encouraging them to be all that He has for them to be.

In verse 2, Christ says, "' I know your deeds and your toil . . .' " Toil sounds like hard work. He sees their perseverance, and the fact that He acknowledges it is like a reward in itself. He observes that they "cannot endure evil men." This does not mean evil men of the community necessarily, but more likely evil men within the body. Matthew 18:15–17 talks about what to do if a brother sins against you. You are to go to him. If he listens to you, you have won a brother; if not, you are to take somebody else with you. If he still will not listen, you are to take him before the church. If he still refuses to listen, he is to be cast out. Unfortunately, I think that this is something that our churches have gotten away from. We are supposed to exercise that kind of judgment over one another. We are not to judge outsiders, but 1 Corinthians 5:9–13 says that we are to judge those of the household of faith.

So if there was a man who claimed to be a brother and persisted in being evil (living in sin), the Christians in this church at Ephesus would not have anything to do with him. Christ says this is a good thing about them—they put to test those claiming to be apostles (verse 2).

There were many people running around claiming to be apostles back in the first century, and there are many people claiming to be apostles today. According to this, we are not just to accept them all carte blanche, but rather we are to try each one to see if he is really an apostle of God. I think that this is something that the church, and we as individuals, should do today.

In verse 3, Christ goes on to say, "you have endured . . . and have not grown weary." He is really telling them that they are in pretty fair shape and that He appreciates them.

Now the bad news, in verse 4. He says *"but,"* which almost

seems to negate much of the positive things He has said. "But I have *this* against you, that you have left your first love." This can be interpreted a number of ways. One way is that we *should* love the Lord our God with all our heart, soul and mind. This is the first and great commandment. Also, we should love our neighbor as ourself. Evidently the Christians at Ephesus had waned from their love of God and from the acts that naturally flow from loving God, and they had waned from loving their brother or their neighbor. Possibly, in their judging of apostles and evil men, they had developed a harshness and abruptness, and a condemning attitude. They seem to have lost the love aspect. There are Christians and even entire churches today that have become this way. They are harsh in discipline and have lost their warmth and love.

Verse 5 says, '"Remember therefore from where you have fallen . . .' " Christ is asking them to think back to how they were when they really loved Jesus and each other. He tells them to get back to that condition, or He will do away with them—wipe out their church. They will no longer have a church unless they get back to that position of love. Those are strong words! Do you think that Christ feels the same way today about churches which are rigid, disciplined and intolerant of evil, but have little real warmth and love? He who has an ear, let him hear what the Spirit is saying to the churches today.

REVELATION 2:8-11

–CHRIST'S LETTER TO THE CHURCH AT SMYRNA

8 "And to the angel of the church in Smyrna write:
The first and the last, who was dead, and has come to life, says this:

9 'I know your tribulation and your poverty (but you are rich), and the blasphemy by those who say they are Jews and are not, but are a synagogue of Satan.

10 'Do not fear what you are about to suffer. Behold, the devil is about to cast some of you into prison, that you may be tested, and you will have tribulation ten days. Be faithful until death, and I will give you the crown of life.

11 'He who has an ear, let him hear what the Spirit says to the churches. He who over comes shall not be hurt by the second death.' . . ."

—Revelation 2

There is no condemnation or criticism in this letter to the church at Smyrna. It is all encouragement. We see a church that is persecuted and some people about to be martyred. Christ, in identifying Himself said, I am the "first and the last, who was dead, and has come to life . . ." Here he is taking the characteristic of Himself that specifically applies to that church. He is saying: "You are going to die, but don't worry. I came back to life and I will bring you back to life." This is a beautiful way in which Christ encourages them.

Verse 9 says, ' "I know your tribulation and your poverty . . ." ' In reflecting, tribulation and poverty evidently go hand in hand. It would be hard to be really persecuted when living in the lap of luxury. This is talking about physical poverty. Christ goes on to say, "but you are rich," referring to spiritual riches. In His letter to the church at Laodicea, Christ tells them that they think they are rich, but they are really poor. Here, in the church at Smyrna, we have the exact opposite. He is telling them that physically they are in poverty and tribulation, but spiritually they are really rich. He tells them that they will be thrown into prison, but for only a short time because they will be killed. He says not to worry about it, but to be faithful until death, and He will give them the crown of life. He encourages them, even though they are persecuted and about to be killed.

Evidently these Christians were being accused by people who went to the Jewish synagogue. They were being accused of some crime—possibly of having another God. Before Christ came, the Jewish synagogue was the synagogue of the Lord, but because the Jews refused to accept Him as the Messiah, I believe that it became a synagogue of Satan. The Jews in the synagogue were accusing these Christians so that the Romans would arrest them and execute them. Romans 2:28, 29 says that a Jew is not one who has been circumcised outwardly, but one who has been circumcised of the heart. Thus, the Christians were the true Jews.

So we have true Jews and the Jews who go to the synagogue (which is no longer the synagogue of God but the synagogue of Satan, because they have overtly rejected Jesus Christ). The latter are not true Jews.

As an aside, we can really get into some beautiful things when we go back and look at the promises to the Jewish people, knowing that we (as Christians) are true Jews, because our hearts have been circumcised. Praise God! Here again, we do not have the space to pursue this subject. I should emphasize that I am in no way anti–Semitic. I love the biological Jew dearly. However, the Christian should realize that he is true Israel and a true Jew, much more so than Abe Goldstein who lives in Jerusalem. If you do wish to pursue this subject, see the cassette entitled "New Covenant versus Old Covenant–Who is Israel?" on the information sheet at the back of this book.

Returning to our consideration of Christ's letter to the believers at Smyrna, we see that Jesus knows all about what is happening to them. In verse 9 He says, " 'I know your tribulation and your poverty (but you are rich) . . .'" He knows what is going on with each individual Christian emotionally, financially, physically and spiritually.

Do you think that Christ knows this about you and me? Of course! He knows and He cares. He cares about our testings and trials, and how we handle them. He is also encouraging us. If we go through a time of real persecution, He will tell us in our hearts, as He told the Christians in Smyrna, "Be faithful until death, and I will give you the crown of life." Praise God!

Isn't it exciting that the book of Revelation is not only understandable, but that it is filled with rich, nourishing spiritual food? You can get such a beautiful picture of Jesus as He functions today, if you will spend some time meditating on His letters to these churches. But for now we must move on; we have five more letters to go, each one packed with things we need to know. (We need to know them or God wouldn't have put them in the Bible.)

REVELATION 2:12–17

–CHRIST'S LETTER TO THE CHURCH AT PERGAMUM

12   "And to the angel of the church in Pergamum write:
The One who has the sharp two–edged sword says this:

13   'I know where you dwell, where Satan's throne is; and you hold fast My name, and did not deny My faith, even in the days of Antipas, My witness, My faithful one, who was killed among you, where Satan dwells.

14   'But I have a few things against you, because you have there some who hold the teaching of Balaam, who kept teaching Balak to put a stumbling block before the sons of Israel, to eat things sacrificed to idols, and to commit *acts of* immorality.

15   'Thus you also have some who in the same way hold the teaching of the Nicolaitans.

16   'Repent therefore; or else I am coming to you quickly, and I will make war against them with the sword of My mouth.

17   'He who has an ear, let him hear what the Spirit says to the churches. To him who overcomes, to him I will give *some* of the hidden manna, and I will give him a white stone, and a new name written on the stone which no one knows but he who receives it.' . . ."

–Revelation 2

In verse 12, the characteristic of Himself that Christ chooses to emphasize is the sword that comes out of His mouth in His appearance to John in Revelation 1. Here, the sharp two–edged sword implies judgment and the piercing of the word of God. Why He chose that characteristic becomes apparent as we study this letter.

In verse 13, we see that the Christians in Pergamum are living in a place where Satan's throne is. There is not total agreement as to exactly what that means. We know that Satan can only be in one place at a time, but perhaps he has several throne rooms in various parts of the world. It is possible, at least for Asia Minor, that that is where Satan's throne actually was. On the other hand, it may mean that the place was a stronghold of Satan. Pergamum was a city of pagan worship and emperor worship. This is one of the characteristics of this city that we know from secular history.

Also in verse 13, Christ praises them because, in spite of the fact that they were living in such a place, they did not deny their faith. Then He points out one Christian martyr, Antipas, by name. Isn't it exciting that Jesus Christ knows each Christian by name! He knows "Jim McKeever" and cares about what is happening to Jim McKeever. He also knows *you* by name and knows what is happening to you, and cares about it.

However, throughout most of this letter Christ is criticizing and judging these Christians in Pergamum, beginning in verse 14. Let us first review who Balaam was. Balaam was a prophet of the Lord. He walked with the Lord and prophesied, but later turned against God. The whole chapter of Numbers 22 deals with Balaam. We read in Numbers 22:

> 18 And Balaam answered and said to the servants of Balak, "Though Balak were to give me his house full of silver and gold, I could not do anything, either small or great, contrary to the command of the LORD my God. . . ."

Balaam started out as a good guy. But now let's look at Numbers 31, which records how he caused the sons of Israel to trespass against the Lord:

> 16 "Behold, these caused the sons of Israel, through the counsel of Balaam, to trespass against the LORD in the matter of Peor, so the plague was among the congregation of the LORD. . . ."
>
> —Numbers 31

Evidently the counsel of Balaam, at this time, was leading the people directly into sin. That should be a warning to any preacher or man of God that although you may start out well, you can fall by the wayside. The result is total disaster.

Verse 14 of Revelation 2 says that the Christians at Pergamum had followed the pagan teachings of Balaam. As a result, they were doing two things. First, they were eating things sacrificed to idols. There are two ways that one can interpret this. One is this: people brought in sacrifices to pagan idols and the priests used some of these carcasses for their own food. The surplus they took down to the city market. This could be purchased cheaper than regular food. Therefore, people would buy it, and take it home and eat it.

There was a big controversy in the early church as to whether Christians should eat this type of meat or not. In the first few verses of Romans 14, Paul deals with a Christian's attitude to this type of meat that had been sacrificed to idols and then sold at the market place. Paul said that those who are more mature know that there is nothing wrong with it, but some of the new Christians (who had just come out of idolatry) wondered how they could possibly eat meat that had been sacrificed to idols. Paul concluded that if, by eating such meat, he was going to hurt a brother, he would not eat it. He said that when he went to somebody's house, he would eat what was set before him. If they pointed out that it had been sacrificed to idols, then he would not eat it, but if he was alone, eating meat that had been sacrificed to idols did not bother him at all.

However, I do not think that this is what Christ is talking about because the eating of meat sacrificed to idols was one of the things that He had *against* this church at Pergamum that He says to repent of or He is going to make war with the people who continue. Christ would not make war against them for something that was alright for Paul.

I think Christ is speaking about people actually participating in the pagan feasts and festivals. They were actually there when the sacrifices were occurring. After the sacrifices, there would usually be a big feast, on the pagan level, somewhat like a Roman orgy. So what Christ is saying here is that, by following these teachings of Balaam, you can be caught up in this type of immoral behavior and commit acts of sexual sin.

Interestingly, in verse 13, He says that they did not deny His faith. They hung in there, but they tolerated among their brothers people who were teaching ungodly practices. This is just the opposite of the first church, Ephesus, where they were not tolerating evil men.

In verse 15, Christ refers to the teaching of the Nicolaitans. We are not exactly sure what this is. Some people say that Nicholas (who was one of the seven deacons appointed in Acts 6) may have wandered off and started a cult, but nobody really knows. Evidently the Nicolaitans had a similar type of teaching to that of Balaam, and were misleading the believers.

In verse 16 Christ tells them to repent and get these teachings and practices out of their midst, or He will make war against them with the sword of His mouth. We know that His sword is extremely sharp, and we would not want to be in a position where He was making war on us with His word. I would be scared to death! If we are even nibbling in some of these areas, I believe that the Lord is saying, "I want you to repent and change your mind and stop doing these kinds of things."

REVELATION 2:18-29

–CHRIST'S LETTER TO THE CHURCH AT THYATIRA

18   "And to the angel of the church in Thyatira write:
The Son of God who has eyes like a flame of fire, and His feet are like burnished bronze, says this:
19   'I know your deeds, and your love and faith and service and perseverance, and that your deeds of late are greater than at first.
20   'But I have *this* against you, that you tolerate the woman Jezebel, who calls herself a prophetess, and she teaches and leads My bond–servants astray, so that they commit *acts of* immorality and eat things sacrificed to idols.
21   'And I gave her time to repent; and she does not want to repent of her immorality.
22   'Behold, I will cast her upon a bed *of sickness*, and those who commit adultery with her into great tribulation, unless they repent of her deeds.
23   'And I will kill her children with pestilence; and all the churches will know that I am He who searches the minds and hearts; and I will give to each one of you according to your deeds.
24   'But I say to you, the rest who are in Thyatira, who do not hold this teaching, who have not known the deep things of Satan, as they call them–I place no other burden on you.
25   'Nevertheless what you have, hold fast until I come.
26   'And he who overcomes, and he who keeps my deeds until the end, TO HIM I WILL GIVE AUTHORITY OVER THE NATIONS;
27   AND HE SHALL RULE THEM WITH A ROD OF IRON, AS THE VESSELS OF THE POTTER ARE BROKEN TO PIECES, as I also have received *authority* from My Father;
28   and I will give him the morning star.

29 'He who has an ear, let him hear what the Spirit says to the churches.' . . ."

                                                                    —Revelation 2

In verse 19, Christ tells the Christians in Thyatira that He knows their deeds, their love, their faith, their service and their perseverance. It sounds like a great church, doesn't it? It is also a growing church, because Christ points out that their recent deeds are greater than the deeds they did when they first became a church. If we just looked at this one verse, we would conclude that this was a healthy, growing church. However, a growing church, such as this one in Thyatira, can also have significant problems.

The church at Pergamum was a faithful church, but it tolerated false teachers. The church at Thyatira is even worse! It is dominated by a false prophetess—a woman named Jezebel. We do not know if that was her actual name, or if she was just like the original Jezebel. You can read in 1 Kings 16 about Jezebel, the queen of Ahab, who was the one who enticed Ahab and Israel to come over and worship Baal. This lady is certainly like that Jezebel. I doubt that this was her name, but she was enticing these people to commit acts of adultery and to eat meat sacrificed to the idols.

Evidently something had happened in the past which we don't know about, because Christ says that He gave her time to repent and that she does not want to repent of her immorality. Since she did not repent, He is now going to take severe wrath against her and cause her and her followers to become sick and possibly die.

This woman may have claimed that the teachings she was giving out were the "deep things of God." Are there "prophets" making similar claims today? We need to test the spirits, to be certain we are hearing from God (1 John 4:1). Christ tells the church at Thyatira to repent and get rid of this false prophetess.

In addressing this church, Christ chooses the description of Himself as having eyes like a flame of fire . . . searching, piercing, light–emitting eyes. He was searching these churches and the hearts of the individuals who composed them. I believe that He is doing the same today.

These last two churches that we have discussed were guilty of too much tolerance. One tolerated false teachers; the other tolerated a false prophetess. We have been taught to be *tolerant:* accept everybody and give everybody a hearing. But that is not really what Christ is saying here, is it? In a sense, He is saying *be intolerant.* If someone comes in who is a false teacher, kick him out! He is telling us to try the spirits. If you know that someone is a false teacher, or a false prophet or prophetess (not of God), do not tolerate that person! I think that we can fall into a lot of errors like these churches did, if we are too tolerant and too accepting of every minister that comes by.

Verse 24 of Revelation 2 is encouraging. Christ knew each individual in the church at Thyatira. He knew that some of them had not accepted the teaching of the false prophetess (and probably opposed her). They did not split off and start another church. They remained as part of that church. Christ commends them for that, and tells them to "hold fast."

How contemporary these letters are! How the Holy Spirit can speak to us through them, if we give Him the chance.

REVELATION 3:1–6
–CHRIST'S LETTER TO THE CHURCH AT SARDIS

1   "And to the angel of the church in Sardis write:
He who has the seven Spirits of God, and the seven stars, says this: I know your deeds, that you have a name that you are alive, and you are dead.

2   'Wake up, and strengthen the things that remain, which were about to die; for I have not found your deeds completed in the sight of My God.

3   'Remember therefore what you have received and heard; and keep it, and repent. If therefore you will not wake up, I will come like a thief, and you will not know at what hour I will come upon you.

4   'But you have a few people in Sardis who have not soiled their garments; and they will walk with Me in white; for they are worthy.

5   'He who overcomes shall thus be clothed in white garments; and I will not erase his name from the book of life, and I will confess his name before My Father, and before His angels.

6 'He who has an ear, let him hear what the Spirit says to the churches.' . . ."

—Revelation 3

In describing Himself in verse 1, Christ chooses the characteristic of having the seven stars (which we know to be the seven angels to the seven individual churches) and the seven Spirits of God. Looking back at Revelation 1, we read:

4 John to the seven churches that are in Asia: Grace to you and peace, from Him who is and who was and who is to come; and from the seven Spirits who are before His throne; . . .

We recall that these seven Spirits are before the throne of God. There are two basic ways that this can be interpreted. One is that these are seven very special angels (for angels are spiritual beings and not physical beings), and the other way is that these are the seven-fold manifestations of the Holy Spirit. Those who hold this latter interpretation would point to Isaiah 11:

2 And the Spirit of the LORD will rest on Him,
The spirit of wisdom and understanding,
The spirit of counsel and strength,
The spirit of knowledge and the fear of the LORD.

The only difficulty with this that I see is that I find only six manifestations listed here. However, this could be a legitimate rendering of this verse. It makes more sense to me to take the point of view that these are seven very special angels. Three verses might help throw some light on this for us:

5 And from the throne proceed flashes of lightning and sounds and peals of thunder. And there were seven lamps of fire burning before the throne, which are the seven Spirits of God; . . .

—Revelation 4

6 And I saw between the throne (with the four living creatures) and the elders a Lamb standing, as if slain, having seven horns and seven eyes, which are the seven Spirits of God, sent out into all the earth.

—Revelation 5

2 And I saw the seven angels who stand before God; and seven trumpets were given to them.

—Revelation 8

From this last verse, we can see that there are seven very special angels who stand before God and that these will blow the trumpets which will initiate certain parts of the Tribulation. In Revelation 5:6, we see that standing around the throne are the elders, and a lamb having seven horns and seven eyes which are the seven Spirits of God. Yet it says that these Spirits were sent out into all the earth. Since "Spirits" is plural, it is hard for me to think of these seven Spirits of God as being the Holy Spirit, or even the manifestations of the Holy Spirit; it is easier for me to conceive of seven special angels.

Christ seems to be saying to this church at Sardis that He is the one who controls the angel messengers and even the special angels who stand before God. Because all of these angels are under His control and work for Him, He knows all of the details about what is going on in that church, and with each individual within that church.

Continuing His letter to this church, Christ says: "'. . . I know your deeds, that you have a name that you are alive . . .'" Evidently everybody was saying things like: "Oh boy, that church in Sardis is really alive! It's a live-wire church. They really know how to clap their hands and stamp their feet!" Christ is saying that they have a reputation of being very "alive," but that they are really dying—in fact, they are almost dead. They are right on the brink. He encourages them to wake up and strengthen what little life remains—to get up off of their death bed, because their deeds are not complete.

If you knew somebody that was just about to die, you might grab his shoulders and say, "Wake up! Don't die!" You would do it because you loved him and were concerned. You would be saying, "Don't give up." That is what Christ is saying here. He is grabbing this church by the shoulders and saying, *wake up,* because He loves them and is concerned about their welfare and growth.

Yet there is another side. Verse 3 says: "'. . . If therefore you will not wake up, I will come like a thief, and you will not know at what hour I will come upon you. . . .'" Christ is saying that if they do not repent, they will lose the life that they have now. He is trying with all of His might to help them to wake up and keep from dying. There are churches today like this one that appear to be alive, but inside the individual members are actually dying spiritually.

However, even in this church at Sardis, there are some who are faithful overcomers. In verse 4, Christ says, "'But you have a few people in Sardis who have not soiled their garments; and they will walk with Me in white; for they are worthy. . . .'" Christ yearns that every Christian will be an overcomer and, therefore, wear white.

Let us take a moment and look at "white linen." The white linen that ultimately the bride of Christ will wear is discussed in Revelation 19:

> 7 "Let us rejoice and be glad and give the glory to Him, for the marriage of the Lamb has come and His bride has made herself ready."
>
> 8 And it was given to her to clothe herself in fine linen bright *and* clean; for the fine linen is the righteous acts of the saints.

We are told that the white linen that the bride will wear is the righteous acts of the saints. Christ seems to be saying to this church: "Wake up; don't die! Get dressed in white." The white that He wants them to get dressed in is righteous acts. Christ is calling us to righteousness. Some Christians are walking around with soiled garments. They need to be washed clean by the blood of Christ. As they walk in righteousness, those garments will get whiter and whiter!

To me, the church at Sardis is the saddest church of all. They didn't have any persecution. There wasn't any Jewish hostility. There were no false teachers—nothing like that. They were on easy street . . . much like us today. And yet, that is the easiest time to get into a downward spiral spiritually. We can get by without praying much or really pressing in to know the mind of God.

If hard times come, then we pray. If your husband, wife or one of your children goes to the hospital and the doctor says that he doesn't know if he or she will live or die, how many hours a day are you going to pray? Many, I'm sure. It's unfortunate that we have to be forced into a position wherein we earnestly pray. God does not want to see us forced into communication with Him; He wants us to talk with Him because we love Him.

REVELATION 3:7-13
—CHRIST'S LETTER TO THE CHURCH AT PHILADELPHIA

7 "And to the angel of the church in Philadelphia write:

He who is holy, who is true, who has the key of David, who opens and no one will shut, and who shuts and no one opens, says this:

8 'I know your deeds. Behold, I have put before you an open door which no one can shut, because you have a little power, and have kept My word, and have not denied My name.

9 'Behold, I will cause *those* of the synagogue of Satan, who say that they are Jews, and are not, but lie—behold, I will make them to come and bow down at your feet, and to know that I have loved you.

10 'Because you have kept the word of My perseverance, I also will keep you from the hour of testing, that *hour* which is about to come upon the whole world, to test those who dwell upon the earth.

11 'I am coming quickly; hold fast what you have, in order that no one take your crown.

12 'He who overcomes, I will make him a pillar in the temple of My God, and he will not go out from it any more; and I will write upon him the name of My God, and the name of the city of My God, the new Jerusalem, which comes down out of heaven from My God, and My new name.

13 'He who has an ear, let him hear what the Spirit says to the churches.' . . ."

—Revelation 3

Philadelphia means brotherly love. This church at Philadelphia is a faithful, witnessing, strong church. Christ has no words of condemnation for these Christians at all.

In this passage, Christ describes Himself as holy and true. Praise God that He is! He is also the possessor of the key of David. In Isaiah we read:

22 "Then I will set the key of the house of David on his shoulder,
When he opens no one will shut,

When he shuts no one will open. . . ."

—Isaiah 22

This is written about Shebna, who was the steward in charge of the household of David. David gave him the key, which meant that he had full authority to run all of the administrative affairs of David. This was a sign of authority. Christ, here in Revelation 3:7, is alluding to that verse. He (a descendant of David) has the key and the authority over the Tribulation, the bottomless pit and the whole messianic kingdom!

As we have said, Christ has no criticism for the Christians in Philadelphia. They have been faithful and have not denied Him. The false Jews (those not spiritual Jews) have gone around accusing them. Christ says that He will make these Jews of Satan bow down at the saints' feet. He is going to protect these Christians when the testing comes.

I believe that testing will also come upon us today. If we live like the brothers and sisters in Philadelphia, God will protect us. However, unlike some of the earlier churches that Christ has written to, wherein He says the Christians will be persecuted and even die, He is going to protect these followers in Philadelphia. This should be an encouragement to us when testing comes. We can be confident of His protection, if we are overcomers like those at Philadelphia.

REVELATION 3:14–22
—CHRIST'S LETTER TO THE CHURCH AT LAODICEA

14   "And to the angel of the church in Laodicea write:
The Amen, the faithful and true Witness, the Beginning of the creation of God, says this:
15   'I know your deeds, that you are neither cold nor hot; I would that you were cold or hot.
16   'So because you are lukewarm, and neither hot nor cold, I will spit you out of My mouth.
17   'Because you say, "I am rich, and have become wealthy, and have need of nothing," and you do not know that you are wretched and miserable and poor and blind and naked,
18   'I advise you to buy from Me gold refined by fire, that you may become rich, and white garments, that you may clothe your-

self, and *that* the shame of your nakedness may not be revealed; and eyesalve to anoint your eyes, that you may see.

19 'Those whom I love, I reprove and discipline; be zealous therefore, and repent.

20 'Behold, I stand at the door and knock; if any one hears My voice and opens the door, I will come in to him, and will dine with him, and he with Me.

21 'He who overcomes, I will grant to him to sit down with Me on My throne, as I also overcame and sat down with My Father on His throne.

22 'He who has an ear, let him hear what the Spirit says to the churches.' "

—Revelation 3

Here we have exactly the opposite of the church at Philadelphia. Christ had only good things to say about the believers in Philadelphia, but He has nothing but bad things to say about this church at Laodicea.

The first part of this passage is probably familiar. Christ says that these Christians are neither hot nor cold, but lukewarm. The Greek then says that He is going to *vomit* them out of His mouth. Many people, when they first become Christians, are really hot for the Lord. As their Christian life progresses, they begin to lose their zeal and excitement and they become lukewarm. Not cold, just lukewarm. Christ says that He doesn't like that at all! A cup of hot tea is nice, as is a glass of iced tea, but anything lukewarm just doesn't taste very nice. Oh God, cause us to be on fire for You!

In verse 17, Christ says that they think that they are rich and wealthy, but spiritually they are really poor and miserable. Now don't get the feeling that these people were hypocrites. A hypocrite knows he is one thing and pretends to be something else. These people really believed that they were spiritually wealthy; Christ says that they didn't even *know* that they were spiritually wretched, miserable, poor, blind and naked. We might pause for a moment to consider whether we think that we are spiritually rich. If we do, it is possible that our hearts have deceived us, as did the hearts of the Christians in Laodicea. Remember, the heart is deceitful and desperately wicked (Jeremiah 17:9). If we are living off the reading and study of the

Bible that we did several years ago; if we are still enjoying the thrill of leading someone to Christ several years ago (but haven't led anyone to the knowledge of Jesus in the last few years); or if we are still proud of the way God used us at one time, it is possible that we have moved from a position of spiritual wealth to spiritual poverty—and haven't even realized it. If you sincerely pray about it and feel that this is your condition, Christ gives you the solution in verse 18.

Christ suggests that the Christians in Laodicea buy from Him gold refined by fire. In those days they would refine gold by heating it up, which would cause the impurities to float to the top. The goldsmith would then scrape off the impurities. However, while scraping it off, some of the impurities would remix with the gold. It would then have to be reheated, the impurities would once again float to the top, and he would scrape them off. But again this would stir it up, causing some impurities to remix with the gold. The process was repeated until the goldsmith could see his reflection in the surface of the gold.

That is what Christ wants to do with you and me, but we must ask Him to do it. He wants to remove the impurities from our lives and see His image perfectly reflected in us! It will be a glorious day when we perfectly reflect the glory of God, twenty-four hours a day!

In 1 Peter 1 we read:

> 6 In this you greatly rejoice, even though now for a little while, if necessary, you have been distressed by various trials.
>
> 7 that the proof of your faith, *being* more precious than gold which is perishable, even though tested by fire, may be found to result in praise and glory and honor at the revelation of Jesus Christ; . . .

Again, this refining is what Christ is desiring to do with us. If we will allow it, it will result in praise and glory and honor to Jesus.

Christ wants these lukewarm Christians in Laodicea to be refined like gold. He wants them to *be like pure gold,* that they might become rich. He also admonishes them to buy from Him white garments, and eye salve that they might see. If they don't have the white garments (the righteous acts of saints), how do they stand? Naked! How I would rather stand in white garments than naked before the world and my God. Even so, purify us Lord Jesus!

Verse 19 says: ' "Those whom I love, I reprove and discipline . . .' " In connection with this, here is the thing that I like to think of. When an orchard keeper (or a husbandman) goes out to prune a tree, so that it will produce more, he trims off the dead parts or those which will never produce fruit. Yet He is never as close to that tree as when he is pruning it. He is looking at every branch. So it is when God is disciplining or "pruning" us—He is never so close to us as He is at that time. Even though it hurts, we can rejoice in the fact that God is right there, pruning out the things that *He* knows will hamper us, so that we can really flourish and bring forth the fruit that He wants us to bring forth. What a beautiful depiction of the loving care of Jesus!

Moving on to verse 20, I don't believe that it was ever meant to be used in connection with non–Christians. This is a powerful message for lukewarm Christians. Many Christians, when witnessing, use this verse: " 'Behold I stand at the door and knock . . .' " Christ may be standing at the door of a non–Christian's heart and knocking, but if you quote Revelation 3:20 in that situation, you are using it incorrectly.

Christ is saying to these lukewarm Christians that He has told them what to do to become hot again. He now says that He is knocking at their life's door. If they will just open the door—and *they* have to do it—He promises that He will come in and they will have a feast together! If we open up our lives completely to His control (and His purifying) we will partake of the rich delights of the spiritual food of the kingdom of God. If you feel that you are lukewarm, open your "door" and let Him in, and you will have a great feast together.

This church at Laodicea had no persecution, immorality or false teachers, yet they were lukewarm. The churches that were being persecuted or accused were the ones with a hot faith. It was the two churches which had no persecution which were the ones that were lukewarm or dying, which is almost two different ways of saying the same thing. They were becoming colder and colder. When something is dead, it is totally cold.

IMPORTANCE OF THESE SEVEN LETTERS

We said at the beginning of this chapter how important we feel these seven letters are. These are not letters of an apostle to these churches—these are letters from *Jesus Christ*, the divine Son of God, to these believers in these seven locations. How very important it is for us to read and study these seven letters. In fact, if one wanted to pick two chapters out of the entire New Testament to memorize, I believe that Revelation 2 and 3 would be at the top of my list. We should make these seven letters not only part of our minds, but also part of our lives. Remember—God said blessed is everyone who reads *and heeds* the words of this revelation.

As you have read through these seven letters of Jesus, it may be that God has spoken to your heart. Praise Him for that, and then prayerfully let it be worked out in your life, giving glory to Him.

GENERAL INTERPRETATIONS OF THESE LETTERS

A few people would say that these seven letters were written just to those seven churches that existed in New Testament times, and that they really don't apply to us. To me that is even more ridiculous than saying we should ignore all of Paul's letters. Most people would say that these letters are also for us to read and benefit by—that they were meant to be a warning, a help, and an encouragement to us also.

There are two basic interpretations of the broad framework of these seven letters. I will give you both of them and then tell you which one I subscribe to.

One says that these letters represent sequential eras since the church was founded. The church at Ephesus was the apostolic church, from roughly 30 to 100 A.D. Smyrna was the persecuted church, from approximately 100 to 313 A.D. Pergamum was the state church, from 313 to 590 A.D. Thyatira was the papal church, from 590 to 1517 A.D. Sardis was the reformed church, from 1517 to 1790. Philadelphia was the missionary church from 1730 to 1900 (some overlap with the reformed church). And in roughly 1900 the Laodicean or the lukewarm church era began.

The other basic interpretation is that these seven churches represent seven different kinds of bodies of believers that have existed in all of these eras. Right after the first century, there were some churches that were lukewarm, some that were dying, some that were faithful and were witnessing and reaching out, some that were being persecuted, and some who had lost their first love. This we know because Christ wrote to them. You can go right through the centuries up until today and find churches which would fit each of these categories.

The persecuted church was Smyrna. If you look at China, Russia and most communist countries today, you see Christians being persecuted. Pergamum was the faithful church, but they tolerated false teachers. There are many churches today which fit this description. The church at Thyatira was dominated by a false prophetess. Today we see some gross false prophets, such as Moon of the Unification Church, and even some generally accepted as Christians who are leading people in some very strange directions.

There are churches today which are spiritually dying, such as the one at Sardis. Philadelphia was the faithful church, and Laodicea represents the lukewarm churches. I find churches like these today, as I travel all over the world, as well as ones like the church at Ephesus, where they had lost their first love.

Personally, I see all of these seven kinds of churches represented in every era. Those of you who wish to believe that it is a sequential thing–God bless you. I'm not going to argue with you. The main thing is to let Christ and the Holy Spirit speak to your heart (and life) through these letters.

If these seven churches are representative of various kinds of churches within our era, the same things are probably also true of various individual Christians within them. There are believers today losing their first love; being persecuted; faithful, but listening to false teachers; faithful, but having false prophets; spiritually dying; faithful and witnessing; and becoming lukewarm. You might want to ask the Lord to show you which category you fit into.

CHRIST'S LETTER TO YOU OR YOUR CHURCH

Below is an outline of a letter that Christ might write to-day. You may want to prayerfully fill one of these out for yourself, and then one for your church.

It will take some prayer and time alone with the Lord to do this. He must speak to you. Put your name after the words "I know you." Then let the Lord show you what He is pleased with about you. After that, let Him show you what He might have you to change or do better, or perhaps a weakness that He wants you to do something about.

Then fill out another one of these, describing your church. What does Christ say that He is pleased with? What does He say needs to be changed? Christ may want you to help bring about these changes in your own church. This needs to be done in a productive, not destructive, way.

The One whose eyes are like a flame of fire (searchlight) says this:

1. I know you _____

2. I know your deeds and am pleased that you_____

_____

_____

_____

3. However, I have this against you _____

_____

_____

_____

4. He who has an ear, let him hear what the Spirit says.

3

HOW THEY PRAISE
IN HEAVEN
(Revelation 4 & 5)

1 **After these things I looked, and behold, a door** *standing* **open in heaven, and the first voice which I had heard, like** *the sound* **of a trumpet speaking with me, said, "Come up here, and I will show you what must take place after these things."**

2 **Immediately I was in the Spirit; and behold, a throne was standing in heaven, and One sitting on the throne.**

—Revelation 4

I would like to amplify on a few things here before we begin this third section of the book of Revelation—"the things which shall take place after these things" (Revelation 1:19).

We saw before, both in the vision and the letters to the churches, that Christ has the keys to the house of David and to the Messianic kingdom. He alone can open and no man can shut, and He can shut and no man open. Christ has opened the door into heaven here and has invited John to come up and see what is happening or, more precisely, what is going to happen in the future.

John says, "Immediately I was in the Spirit . . . in heaven . . ." He was not necessarily there in bodily form. The One sitting on the throne is God the Father. We will see later the scriptural basis for this.

If I asked you to describe Christ, you might have an idea of what He looks like. However, if I were to ask a group of Christians what God the Father was like, there would probably be a great diversity of opinion. Does God the Father have hands and a face, or a front and a back? Have you ever thought about it? I believe that the Bible says He does. Yet we don't really think of Him in this Father–image way. We tend to think of Him more as a bright, glowing, unapproachable thing. We feel we can approach Christ because He has arms and legs and a head, and so on, and we can identify with Him. But God the Father is something else. That is why we have a tendency to pray to Jesus. We don't quite know how to relate to God the Father, because our image of Him is vague.

In Revelation 5 John says:

> 1 And I saw in the right hand of Him who sat on the throne a book written inside and on the back, sealed up with seven seals.

This says that God the Father has a scroll in His right hand; thus, we know that God has hands.

In Exodus 33 we read:

> 18 Then Moses said, "I pray Thee, show me Thy glory!"
> 19 And He said, "I Myself will make all My goodness pass before you, and will proclaim the name of the LORD before you; and I will show compassion on whom I will show compassion."
> 20 But He said, "You cannot see My face, for no man can see Me and live!"
> 21 Then the LORD said, "Behold, there is a place by Me, and you shall stand *there* on the rock;
> 22 and it will come about, while My glory is passing by, that I will put you in the cleft of the rock and cover you with My hand until I have passed by.
> 23 "Then I will take My hand away and you shall see My back, but My face shall not be seen."

In this passage, God the Father says that He has a face, He has a hand, and He has a back. Hopefully your image of God is becoming a little clearer. How big is God's hand? According to verse 22 of Exodus 33, His hand is big enough to cover Moses. You can draw your own conclusions from that.

Recently there was a case wherein a young girl had a vision or a visitation from Christ. He sat and talked with her for about thirty minutes or an hour. One of the things that He told her several times within that time was, "Don't pray to Me; pray to My Father. Pray in My name, but pray to the Father." Christ never says, "If you ask Me anything I will do it." *Never.* Yet over and over again He says, "Anything you ask God the Father in My name, I will do." (See John 14:13; 15:16.)

Sometimes we have gone overboard in emphasizing Christ, such that we have ignored God the Father. On one hand, God the Father is an infinite person, beyond the limits of our imagination. He is all-powerful, and yet, on the other hand, He is loving and *approachable, as our Father.* This is really beautiful if you can grasp it.

There are two or three instances where the Bible says that God's throne is in heaven. Revelation 4 is one of them. Daniel 7 is another. But there are also a number of scriptures that say heaven is too small to hold God's throne. Let's look at a couple of those:

> 1 Thus says the LORD,
> "Heaven is My throne, and the earth is My footstool.
> Where then is a house you could build for Me?
> And where is a place that I may rest? . . ."
>
> —Isaiah 66

God says that heaven is His throne and the earth His footstool. That is a gigantic God! Here is another:

> 27 "But will God indeed dwell on the earth? Behold, heaven and the highest heaven cannot contain Thee, how much less this house which I have built! . . ."
>
> —1 Kings 8

All of heaven cannot contain God. Yet conversely, He is "condensible" enough (if that's the right word), that He can fit on a throne and be a person that we can approach. I can think of a couple of crude analogies to illustrate this. A balloon can expand and contract, varying its size. In some senses, God seems to have this ability. He fills the whole universe, and yet we also have the *fullness* of God dwelling inside of us!

14 For this reason, I bow my knees before the Father,

15 from whom every family in heaven and on earth derives its name,

16 that He would grant you, according to the riches of His glory, to be strengthened with power through His Spirit in the inner man;

17 so that Christ may dwell in your hearts through faith; *and* that you, being rooted and grounded in love,

18 may be able to comprehend with all the saints what is the breadth and length and height and depth,

19 and to know the love of Christ which surpasses knowledge, that you may be filled up to all the fulness of God.

—Ephesians 3

With our laws of physics, it is inconceivable to us to be filled with all the fullness of God while He fills all the universe. Yet the Bible says that both are true.

I do not want to detract at all from God, as we look at Him as a person Who does have a face, hands, a back, a front, and other parts of a body. This is not an attempt to make God in our image; remember, we were made in His image! He is an incredible, fantastic person, who loves you and me and was willing to sacrifice His Son that you and I might have eternal life. Praise You, Father!

We need to pray and ask God the Father to show us what He is like and how to relate to Him, because we want to love Him and serve Him. He will do it, if we only ask Him. He will make Himself very real and precious to us if we just wait on Him and let Him reveal Himself to us.

Evidently John is now in heaven in his spirit, and remains there through Revelation 9. In Revelation 10, John apparently comes back to earth, because he says, "I saw an angel descending out of heaven." So roughly from this point through Chapter 9, John is going to be in heaven observing things which are occurring there, in a preview sense.

REVELATION 4:3-6
-THE THRONE ROOM

3 And He who was sitting *was* like a jasper stone and a sardis in appearance; and *there was* a rainbow around the throne, like an emerald in appearance.

4 And around the throne *were* twenty-four thrones; and upon the thrones I *saw* twenty-four elders sitting, clothed in white garments, and golden crowns on their heads.

5 And from the throne proceed flashes of lightning and sounds and peals of thunder. And *there were* seven lamps of fire burning before the throne, which are the seven Spirits of God;

6 and before the throne *there was,* as it were, a sea of glass like crystal; and in the center and around the throne, four living creatures full of eyes in front and behind.

—Revelation 4

In verse 3, it mentions three stones: jasper (sometimes called crystal or diamond), sardis (which is very red), and a rainbow which appeared like an emerald (green). In Exodus 18:17, these were the three jewels on the first row of the breastplate of the priests. Also, these are three of the jewels that are the foundation for the holy city (Revelation 21:19-20). Why God chose these particular three has had much speculation. Some people believe that He chose the jasper, or diamond, because God is light and emits light; the sardis (red) for the blood of Christ or to imply justice or judgment; and the emerald (green) to imply mercy. We can come up with a lot of conjecture, but we really don't know why He chose these three.

The rainbow could be a reference back to the promise to Noah, which is really a promise of mercy on God's part. A legitimate translation of the word "rainbow" from the Greek would be "halo." I would probably lean toward this latter translation a little more—that is, that which John saw around the throne was an emerald-colored halo.

In verse 5, we read: "And from the throne proceed flashes of lightning and sounds and peals of thunder. . . ." I don't think that these flashes of lightning are the jaggedy lightning bolts that streak through the sky, but rather what is called blanket or area lightning, where the whole sky lights up. I can imagine this blanket lightning continually surging out from the throne, like a giant halo. God is light, and He would be emitting a tremendously brilliant light.

Sounds like peals of thunder are also said to proceed from the throne. Those of you who have hi–fi equipment and can get down into the very low cycles with a real big base speaker, know that the walls and floors vibrate with the sound. I know one hi-fi "nut" who had a cement slab floor with a big base speaker mounted in it. It carried sound so low that you could not hear it, but you could feel it. I think that this may be the vibrating sense of the sound coming from God's throne, which accompanies the flashes of blanket lightning. I am sure that John had an awesome sense of God's power as he viewed the throne. I would have a similar feeling if I were looking at a glowing atomic reactor, yet what John saw would make the atomic reactor look like a candle in comparison. John probably had a desire to fall on his face and worship the Lord as he viewed this awesome scene.

Much of what is contained in the book of Revelation also appears in the Old Testament. Lightning and thunder are normal manifestations when God makes His presence known on the earth. That is what Moses and the sons of Israel experienced when God manifested Himself to them on Mt. Sinai, so that the people might believe in Moses (Exodus 19:16, 19). There is also a reference to it in Psalm 18:

> 13 **The LORD also thundered in the heavens,**
> **And the Most High uttered His voice,**
> **Hailstones and coals of fire.**
> 14 **And He sent out His arrows, and scattered them,**
> **And lightning flashes in abundance, and routed them.**

In this case, the Lord was driving out an enemy. In Job 37 we read this:

> 2 **"Listen closely to the thunder of His voice,**
> **And the rumbling that goes out from His mouth.**
> 3 **"Under the whole heaven He lets it loose,**
> **And His lightning to the ends of the earth.**

> 4 "After it, a voice roars;
>   He thunders with His majestic voice;
>   And He does not restrain *the lightnings* when His voice is
>   heard.
> 5 "God thunders with His voice wondrously,
>   Doing great things which we cannot comprehend. . . ."

We begin to see that this is not something unique to the book of Revelation. Historically, this is the way that God has been described when making a personal appearance on the earth. This is something that is normal and common in the Bible, as is most of the symbolism used in the book of Revelation. If you say that you cannot understand Revelation, then you are saying you cannot understand Job, Psalms, Exodus, and the other books of the Bible that use the same language and symbols.

In reference to Revelation 4:6, which says: ". . . and before the throne *there was,* as it were, a sea of glass like crystal . . .", let's turn to Exodus 24:

> 10 and they saw the God of Israel; and under His feet there ap-
> peared to be a pavement of sapphire, as clear as the sky itself.

The sea of glass has been there at least since Exodus! This is not some "weird" symbol, unique to Revelation. Concerning this sea of glass, in the ancient days, many of the kings had a moat before their throne so that their enemies could not just come charging up and kill them. This was typically a body of water some forty or fifty feet wide. If they wanted somebody to approach the throne, they would let down a little bridge and the person would go forward. But the king could control the access to his throne by that "little sea."

What I perceive the scripture to be saying here is that God has made that sea solid, so *we are free to approach Him at any time.* Isn't that beautiful! We can come freely to the throne of grace, because of Jesus!

This sea is not like regular glass, but like cut crystal, sparkling like prisms. How beautiful is the approach to our God! (If there is a bridge across this sea at all, it is probably in the shape of a cross.)

REVELATION 4:6–8
–THE FOUR CREATURES

6 and before the throne *there was,* as it were, a sea of glass like crystal; and in the center and around the throne, four living creatures full of eyes in front and behind.

7 And the first creature *was* like a lion, and the second creature like a calf, and the third creature had a face like that of a man, and the fourth creature *was* like a flying eagle.

8 And the four living creatures, each one of them having six wings, are full of eyes around and within; and day and night they do not cease to say,

"HOLY, HOLY, HOLY, *is* THE LORD GOD, THE ALMIGHTY, who was and who is and who is to come."

As we just read, the first creature was like a lion, the second like a calf, the third had a face like a man, and the fourth was like a flying eagle. Each of them had six wings and many, many eyes.

You can look at this on one level, and say that the lion represents the wild beast, the calf (or the ox) represents the domestic beasts, the man represents man, and the eagle represents birds. With the exception of the fish, these creatures could represent, in a sense, the flesh and blood part of God's creation, and thus that all of His creation was praising Him.

It is interesting that there is an incredible similarity in these creatures to some that are described in the Old Testament. Let's look first at the easiest one, which is found in Isaiah 6:

1 In the year of King Uzziah's death, I saw the Lord sitting on a throne, lofty and exalted, with the train of His robe filling the temple.

2 Seraphim stood above Him, each having six wings; with two he covered his face, and with two he covered his feet, and with two he flew.

3 And one called out to another and said, "Holy, Holy, Holy, is the LORD of hosts, the whole earth is full of His glory."

Here we see the seraphim above God's throne. We will see something that is below God's throne in a minute. Each of them had six wings and they were praising and giving glory to God.

God created the seraphim explicitly to glorify Him night and day. Do you think they did it in a perfect way? Yes. And for whatever reason, they can do it better with six wings than two, or none. This is the way God created them, and for me to ask why He didn't make them with, say, four wings, is really a ridiculous question.

There is another thing in Ezekiel called the cherubim (cherub is singular), as we see in the following:

> 1 Now it came about in the thirtieth year, on the fifth *day* of the fourth month, while I was by the river Chebar among the exiles, the heavens were opened and I saw visions of God. . . .
>
> 4 and as I looked, behold, a storm wind was coming from the north, a great cloud with fire flashing forth continually and a bright light around it, and in its midst something like glowing metal in the midst of the fire.
>
> 5 And within it there were figures resembling four living beings. And this was their appearance: they had human form.
>
> 6 Each of them had four faces and four wings.
>
> 7 And their legs were straight and their feet were like a calf's hoof, and they gleamed like burnished bronze.
>
> 8 Under their wings on their four sides *were* human hands. As for the faces and wings of the four of them,
>
> 9 their wings touched one another; their *faces* did not turn when they moved, each went straight forward.
>
> 10 As for the form of their faces, *each* had the face of a man, all four had the face of a lion on the right and the face of a bull on the left, and all four had the face of an eagle.
>
> —Ezekiel 1

We will find out later that these were cherubim. It says they had four faces—one on each side—which are identical to the faces that John saw on the living creatures in Revelation. One of the reasons for the wings probably is that they moved quickly, as we see reading further in Ezekiel 1:

> 14 And the living beings ran to and fro like bolts of lightning.

This chapter goes on to describe an expanse of crystal over the heads of the cherubim, above which was a throne. This sounds more than slightly like John's description of the sea of glass that is before the throne of God:

22 Now over the heads of the living beings there was something like an expanse, like the awesome gleam of crystal, extended over their heads. . . .

26 Now above the expanse that was over their heads there was something resembling a throne . . .

—Ezekiel 1

Turning to Ezekiel 10, we find further details on the cherubim:

1 Then I looked, and behold, in the expanse that was over the heads of the cherubim something like a sapphire stone in appearance resembling a throne, appeared above them.

2 And He spoke to the man clothed in linen and said, "Enter between the whirling wheels under the cherubim, and fill your hands with coals of fire from between the cherubim, and scatter *them* over the city." And he entered in my sight.

3 Now the cherubim were standing on the right side of the temple when the man entered, and the cloud filled the inner court.

4 Then the glory of the LORD went up from the cherub to the threshold of the temple, and the temple was filled with the cloud, and the court was filled with the brightness of the glory of the LORD.

5 Moreover, the sound of the wings of the cherubim was heard as far as the outer court, like the voice of God Almighty when He speaks.

6 And it came about when He commanded the man clothed in linen, saying, "Take fire from between the whirling wheels, from between the cherubim," he entered and stood beside a wheel.

7 Then the cherub stretched out his hand from between the cherubim to the fire which *was* between the cherubim, took some and put it into the hands of the one clothed in linen, who took *it* and went out. . . .

14 And each one had four faces. The first face *was* the face of a cherub, the second face *was* the face of a man, the third the face of a lion, and the fourth the face of an eagle. . . .

18 Then the glory of the LORD departed from the threshold of the temple and stood over the cherubim.

19 When the cherubim departed, they lifted their wings and rose up from the earth in my sight with the wheels beside them; and they stood still at the entrance of the east gate of the LORD'S house. And the glory of the God of Israel hovered over them.

20 These are the living beings that I saw beneath the God of Israel by the river Chebar; so I knew that they *were* cherubim.

21 Each one had four faces and each one four wings, and beneath their wings *was* the form of human hands.

22 As for the likeness of their faces, they were the same faces whose appearance I had seen by the river Chebar. Each one went straight ahead.

—Ezekiel 10

I believe that these four creatures are the same creatures described in Revelation. God's throne is above these cherubim, and above God's throne are the seraphim. So there are creatures to glorify the Lord both above and below His throne!

The cherubim also appear in Exodus. The tabernacle contained the holy of holies and the main thing in the holy of holies was the ark. Inside the ark were the tablets of the Ten Commandments. What was on top of the ark?—*cherubim:*

16 "And you shall put into the ark the testimony which I shall give you.

17 "And you shall make a mercy seat of pure gold, two and a half cubits long and one and a half cubits wide.

18 "And you shall make two cherubim of gold, make them of hammered work at the two ends of the mercy seat.

19 "And make one cherub at one end and one cherub at the other end; you shall make the cherubim *of one piece* with the mercy seat at its two ends.

20 "And the cherubim shall have *their* wings spread upward, covering the mercy seat with their wings and facing one another; the faces of the cherubim are to be *turned* toward the mercy seat.

21 "And you shall put the mercy seat on top of the ark, and in the ark you shall put the testimony which I shall give to you.

22 "And there I will meet with you; and from between the cherubim which are upon the ark of the testimony, I will speak to you about all that I will give you in commandment for the sons of Israel. . . ."

—Exodus 25

The mercy seat is where God met the high priest. His presence and His glory were manifested there, between the two cherubim. For whatever reason, that is the place and the way in which God chose to meet with His people in those days.

In Revelation, John is looking at God's throne, whereat the nations will eventually be meeting God. The cherubim are going to be there, representing all living beings glorifying God. In Revelation 4:8 they are worshiping the Lord and magnifying Him, not for anything that He has done, but simply for who He is. They are involved with the person of God the Father. Day and night they do not cease to say: "HOLY, HOLY, HOLY, *is* THE LORD GOD, THE ALMIGHTY, who was and who is and who is to come" (Revelation 4:8).

In Revelation 4:10-11, the 24 elders are praising God for what He has done. Some people almost always praise God for what He does and not for who He is. I think we need to find a balance between the two. Much of our praise and adoration should be simply because of who He is. True love is not dependent upon performance.

REVELATION 4:9-11
—THE 24 ELDERS

9 And when the living creatures give glory and honor and thanks to Him who sits on the throne, to Him who lives forever and ever,

10 the twenty-four elders will fall down before Him who sits on the throne, and will worship Him who lives forever and ever, and will cast their crowns before the throne, saying,

11 "Worthy art Thou, our Lord and our God, to receive glory and honor and power; for Thou didst create all things, and because of Thy will they existed, and were created."

—Revelation 4

This is a tough section, and there is probably more disagreement as to who the 24 elders are than on just about anything else in Revelation. There are some who say they are the 12 disciples and the 12 patriarchs of the Old Testament. Some say they represent the church. Others say that they are all from Israel. We could examine many of these theories and why I do not think they are valid, but let me instead simply share what I believe is the best interpretation.

The best thing that I can come up with is that the 24 elders are leaders of angels—generals or elders of the angels, if I can use this term. Let me give you several reasons why I believe this.

Further in the book of Revelation, we read this:

> 8 And when He had taken the book, the four living creatures and the twenty-four elders fell down before the Lamb, having each one a harp, and golden bowls of incense, which are the prayers of the saints.
>
> 9 And they sang a new song, saying,
> "Worthy art Thou to take the book, and to break its seals; for Thou was slain, and didst purchase for God with Thy blood *men* from every tribe and tongue and people and nation.
>
> 10 "And Thou hast made them *to be* a kingdom and priests to our God; and they will reign upon the earth."
>
> —Revelation 5

In verse 10, the elders are talking about the Christians as *them*, not *us*. Three chapters later, we read this:

> 3 And another angel came and stood at the altar, holding a golden censer; and much incense was given to him, that he might add it to the prayers of all the saints upon the golden altar which was before the throne.
>
> —Revelation 8

Note that an angel is handling the golden bowls that contained the prayers of the saints. So here an angel is doing what the 24 elders are doing in Revelation 5. Let's look further:

> 9 After these things I looked, and behold a great multitude, which no one could count, from every nation and all tribes and peoples and tongues, standing before the throne and before the Lamb, clothed in white robes, and palm branches were in their hands;
>
> 10 and they cry out with a loud voice, saying,
> "Salvation to our God who sits on the throne, and to the Lamb."
>
> 11 And all the angels were standing around the throne and *around* the elders and the four living creatures; and they fell on their faces before the throne and worshiped God.
>
> 12 saying,
> "Amen, blessing and glory and wisdom and thanksgiving and honor and power and might, *be* to our God forever and ever. Amen."

13   And one of the elders answered, saying to me, "These who are clothed in the white robes, who are they, and from where have they come?"

14   And I said to him, "My lord, you know." And he said to me, "These are the ones who come out of the great tribulation, and they have washed their robes and made them white in the blood of the Lamb. . . ."

—Revelation 7

John called one of these elders "My lord," which would also lead me to believe that these were angelic leaders of some type, since John would not call another Christian that. Verse 9 deals with the Christians, while verse 11 deals with angels, the elders, and the four creatures. Thus, the elders are grouped with the angels and not with the Christians.

Ephesians 3 talks about the rulers in the heavenly places (angelic rulers):

8   To me, the very least of all saints, this grace was given, to preach to the Gentiles the unfathomable riches of Christ,

9   and to bring to light what is the administration of the mystery which for ages has been hidden in God, who created all things;

10   in order that the manifold wisdom of God might now be made known through the church to the rulers and the authorities in the heavenly *places.*

Let me restate that I do not believe that is absolute scriptural proof as to who the elders really are. I feel that there is more scriptural evidence that they are angel leaders than anything else. Therefore, we will consider them to be such for the remainder of this book.

REVELATION 5:1–14
–WORTHY IS THE LAMB

As we begin this exciting chapter, we need to remember that the Greek word translated "book" should more accurately be translated "scroll."

1   And I saw in the right hand of Him who sat on the throne a book written inside and on the back, sealed up with seven seals.

2   And I saw a strong angel proclaiming with a loud voice, "Who is worthy to open the book and to break its seals?"

3   And no one in heaven, or on the earth, or under the earth, was able to open the book, or to look into it.

4   And I *began* to weep greatly, because no one was found worthy to open the book, or to look into it;

5   and one of the elders said to me, "Stop weeping; behold, the Lion that is from the tribe of Judah, the Root of David, has overcome so as to open the book and its seven seals."

6   And I saw between the throne (with the four living creatures) and the elders a Lamb standing, as if slain, having seven horns and seven eyes, which are the seven Spirits of God, sent out into all the earth.

7   And He came, and He took *it* out of the right hand of Him who sat on the throne.

8   And when He had taken the book, the four living creatures and the twenty-four elders fell down before the Lamb, having each one a harp, and golden bowls of incense, which are the prayers of the saints.

9   And they sang a new song, saying,

"Worthy art Thou to take the book, and to break its seals; for Thou wast slain, and didst purchase for God with Thy blood *men* from every tribe and tongue and people and nation.

10   "And Thou hast made them *to be* a kingdom and priests to our God; and they will reign upon the earth."

11   And I looked, and I heard the voice of many angels around the throne and the living creatures and the elders; and the number of them was myriads of myriads, and thousands of thousands,

12   saying with a loud voice,

"Worthy is the Lamb that was slain to receive power and riches and wisdom and might and honor and glory and blessing."

13   And every created thing which is in heaven and on the earth and under the earth and on the sea, and all things in them, I heard saying,

"To Him who sits on the throne, and to the Lamb, *be* blessing and honor and glory and dominion forever and ever."

14   And the four living creatures kept saying, "Amen." And the elders fell down and worshiped.

—Revelation 5

If you viewed the whole Bible as a drama, in the drama you would have a climax and an anti–climax, which is the action that takes place after the climax. I am not saying that this scene is more important than the crucifixion, the resurrection, the ascension or the new heaven and new earth; what I am saying is that in viewing the Bible as a play or drama, this is the climax. I can almost see on the stage millions of people all shouting in unison, and thousands of angels praising God, and the trumpets blasting! At last, our dilemma has been solved, and there is someone who is *worthy* to open the scroll! Every created being is proclaiming praises to God! What a scene that will be!

Turning from the grand, general view of this scene, let us look at some of the specifics. One of the reasons that the word should be translated "scroll" and not "book" is because in those days they had no leaf–type books. Everything written was on a scroll.

As I mentioned in my previous book, *CHRISTIANS WILL GO THROUGH THE TRIBULATION—And how to prepare for it,* if somebody very important were sending a message to another very high official, he would write out his message and seal the scroll at that point. Then he might write instructions to perhaps a lieutenant, roll it further and seal it at that point. He may include instructions to a doorman, roll it up and seal it there. So when the scroll arrived at this high official's house, the lowest official would open the first seal and roll it back to the second seal. The message between those two seals might say, "Please deliver this to the governor's lieutenant." The governor's lieutenant would then break the next seal. (The lower official would not dare to break it, because he was not authorized—he wasn't *worthy.*) So the lieutenant would roll the scroll back to the third seal, but would not break that one. This would continue until the scroll reached the high official. A person had to be *worthy* or authorized to break these seals as he unrolled the scroll. We will see this occurring in the next chapters.

Now God the Father has, in His hand, a scroll which holds the end–time events of this age and eternity. No one can take it out of God's hand. So the timing of the starting of these events is up to God the Father. Satan is in charge of the earth (and he seems to be gaining ground every day). If no one were ever worthy to open the scroll, there would never be any end to Satan's control of earth. In the scroll are contained God's judgments of evil and what He is going to do to purify the earth. If that scroll were never opened, those events would never take place, and Satan would continue in his dominion—the earth would get deeper and deeper in sin.

This might be why John was weeping. I can just see everyone groaning and wondering if Satan's rule is going to go on for thousands or perhaps millions of years. *Somebody* must be worthy to open the scroll so that the events can be triggered to begin purification of the earth and to end Satan's rule. In a sense, this scroll is almost like the title deed to the earth.

If Christ had not been slain, He would not have been worthy to open the scroll. He had to become a slain Lamb in order to be worthy. At some point Christ shifts from the slain Lamb to the Lion, which is the King and the Master. We see that happen in Revelation 5. When He takes that scroll from God's hand, He switches from a suffering Savior to *King* of the earth, and from that point on He directs the judgments against the earth, in preparation for His return when He is going to totally defeat Satan. We are looking at the point in time when the transference actually takes place. The timing is in God's hands. Christ is worthy! He is today still sitting as our mediator and intercessor. Someday He is going to switch from that role to one of *King,* and take His property—the earth—for which God is holding the title deed in His hands.

Christ had the heart attitude of someone who had sacrificed His life. He said: ". . . learn of me; for I am meek and lowly . . ." (Matthew 11:29 *KVJ).* Sheep are meek and lowly. I am sure that He had the marks on Him from the death that He had experienced. Yet in His humility, He comes up and takes the scroll, and then becomes in full essence the *Lion of Judah*—the King of the earth! Now those standing nearby can see that Satan's reign is coming to an end, and they begin to rejoice! There is then a time of exultation and praise! They sing a new song that they have never sung before, recorded in verses 9 and 10.

Do you believe that Christ's work is finished? You hear people talk about the finished work of Christ. Absolutely not! The Lamb part is finished, but there is another whole part yet to come. His work is not completed by any means. It is exciting to think that possibly at this minute, the Lamb is taking the scroll out of God's hands, and all the angels of heaven are rejoicing with a new song! As we will see, as He breaks each seal and opens the scroll and reads what is there, the events recorded in each portion simultaneously occur on the earth.

As the Lamb, Christ had seven horns. The horn was a sign of authority in the Old Testament. In Psalm 18 we read:

> 2 **The LORD is my rock and my fortress and my deliverer,**
> **My God, my rock, in whom I take refuge;**
> **My shield and the horn of my salvation, my stronghold.**

This is not something that you or I would say. "Horn" is a term that is foreign to us, yet back then it was a common expression. Let's look at another Psalm, which talks about the Lord's horn being exalted.

> 9 **He has given freely to the poor;**
> **His righteousness endures forever;**
> **His horn will be exalted in honor.**
> 10 **The wicked will see it and be vexed;**
> **He will gnash his teeth and melt away;**
> **The desire of the wicked will perish.**

> —Psalm 112

Revelation 5:10 says that the kingdom of priests will reign on the earth. Reflect back on the beatitudes. Who is going to inherit the earth? . . . *the meek*. There is a sense of meekness in recognizing that we are priests before God. If we want to rule and reign with Christ, we must be meek. I don't believe that the proud and haughty are going to be among this group.

To me, this whole chapter of Revelation presents a glorious picture of the way God has everything in His hands; the timing is His, the Lamb is worthy to open the scroll, God has created beings just for His glory, and He has created us to be as a nation of priests! One day soon, God is going to hand that scroll to the Lamb, and He will judge the earth and purge it of evil. Hallelujah!

4

THE RAPTURE
AND THE TRIBULATION

In Chapter 5 of Revelation, we saw real rejoicing because Christ was worthy to take the scroll and open it. In Chapter 6, I believe that the Tribulation itself, or at least the "time of sorrows" that we read about in Matthew 24, begins.

Before we get into the events that are going to occur during the Tribulation, I think that it is important to explore briefly the question of the Rapture of the church. The reason that this is important is that you will view Chapters 6 through 19 of Revelation very differently, depending on how you feel about whether or not Christians will go through the Tribulation. If you think that they are going to experience this period, then you need to look at the events we will read about in the next chapters as things that are very possibly going to happen to you, and you will need to prayerfully consider how you should prepare for them. If you believe that the church will be raptured out beforehand, you then would consider yourself to be up in heaven looking down at these poor people going through these things. That is a very important question which will determine not only how you view the book of Revelation, but many of your own daily decisions, such as what job to take, where to live, how to structure your house, and things of this nature.

The second important question (particularly if you have decided that Christians will go through the Tribulation) is, "how near is it?" If it is hundreds of years away, or even several decades, we need not be very concerned about preparation. On the other hand, if it appears to be fairly close, we probably should be making some preparation or at least be praying about what preparations God would have us to make. He may say to do nothing, He may guide you to make extensive preparations, or anything in between.

THE RAPTURE

The word Rapture is not used in the English translations of the Bible (but is in the Latin). Hal Lindsey, whom I know personally, author of *The Late Great Planet Earth*, uses the expression "the great snatch" to describe the time when Christians will be caught up in the air to meet the Lord. We will be using the word "Rapture" since it is a common term used to refer to this event. What we will primarily be discussing in this chapter is *when* the Rapture is going to occur. In 1 Thessalonians 4, we read:

> 16 For the Lord Himself will descend from heaven with a shout, with the voice of *the* archangel, and with the trumpet of God; and the dead in Christ shall rise first.
> 17 Then we who are alive and remain shall be caught up together with them in the clouds to meet the Lord in the air, and thus we shall always be with the Lord.

Whenever this event occurs, from that point through all eternity, Jesus and I will never be separated! Praise God!

In those two verses we have a listing of things characteristic of the Rapture: the Lord descends from heaven; He is in the clouds; there is a trumpet and a shout (loud voice); the dead rise first (resurrection); then the Christians who are alive are caught up together with Him in the air.

Figure 2 lists these characteristics, and provides a matrix showing which of these characteristics are found in other passages dealing with the Rapture.

THE OLIVET DISCOURSE

Christ's greatest discourse on the future, the Tribulation and His Second Coming is found in Matthew 24. Let us see what gave rise to this revelation:

MATT. 24	1 COR. 15	1 THES. 4	REV. 11	EVENT
X		X		LORD IN AIR
		X	X	SHOUT
	X	X	X	TRUMPET
X	X	X	X	DEAD RISE
X	X	X.	X	ALIVE CHRISTIANS CAUGHT UP (CHANGED)

Figure 2

3 And as He was sitting on the Mount of Olives, the disciples came to Him privately, saying, "Tell us, when will these things be, and what *will* be the sign of Your coming, and of the end of the age?"

Here we see that the disciples have asked Jesus a very straightforward question: "What will be the sign of Your coming and of the end of the age?" I believe that He gave them a no-nonsense, straightforward answer. He always did this with His disciples; when they asked Him something privately about a parable He had just told, He would explain it to them.

Now let us look at Christ's answer to the question about what the sign of His coming and the end of this age would be. Reading again in Matthew 24, we see this:

4 And Jesus answered and said to them, "See to it that no one misleads you.

5 "For many will come in My name, saying, 'I am the Christ,' and will mislead many.

6 "And you will be hearing of wars and rumors of wars; see that you are not frightened, for *those things* must take place, but *that* is not yet the end.

7 "For nation will rise against nation, and kingdom against kingdom, and in various places there will be famines and earthquakes.

8 "But all these things are *merely* the beginning of birth pangs.

9 "Then they will deliver you to tribulation, and will kill you, and you will be hated by all nations on account of My name.

10 "And at that time many will fall away and will deliver up one another and hate one another.

11 "And many false prophets will arise, and will mislead many.

12 "And because lawlessness is increased, most people's love will grow cold.

13 "But the one who endures to the end, he shall be saved.

14 "And this gospel of the kingdom shall be preached in the whole world for a witness to all the nations, and then the end shall come.

15 "Therefore when you see the ABOMINATION OF DESOLATION which was spoken of through Daniel the prophet, standing in the holy place (let the reader understand),

16 then let those who are in Judea flee to the mountains.

17 let him who is on the housetop not go down to get the things out that are in his house;

18 and let him who is in the field not turn back to get his cloak.

19 "But woe to those who are with child and to those who nurse babes in those days!

20 "But pray that your flight may not be in the winter, or on a Sabbath; . . ."

All that we have read thus far is just the *birth pangs* (a time of sorrows). There is war, persecution, famine and the preaching of the gospel to the whole world. Verse 21 begins the description of the great Tribulation. Regardless of what a person might believe about when the Rapture will occur, we are all going through the very rough times known as "birth pangs." *After* the birth pangs comes the great Tribulation:

21 ". . . for then there will be a great tribulation, such as has not occurred since the beginning of the world until now, nor ever shall. . . ."

—Matthew 24

The Tribulation discussed here has never happened before, and it will never happen again. Many people and countries have experienced tribulations, but not the "great Tribulation." This great Tribulation could be three and a half years in length, or seven, or ten and a half. The most common view is that it will last seven years. Christ then goes on to discuss this great Tribulation:

22   "And unless those days had been cut short, no life would have been saved; but for the sake of the elect those days shall be cut short.
—Matthew 24

Here Christ uses the word *elect* to describe Christians. He is stating that there are going to be Christians on earth during the Tribulation. It will be cut short for their sake; otherwise no one would make it through. Christ then describes what the Christians (elect) will encounter during the great Tribulation:

23   "Then if anyone says to you, 'Behold, here is the Christ,' or 'There *He is,'* do not believe *him.*

24   "For false Christs and false prophets will arise and will show great signs and wonders, so as to mislead, if possible, even the elect.

25   "Behold, I have told you in advance.

26   "If therefore they say to you, 'Behold, He is in the wilderness,' do not go forth, *or,* 'Behold, He is in the inner rooms,' do not believe *them.*

27   "For just as the lightning comes from the east, and flashes even to the west, so shall the coming of the Son of Man be.

28   "Wherever the corpse is, there the vultures will gather.

29   "But immediately after the tribulation of those days THE SUN WILL BE DARKENED, AND THE MOON WILL NOT GIVE ITS LIGHT, AND THE STARS WILL FALL from the sky, and the powers of the heavens will be shaken.

30   and then the sign of the Son of Man will appear in the sky, and then all the tribes of the earth will mourn, and they will see the SON OF MAN COMING ON THE CLOUDS OF THE SKY with power and great glory.

31   "And He will send forth His angels WITH A GREAT TRUMPET and THEY WILL GATHER TOGETHER His elect FROM THE FOUR WINDS, FROM ONE END OF THE SKY TO THE OTHER.
—Matthew 24

Verses 29–31 talk about Christ's Second Coming. At the time of His Second Coming, there is a gathering of the elect (the Christians). The elect, who are gathered together from the four winds (which is one way to describe the four corners of the earth) would be the Christians who had gone through the Tribulation and were still alive. The Christians gathered from one end of the sky to the other would represent the dead Christians. Here we see that the angels will gather together to Christ in the air both the alive Christians and those who have died. Christ is in the clouds, and there is a trumpet.

1 Thessalonians 4:16–17 could be describing this same event. Certainly all of the factors, except the shout, are identical.

If an event as big as a Rapture were going to occur earlier, before the Tribulation, Christ surely would have mentioned it. There is no reason that He would omit it in discussing the beginning of the Tribulation and include it at the end of the Tribulation. To place the Rapture before the Tribulation, it would be necessary to cut out verses 29 to 31, and put them between verses 20 and 21. One would have to do some juggling of scriptures in order to achieve this.

Based on the list in Figure 2, I would say that verses 29–31 are exactly the same things described in 1 Thessalonians 4. It appears that these two passages are describing the same event.

Before looking at another of Paul's descriptions of the Rapture, it is interesting to note that no one claims that Jesus Christ taught a pre–Tribulation Rapture. To me it doesn't make sense that God would "reveal" this to Paul, and not to His own Son!

THE RAPTURE IN CORINTHIANS

In his first letter to the Christians at Corinth, Paul gives some additional insights on the Rapture:

> **50** Now I say this, brethren, that flesh and blood cannot inherit the kingdom of God; nor does the perishable inherit the imperishable.
>
> **51** Behold, I tell you a mystery; we shall not all sleep, but we shall all be changed,
>
> **52** in a moment, in the twinkling of an eye, at the last trumpet; for the trumpet will sound, and the dead will be raised imperishable, and we shall be changed.
>
> –1 Corinthians 15

We will discuss "the mystery" later. Here it is sufficient to note that the word *mystery* is talked about in the future tense. It is something that has not yet been fulfilled. The word for *sleep* used here is one of the Biblical words for *die*.

In verse 52, we have the sounding of the trumpet and the dead being raised. As we are caught up in the air with the dead people, we will all be transformed. The main thing isn't being caught up in the air; the main thing is that we will all be changed so that our bodies will be like Christ's resurrected body and our spirits will be perfected.

One new thing that we are told here is *when* this is going to occur—at the last trumpet. The definition of "first" means there cannot be anything before it, or it wouldn't be the first. "Last" means that there cannot be any after it, or it wouldn't be the last. The Bible says that we will be changed and the dead will be raised *at the last trumpet*. There cannot be any more trumpets talked about in the Bible after the last one, or it would not be the last one.

Let's turn to Revelation 8:

> 1 And when He broke the seventh seal, there was silence in heaven for about half an hour.
>
> 2 And I saw the seven angels who stand before God; and seven trumpets were given to them.

These are God's trumpets that He gives to these seven angels to blow at His command. If you read further, in verse 7 the first trumpet sounds, in verse 8 the second, in verse 10 the third, and in verse 12 the fourth trumpet sounds. In Revelation 7:1 the fifth trumpet is sounded, and in verse 13 the sixth trumpet is sounded. Then in Revelation 11 we read this:

> 15 And the seventh angel sounded; and there arose loud voices in heaven, saying,
>
> "The kingdom of the world has become *the kingdom* of our Lord, and of His Christ; and He will reign forever and ever."
>
> 16 And the twenty-four elders, who sit on their thrones before God, fell on their faces and worshiped God,
>
> 17 saying,
>
> "We give Thee thanks, O Lord God, the Almighty, who art and who wast, because Thou hast taken Thy great power and hast begun to reign.
>
> 18 "And the nations were enraged, and Thy wrath came, and the time came for the dead to be judged, and *the time* to give their reward to Thy bond-servants the prophets and to the saints and to

those who fear Thy name, the small and the great, and to destroy
those who destroy the earth."

19 And the temple of God which is in heaven was opened; and
the ark of His covenant appeared in His temple, and there were
flashes of lightning and sounds and peals of thunder and an earthquake and a great hailstorm.

In verse 18, we see that this is a time for giving reward
to the Christians, the bond-servants and the prophets. We also
have the lightning and peals of thunder which are characteristic
of God, as we discussed in the last chapter.

Let's pause and summarize what happens at the seventh
trumpet, which is the last trumpet mentioned in the Bible:
Christ begins to reign, the dead are going to be judged, the
Christians are going to be rewarded, and Christ is going to destroy evil.

In Revelation 11:15, it says that the seventh angel sounded,
which is the trumpet. It says there arose loud voices; that is the
shout that we mentioned earlier. The dead then rise and the
Christians are caught up. So here we have the same list of things
occurring as we read in Matthew 24, 1 Thessalonians 4, and
1 Corinthians 15. Whenever the seventh trumpet sounds, all of
this will occur. If that trumpet sounds in the middle of the Tribulation, then the Rapture will occur at that point. If it sounds
at the end of the Tribulation, then it will occur at the end of
the Tribulation. The Rapture will occur at the last trumpet,
which places it in the middle or at the end of the Tribulation.
Matthew 24 places it at the end, rather than in the middle.

If the last trumpet had been a plague of grasshoppers, then
this interpretation would not be valid. But the events of the
seventh (last) trumpet are exactly what *should* occur at the
Rapture.

I do not believe that the book of Revelation is sequential,
because here in Revelation 11 it says that Christ begins to reign,
and everything else we see in scripture says that the reign is a
thousand-year reign, yet the chapters of Revelation immediately following the sounding of the seventh trumpet do not depict
this peaceful thousand-year reign. What the Lord has shown
me, which He may or may not show you, is that basically Chap-

ters 12 through 19 are snapshots or flashbacks of some of the events of the Tribulation.

REVELATION 20:1-6
–RESURRECTION

Let's consider one other thing here: is there a resurrection in connection with the Rapture? The answer is a definite *yes.* In the previous passages of scripture concerning the Rapture, we see that the dead are raised.

I place the following passage in the same time sequence as the seventh trumpet. I believe this is an amplification of it:

1   And I saw an angel coming down from heaven, having the key of the abyss and a great chain in his hand.

2   And he laid hold of the dragon, the serpent of old, who is the devil and Satan, and bound him for a thousand years,

3   and threw him into the abyss, and shut *it* and sealed *it* over him, so that he should not deceive the nations any longer, until the thousand years were completed; after these things he must be released for a short time.

4   And I saw thrones, and they sat upon them, and judgment was given to them. And I *saw* the souls of those who had been beheaded because of the testimony of Jesus and because of the word of God, and those who had not worshiped the beast or his image, and had not received the mark upon their forehead and upon their hand; and they came to life and reigned with Christ for a thousand years.

5   The rest of the dead did not come to life until the thousand years were completed. This is the first resurrection.

–Revelation 20

It says here that this resurrection, at the end of the Tribulation, is the *first* resurrection. If there had been a resurrection seven years before, this would not have been the first one. We know that there is a resurrection as part of the Rapture (which occurs at the *last* trumpet). It says specifically that this is the first resurrection. There may be some after it, but there can be none before it. I feel that this clearly places the Rapture at the end of the Tribulation.

Earlier in this chapter, we made reference to a mystery,

spoken of in 1 Corinthians 15, that was yet future. If we are right in our interpretation, that mystery should be solved at the seventh trumpet. In Revelation 10 we read about the finishing of this mystery, in connection with the last trumpet.

> 7 . . . but in the days of the voice of the seventh angel, when he is about to sound, then the mystery of God is finished, as He preached to His servants the prophets.
>
> —Revelation 10

As you can see, if you interpret the Scriptures simply and straightforwardly, the overwhelming preponderance of evidence is that Christians will indeed go through the Tribulation, and that the Rapture is a part of Christ's return in power and glory at the end of the Tribulation. There is much more evidence that we could have looked at, and we could have considered the points, weak as they are, that would lead a person to believe in a pre–Tribulation Rapture. All of this was done in my book *CHRISTIANS WILL GO THROUGH THE TRIBULATION— And how to prepare for it.* If you are interested in pursuing this subject further, I would suggest that you read that book. (See order form at the back of this book.)

Before we leave this subject, however, we need to consider one other aspect. During the plagues in Egypt, the instance of Daniel in the lion's den, or Shadrach, Meshach and Abed-nego in the fiery furnace, God did not deliver them out of the difficulty, but protected them in it. I believe that He will do the same during the great Tribulation. Many of the plagues in Egypt basically did not affect the children of Israel. For example, we read in Exodus:

> 20 Now the LORD said to Moses, "Rise early in the morning and present yourself before Pharaoh, as he comes out to the water, and say to him, 'Thus says the LORD, "Let My people go, that they may serve Me.
>
> 21 "For if you will not let My people go, behold, I will send swarms of insects on you and on your servants and on your people and into your houses; and the houses of the Egyptians shall be full of swarms of insects, and also the ground on which they *dwell.*
>
> 22 "But on that day I will set apart the land of Goshen, where My people are living, so that no swarms of insects will be there, in order that you may know that I, the LORD, am in the midst of the land.

23   "And I will put a division between My people and your people. Tomorrow this sign shall occur."'"

—Exodus 8

1   Then the LORD said to Moses, "Go to Pharaoh and speak to him, 'Thus says the LORD, the God of the Hebrews, "Let My people go, that they may serve Me.

2   "For if you refuse to let *them* go, and continue to hold them,

3   behold the hand of the LORD will come *with* a very severe pestilence on your livestock which are in the field, on the horses, on the donkeys, on the camels, on the herds, and on the flocks.

4   "But the LORD will make a distinction between the livestock of Israel and the livestock of Egypt, so that nothing will die of all that belongs to the sons of Israel."'"

5   And the LORD set a definite time, saying, "Tomorrow the LORD will do this thing in the land."

6   So the LORD did this thing on the morrow, and all the livestock of Egypt died; but of the livestock of the sons of Israel, not one died.

7   And Pharaoh sent, and behold, there was not even one of the livestock of Israel dead. But the heart of Pharaoh was hardened, and he did not let the people go. . . .

22   Now the LORD said to Moses, "Stretch out your hand toward the sky, that hail may fall on all the land of Egypt, on man and on beast and on every plant of the field, throughout the land of Egypt."

23   And Moses stretched out his staff toward the sky, and the LORD sent thunder and hail, and fire ran down to the earth. And the LORD rained hail on the land of Egypt.

24   So there was hail, and fire flashing continually in the midst of the hail, very severe, such as had not been in all the land of Egypt since it became a nation.

25   And the hail struck all that was in the field through all the land of Egypt, both man and beast; the hail also struck every plant of the field and shattered every tree of the field.

26   Only in the land of Goshen, where the sons of Israel *were,* there was no hail.

—Exodus 9

21   Then the LORD said to Moses, "Stretch out your hand toward the sky, that there may be darkness over the land of Egypt, even a darkness which may be felt."

22 So Moses stretched out his hand toward the sky, and there was thick darkness in all the land of Egypt for three days.

23 They did not see one another, nor did anyone rise from his place for three days, but all the sons of Israel had light in their dwellings.

—Exodus 10

Also, when the death angel passed over to kill the first born of all families and animals, the children of Israel were protected. However, they were only protected *if* they did what God had told them to do, which was to sprinkle the blood of the lamb over their door post. Similarly, God will protect us through the Tribulation *if* we do what He tells us to in preparation.

TRIBULATION, BUT NOT WRATH

Even though the Christians may experience the Tribulation, they will never experience the wrath of God (Romans 5:9, 1 Thessalonians 5:9,10). All the way through the Scriptures we are told that Christians *will* experience tribulation. For example, Jesus has this to say to us in John 16:

33 "These things I have spoken to you, that in Me you may have peace. In the world you have tribulation, but take courage; I have overcome the world."

Here He clearly informs us that we are going to have tribulation, but He tells us to have courage for He will give us victory over the world.

The apostle Paul said that we would enter the kingdom of God through tribulations:

21 And after they had preached the gospel to that city and had made many disciples, they returned to Lystra and to Iconium and to Antioch,

22 strengthening the souls of the disciples, encouraging them to continue in the faith, and *saying,* "Through many tribulations we must enter the kingdom of God."

—Acts 14

In Chapter 5 of his letter to the Romans, Paul amplifies on the subject of tribulation:

3 And not only this, but we also exult in our tribulations, knowing that tribulation brings about perseverance;

4 and perseverance, proven character; and proven character,
hope;

5 and hope does not disappoint, because the love of God has
been poured out within our hearts through the Holy Spirit who was
given to us.

–Romans 5

Paul expands further on this subject in a very precious way
in Romans 8:

35 Who shall separate us from the love of Christ? Shall tribulation,
or distress, or persecution, or famine, or nakedness, or peril, or
sword?

36 Just as it is written,

"FOR THY SAKE WE ARE BEING PUT TO DEATH ALL
     DAY LONG;
WE WERE CONSIDERED AS SHEEP TO BE SLAUGH-
     TERED."

37 But in all these things we overwhelmingly conquer through
Him who loved us.

38 For I am convinced that neither death, nor life, nor angels,
nor principalities, nor things present, nor things to come, nor powers,

39 nor height, nor depth, nor any other created thing, shall be
able to separate us from the love of God, which is in Christ Jesus
our Lord.

It is wonderful that all of the terrible things that will come
upon the earth during the Tribulation cannot separate us from
the love of Christ!

We have seen that Christians are expected to go through
tribulation; this does *not* mean that we will experience the wrath
of God. In Romans 5, Paul tells us that we will not:

9 Much more then, having now been justified by His blood, we
shall be saved from the wrath *of God* through Him.

By negative implication, we see the same thing in John 3:

36 "He who believes in the Son has eternal life; but he who does
not obey the Son shall not see life, but the wrath of God abides on
him."

This says that those who believe in the Son have eternal life, but those who do not obey Him not only will not have life, but the wrath of God abides on them. The implication is that those who believe in the Son will not experience the wrath of God.

The wrath of God will be poured out against the world. We can rejoice because we are not part of the world. Revelation 7:2-3 tells us that God will seal the foreheads of His bond-servants to protect them. Remember, God did not remove the children of Israel from Egypt during the plagues. If they obeyed Him, He protected them from the disasters being poured out upon the earth. Similarly, we can go through the Tribulation victoriously by following and obeying God.

PURPOSE OF THE TRIBULATION

What is the purpose of the Tribulation? If Christ were to come back tomorrow and begin His reign, He would have to destroy all the evil in the earth: the houses of prostitution, pornography, criminals, and so forth. He would have to get rid of all of the armies and governments because He will be the government. That would be a messy way to start His thousand-year reign of peace, love and joy. So the purpose of the Tribulation is to get rid of all this evil, and to plow up the earth so that it can become a garden once again. Some of the mountains, which keep the coastal winds from carrying water to the desert, will have to be flattened. To become a garden, the earth must be plowed up and be rid of all of the evil.

Through all the centuries, God has used His people to achieve His ends. I believe that the Christians will be mightily used of God during the Tribulation as His tools to get rid of evil. Later in Revelation, we will see people come against the two witnesses; when this happens, fire comes out of their mouths and their enemies are consumed. I think that it will be *fabulous* to see God use you and me to help purify the earth.

5

THE FIRST SIX SEALS
AND AN INTERLUDE
(Revelation 6 & 7)

In the last chapter we looked at whether or not Christians will go through the Tribulation. To me the most reasonable interpretation of the Scriptures, without trying to bend and hammer them, is that we will most likely go through the Tribulation. If the Tribulation and the coming of Christ are within our generation, what this chapter deals with will be events which we will be experiencing.

REVELATION 6:1–2
–THE FIRST SEAL

1 And I saw when the Lamb broke one of the seven seals, and I heard one of the four living creatures saying as with a voice of thunder, "Come."
2 And I looked, and behold, a white horse, and he who sat on it had a bow; and a crown was given to him; and he went out conquering, and to conquer.

–Revelation 6

Some translations read, "Come and see" at the end of verse 1. This has been added because the translators thought that the living creature was talking to John. The living creature is really calling forth the horse, as we will see when we get into the next three horses. He is saying to the horse, "Come forth."

The white horse had always bothered me. We know that this is not Christ. Christ comes on a white horse in Revelation 19. I could not understand who it represents until the Lord showed me that it is Christians on the white horse. Christians will be dressed in white robes because Christ is going to give us these robes, as we will see later. White is usually the color associated with a Christian, rather than with war and bloodshed. I believe that the rider on the white horse going out to conquer represents the gospel being spread to all the nations. To the Christians God has given a crown and authority, and He has given us a bow. Christ obviously doesn't need a bow to conquer. His only weapon is the word of His mouth.

Let's look at Mark to see why this interpretation might fit in. All of the seals are covered in Matthew 24 and Mark 13.

> 7 "And when you hear of wars and rumors of wars, do not be frightened; *those things* must take place; but *that is* not yet the end.
>
> 8 "For nation will arise against nation, and kingdom against kingdom; there will be earthquakes in various places; there will *also* be famines. These things are *merely* the beginning of birth pangs.
>
> 9 "But be on your guard; for they will deliver you up to *the* courts, and you will be flogged in *the* synagogues, and you will stand before governors and kings for My sake, as a testimony to them.
>
> 10 "And the gospel must first be preached to all the nations.
>
> 11 "And when they arrest you and deliver you up, do not be anxious beforehand about what you are to say, but say whatever is given you in that hour; for it is not you who speak, but *it is* the Holy Spirit.
>
> 12 "And brother will deliver up brother to death, and a father *his* child; and children will rise up against parents and have them put to death.
>
> 13 "And you will be hated by all on account of My name, but the one who endures to the end, he shall be saved. . . ."
>
> —Mark 13

If all of the things mentioned here are covered in the seals, verse 10—"and the gospel must first be preached to all the nations"—is absent in the seals *unless* it is fulfilled in the white horse. I believe that it is.

Let's now look at Zechariah 9:

11 As for you also, because of the blood of *My* covenant with
     you,
     I have set your prisoners free from the waterless pit.
12 Return to the stronghold, O prisoners who have the hope;
     This very day I am declaring that I will restore double to you.
13 For I will bend Judah as My bow,
     I will fill the bow with Ephraim.
     And I will stir up your sons, O Zion, against your sons, O
       Greece;
     And I will make you like a warrior's sword.
14 Then the LORD will appear over them,
     And His arrow will go forth like lightning;
     And the Lord GOD will blow the trumpet,
     And will march in the storm winds of the south.
15 The LORD of hosts will defend them.
     And they will devour, and trample on the sling stones;
     And they will drink, *and* be boisterous as with wine;
     And they will be filled like a *sacrificial* basin,
     Drenched like the corners of the altar.

Verse 13 tells us that God uses His people as His *bow*. As
we go out to conquer for Christ, in a spiritual sense, He uses us
as His bow to deliver arrows and to preach the gospel unto all
nations.

We can therefore appropriately say that the Tribulation is
going to start with Christians spreading the gospel. It could have
started yesterday or last week. There is no definite event that
we can look on, as I had previously thought, to begin the Tribulation. I don't believe we will know the day that the Tribulation
starts.

REVELATION 6:3–4
–THE SECOND SEAL

3 And when He broke the second seal, I heard the second living
creature saying, "Come."

4 And another, a red horse, went out; and to him who sat on it,
it was granted to take peace from the earth, and that *men* should
slay one another; and a great sword was given to him.

–Revelation 6

This, I think you would agree, is *war*. How extensive is the war? ". . . it was granted to take peace from the earth . . ." It sounds like a world war. We have never really had a world war. For example, South America and Australia have never really been involved in a war—nor has much of the rest of the southern hemisphere. World War I and World War II were basically northern hemisphere wars.

Let's take a look at Zechariah 6:

1 Now I lifted up my eyes again and looked, and behold, four chariots were coming forth from between the two mountains; and the mountains were bronze mountains.

2 With the first chariot *were* red horses, with the second chariot black horses,

3 with the third chariot white horses, and with the fourth chariot strong dappled horses.

4 Then I spoke and said to the angel who was speaking with me, "What are these, my lord?"

5 And the angel answered and said to me, "These are the four spirits of heaven, going forth after standing before the Lord of all the earth,

6 with one of which the black horses are going forth to the north country; and the white ones go forth after them, while the dappled ones go forth to the south country.

7 "When the strong ones went out, they were eager to go to patrol the earth." And He said, "Go, patrol the earth." So they patrolled the earth.

8 Then He cried out to me and spoke to me saying, "See, those who are going to the land of the north have appeased My wrath in the land of the north."

It is interesting that in Zechariah, two horses go north and two go south. I believe that this represents the two hemispheres. The entire globe will be enveloped in this war that is coming.

One thing that I pondered was how the northern and southern hemispheres could both be totally involved in war. There aren't enough foot soldiers and tanks around to have a conventional war. About the only way that I can see the entire world being involved is if it were a nuclear war. If enough bombs were set off, you would get radioactivity over the entire globe, and experience the upheavals that come with that type of war. The

Bible says that not just a sword was given to the rider, but a *great* sword. I think John was trying to say that it was the biggest weapon that he had ever seen! If you were to ask someone today what the biggest or most destructive weapon is that he has ever seen, he would probably say a hydrogen bomb. With what we know today, it seems to me that this is the most likely explanation for what is being shown here. It would cause many deaths and would take peace from the entire earth.

REVELATION 6:5–6
–THE THIRD SEAL

5 And when He broke the third seal, I heard the third living creature saying, "Come." And I looked, and behold, a black horse; and he who sat on it had a pair of scales in his hand.

6 And I heard as it were a voice in the center of the four living creatures saying, "A quart of wheat for a denarius, and three quarts of barley for a denarius; and do not harm the oil and the wine."

–Revelation 6

Here we see definite famine and food shortage. The denarius was a silver coin worth about 18 cents, which was then equivalent to a day's wage. It takes about a quart of wheat a day for a family to live on, at a bare minimum subsistence, almost starvation level. So what this says is that 100 percent of a working man's wage will have to go for food. The social implications of that are incredible. It would mean that you could not pay for your housing, automobile, or anything else. This is something that you and I are *likely* to experience! (We won't get into how to prepare for a nuclear war or this food shortage here, for this is dealt with in my book, *CHRISTIANS WILL GO THROUGH THE TRIBULATION–And how to prepare for it.* If you read this, don't immediately go out and make preparation, but bring the matter before God and ask Him what He would have *you* to do.)

There are two ways to interpret the latter part of verse 6: ". . . and do not harm the oil and the wine." Probably the majority of commentators and biblical scholars look at it this way: they feel that the oil and wine were used more by the rich than by the average person and that the rich will therefore fare all right during this time and will have enough money to buy whatever they need. I think that is probably the best interpretation.

The other interpretation is that all the way through the Old Testament grain, wine and oil are used to define the necessities of life.

> **13** "And He will love you and bless you and multiply you; He will also bless the fruit of your womb and the fruit of your ground, your grain and your new wine and your oil, the increase of your herd and the young of your flock, in the land which He swore to your forefathers to give you.
>
> —Deuteronomy 7

Let's also look at Deuteronomy 11:

> **13** "And it shall come about, if you listen obediently to my commandments which I am commanding you today, to love the LORD your God and to serve Him with all your heart and all your soul,
>
> **14** that 'I will give the rain for your land in its season, the early and late rain, that you may gather in your grain and your new wine and your oil.
>
> **15** 'And I will give grass in your fields for your cattle, and you shall eat and be satisfied.' . . ."

Considering this interpretation for a moment—that these are the essential things needed to live—the oil was basically for their lighting; it was their energy. The wine was primarily their drink, since much of the water was contaminated. So if you took that interpretation, you could say that we are going to have enough energy and drink, but not enough food. No matter how you come at it, there is going to be a food shortage.

The oil came from squeezing the olives, so if grain is in short supply, it would seem improbable that the olive trees would bring forth oil. Therefore it would likely be in short supply also, and only the very rich could afford it. This is why I feel that the first interpretation is probably correct—that we will have a food shortage but the rich will make out okay. It is the average person that will be destitute.

It is also interesting to note that this famine could have been brought on by the nuclear World War III of the second seal. The fire storms created by nuclear explosions could burn up the crops in the fields.

REVELATION 6:7-8
—THE FOURTH SEAL

7 And when He broke the fourth seal, I heard the voice of the fourth living creature saying, "Come."

8 And I looked, and behold, an ashen horse; and he who sat on it had the name "Death"; and Hades was following with him. And authority was given to them over a fourth of the earth, TO KILL WITH SWORD AND WITH FAMINE AND WITH PESTILENCE AND BY THE WILD BEASTS OF THE EARTH.

—Revelation 6

Right on the heels of the famine is going to be death. A lot of people will die from the famine. Let me take you through a couple scenarios.

Let's say that all trucks and trains stopped coming into Los Angeles because of a strike, and there were only a two-week supply of food in the grocery stores. Pretty soon, a person hears of the strike so he loads up three or four weeks' worth of food. Soon, someone else does the same thing, and so on, so that everyone has enough food for a week or two. At some point, somebody's food is going to run out. If just I were hungry, it would be one thing, but if I had two children crying from hunger, I would want to provide for them.

So let's say that the average non-Christian saw Joe Blow down the street carry bags and bags of groceries into his house. He decides to go see Joe and convince him that he should share. He walks down the sidewalk and there is a shot fired over his head. Joe tells him to hold it right there, because he knows why he is coming. So he goes home, calls a friend, and says, "Joe must really have the food at his place because he's really defending it. Let's all get our rifles and go to Joe's. We will split up the food that we get." Joe eventually loses. There is no way the other people in the neighborhood would let him get away with hoarding all the food.

If you carry this further, people will have pets which they won't be able to feed. When there is no food, most people would not kill their dog or cat. Instead they would turn them loose. I have seen a group of domesticated dogs go wild. If they get hungry enough, they will attack anything that moves, including human beings.

The killing of the sword that is mentioned here in the fourth seal I do not believe is a war. I think this is "people shooting Joe," rioting, looting, and people defending what they have. I think this means "murder," in a sense. Some people will die of the famine (starvation) and some by wild beasts of the earth. This could mean lions and tigers, if you were in Africa, but it could also mean domesticated animals gone wild. It also says that some will die with pestilence. If you have millions of people dying with no one to bury them, with the rats and such, you could have all sorts of disease. It says that Hades follows death. All of the non-Christians that die will go to Hades (the rich man went to Hades and Lazarus went to Paradise to be in Abraham's bosom—Luke 16:19-31).

Looking back at the first four seals, we have four horses. The colors are significant. They match with Zechariah's vision (Zechariah 6:1-8). We have seen that both the southern and northern hemispheres will be affected by them.

REVELATION 6:9-11
—THE FIFTH SEAL

9 And when He broke the fifth seal, I saw underneath the altar the souls of those who had been slain because of the word of God, and because of the testimony which they had maintained;

10 and they cried out with a loud voice, saying, "How long, O Lord, holy and true, wilt Thou refrain from judging and avenging our blood on those who dwell on the earth?"

11 And there was given to each of them a white robe; and they were told that they should rest for a little while longer, until *the number* of their fellow servants and their brethren who were to be killed even as they had been, should be completed also.

—Revelation 6

In this seal, we see persecution of the Christians and martyrdom. Some of these martyrs might have died in some of the other holocausts. But it says that they died because of "the word of God, and because of the testimony which they had maintained." They are spreading the word of their testimony and will be killed because of the message that they are actually preaching.

Verse 9 talks about an altar. This altar is in the heavenly temple of God, so evidently these martyrs are very close to God. Also, when sacrifices are made, the majority of blood winds up at the base of the altar. As these people were martyred for Christ and shed their blood symbolically on the altar, it ran down to the base of the altar. So, in a sense, it is through their blood, which has soaked down into the altar, that they are crying out to God.

In the Old Testament, the Lord says, "Vengeance is Mine" (Deuteronomy 32:35). He tells us over and over not to avenge ourselves. To leave vengeance to God is very difficult for some of us. This is something we need to pray about. If somebody were to murder or execute our spouse because of her testimony for Christ, we would immediately want to kill the guy. That would be a natural human reaction. But if we do, we are forgetting that vengeance belongs to the Lord. Here in Revelation the martyrs are not trying to take their own vengeance, but they cry out to God asking when He will take the vengeance for them.

In Luke 18 we see a similar thing. Christ had just given the parable of the widow who kept going to the judge and pestering him until he finally gave her what she wanted—not because she deserved it, but because of her persistence. Then He says this:

> 6 And the Lord said, "Hear what the unrighteous judge said;
>
> 7 now shall not God bring about justice for His elect, who cry to Him day and night, and will He delay long over them?
>
> 8 "I tell you that He will bring about justice for them speedily. However, when the Son of Man comes, will He find faith on the earth?"
>
> —Luke 18

When the Son of Man comes, will He find faithful people on the earth? The timing is His, but the Lord *will* avenge those who are martyred for His sake during the Tribulation.

REVELATION 6:12–17
–THE SIXTH SEAL

12 And I looked when He broke the sixth seal, and there was a great earthquake; and the sun became black as sackcloth *made* of hair, and the whole moon became like blood;

13 and the stars of the sky fell to the earth, as a fig tree casts its unripe figs when shaken by a great wind.

14 And the sky was split apart like a scroll when it is rolled up; and every mountain and island were moved out of their places.

15 And the kings of the earth and the great men and the commanders and the rich and the strong and every slave and free man, hid themselves in the caves and among the rocks of the mountains;

16 and they said to the mountains and to the rocks, "Fall on us and hide us from the presence of Him who sits on the throne, and from the wrath of the Lamb;

17 for the great day of their wrath has come; and who is able to stand?"

–Revelation 6

Quake means to shake, and an earthquake is when the earth shakes. An earth *upheaval* is something much more gigantic than the earth shaking. There are a number of gigantic upheavals recorded in the Bible. When Joshua was fighting against the Amorites at Gibeon, the Bible records that the sun stood still for about a whole day (Joshua 10:12–14). What must happen for the sun to stand still? The earth has to stop rotating. In the historical writings of South America and China, a night which was almost twice as long as the normal night was recorded at about the same time this was happening with Joshua. If the earth stopped rotating, what would happen to the water? It would still keep going. The inside of the earth, which is molten, would also keep going. Volcanoes, which are fissures in the earth where the molten core spews out, would occur in great magnitude.

The earth's shaking (it says that every mountain and island were "moved out of their places") can be interpreted in one of two ways. One is that the earth's axis will be tilted, or the earth will be kicked out of its present orbit. This would cause every mountain and island to move out of its place. The other interpretation is that they will be moved on the crust of the earth, with the earth retaining its orbit and its present tilted axis.

One of the things that happens when you get this kind of an earth upheaval is that there is so much ash in the air that you cannot view the sun in its full strength. If you have things like this happening all over the earth, the atmosphere will be so contaminated with ash that the sun will appear "black as sackcloth made of hair, and the whole moon . . . like blood."

This has been predicted all through the Old Testament. It is nothing new with Revelation. Let's look at a couple of places where the Bible deals with this. We are already familiar with part of this prophecy in Joel 2, because Peter quoted it.

> 28 "And it will come about after this
>   That I will pour out My Spirit on all mankind;
>   And your sons and daughters will prophesy,
>   Your old men will dream dreams,
>   Your young men will see visions.
> 29 "And even on the male and female servants
>   I will pour out My Spirit in those days.
> 30 "And I will display wonders in the sky and on the earth,
>   Blood, fire, and columns of smoke.
> 31 "The sun will be turned into darkness,
>   And the moon into blood,
>   Before the great and awesome day of the LORD comes.
> 32 "And it will come about that whoever calls on the name of the
>   LORD
>   Will be delivered;
>   For on Mount Zion and in Jerusalem
>   There will be those who escape,
>   As the LORD has said,
>   Even among the survivors whom the LORD calls.
>
>   —Joel 2

We can look at other places where it is also prophesied that the sun will be darkened and the moon will appear as blood.

Such instances appear all through the Old Testament. From all indications, it appears that the super earthquake spoken of in Revelation 6:12 will cause this to occur.

Is this going to affect crop production? Yes indeed! That will in turn amplify the famine problem that already will exist.

The word of God so beautifully fits together! Let's take a look at Isaiah 2:

12   For the LORD of hosts will have a day of reckoning
      Against everyone who is proud and lofty,
      And against everyone who is lifted up,
      That he may be abased.

13   And *it will be* against all the cedars of Lebanon that are lofty
          and lifted up,
      Against all the oaks of Bashan,

14   Against all the lofty mountains,
      Against all the hills that are lifted up,

15   Against every high tower,
      Against every fortified wall,

16   Against all the ships of Tarshish,
      And against all the beautiful craft.

17   And the pride of man will be humbled,
      And the loftiness of men will be abased,
      And the LORD alone will be exalted in that day.

18   But the idols will completely vanish.

19   And *men* will go into caves of the rocks,
      And into holes of the ground
      Before the terror of the LORD,
      And before the splendor of His majesty,
      When He arises to make the earth tremble.

20   In that day men will cast away to the moles and the bats
      Their idols of silver and their idols of gold,
      Which they made for themselves to worship,

21   In order to go into the caverns of the rocks and the clefts of
          the cliffs,
      Before the terror of the LORD and the splendor of His majesty,
      When He arises to make the earth tremble.

22   Stop regarding man, whose breath *of life* is in his nostrils;
      For why should he be esteemed?

                                                        —Isaiah 2

When this super earthquake happens, the fortified walls will come tumbling down, ships will be destroyed (probably by tidal waves), and men will hide in caves, just as Revelation predicts. Let's look further in Isaiah:

> 9 Behold, the day of the LORD is coming,
> Cruel, with fury and burning anger,
> To make the land a desolation;
> And He will exterminate its sinners from it.
> 10 For the stars of heaven and their constellations
> Will not flash forth their light;
> The sun will be dark when it rises,
> And the moon will not shed its light.
> 11 Thus I will punish the world for its evil,
> And the wicked for their iniquity;
> I will also put an end to the arrogance of the proud,
> And abase the haughtiness of the ruthless.
> 12 I will make mortal man scarcer than pure gold,
> And mankind than the gold of Ophir.
> 13 Therefore I shall make the heavens tremble,
> And the earth will be shaken from its place
> At the fury of the LORD of hosts
> In the day of His burning anger.

—Isaiah 13

In verse 13 it says that the earth will be shaken from its place! That means more than just earth upheavals. I believe we have five recorded reversals of the North and South Poles within geologic history. There could be another one coming up during the Tribulation.

REVELATION 7:1-8
—THE 144,000

Chapter 7 is an interlude between the breaking of the sixth and seventh seals; the seventh seal isn't broken until verse 1 of Chapter 8. We begin here by looking at two multitudes. The first multitude is discussed in the first eight verses of Chapter 7:

> 1 After this I saw four angels standing at the four corners of the earth, holding back the four winds of the earth, so that no wind should blow on the earth or on the sea or on any tree.

2 And I saw another angel ascending from the rising of the sun, having the seal of the living God; and he cried out with a loud voice to the four angels to whom it was granted to harm the earth and the sea,

3 saying, "Do not harm the earth or the sea or the trees, until we have sealed the bond-servants of our God on their foreheads."

4 And I heard the number of those who were sealed, one hundred and forty-four thousand sealed from every tribe of the sons of Israel:

5 from the tribe of Judah, twelve thousand *were* sealed, from the tribe of Reuben twelve thousand, from the tribe of Gad twelve thousand,

6 from the tribe of Asher twelve thousand, from the tribe of Naphtali twelve thousand, from the tribe of Manasseh twelve thousand,

7 from the tribe of Simeon twelve thousand, from the tribe of Levi twelve thousand, from the tribe of Issachar twelve thousand,

8 from the tribe of Zebulun twelve thousand, from the tribe of Joseph twelve thousand, from the tribe of Benjamin, twelve thousand *were* sealed.

—Revelation 7

Before we discuss the multitude who are sealed, let's discuss the sealing on the foreheads referred to in a prior chapter. I rejoice that we will be sealed on our foreheads by God's protective seal. The mark of the beast does not occur until Revelation 13. Thus, Christians, who are bond-servants, do not have to worry about taking on the mark of the beast. Our foreheads will already be occupied with God's seal, and therefore there will be no room for the beast's mark.

Now let's look at the purpose of God's seal, as stated in Revelation 9:

4 And they were told that they should not hurt the grass of the earth, nor any green thing, nor any tree, but only the men who do not have the seal of God on their foreheads.

"They" refers to locusts with the power of scorpions. We see that the purpose for the seal of God on the foreheads is for protection. The locusts, which could sting like scorpions, could not hurt anyone who had the seal of God on his forehead. Praise the Lord!

Later in Revelation we see similar protection, in connection with the first bowl of wrath.

2 And the first *angel* **went and poured out his bowl into the earth; and it became a loathsome and malignant sore upon the men who had the mark of the beast and who worshiped his image.**

–Revelation 16

The Christians would not be affected by this because they would have God's mark on the forehead. So again we see that the purpose of the seal is for God's protection of the believers.

I think that the Christians will go through the first six seals, but then we will receive God's seal and be exempt or protected from the things that will follow, *if* we are His bond–servants (bond–slaves).

In Chapter 1 we discussed what it meant in Old Testament times to be a bond–slave. As a Christian, we can come to a point whereat we tell Christ that we want to permanently be His slave, with no rights and no property of our own. This is a permanent transaction with the Lord. (Of course we can always attempt to steal the things that were formerly ours and try to run away with them.) When we become God's bond–slave, voluntarily, He then takes on the responsibility of feeding us and caring for us as long as we live. It is a beautiful, but permanent relationship. Thank You, Master!

I do not believe that all Christians have committed themselves to be bond–slaves of Christ. We see in Revelation 7 that the bond–slaves of God are sealed in their foreheads. We do not know what happens to those who are Christians but are not bond–slaves. The important thing for you, dear reader, is to be sure that you are a bond–slave of the Lord. If you are not sure, then I would encourage you to pause in reading this book and right now commit yourself to becoming a bond–slave of Christ.

WHO IS SEALED?

Do you think that Christ would seal the foreheads of the Israelite Christians on the earth, but not the Gentile Christians? No way! We need to realize that the Israel we are speaking of here in Revelation 7 is not the land of Israel that we know today.

Basically the land of Israel today is primarily the tribe of Judah, which is *biologically* a very impure tribe. As they came out of the Babylonian captivity, many had intermarried. Ten of the tribes of biological Israel are what they call "the 10 lost tribes." They were taken into captivity and never heard of again. Many people say that they wound up in Germany, England and many other places. So we know that this multitude is more than just what we call "Jewish" Christians. At least it is from the entire 12 tribes.

It is also interesting that this list of the 12 tribes in Revelation 7:4-8 does not match with any other list of the 12 tribes in the Bible. Genesis 49 lists the original 12 tribes and Ezekiel 48 lists the tribes that are going to be redeemed. Both of those include the tribe of Dan. The tribe of Dan, however, is not included in this passage in Revelation. Joseph was the father of Manasseh and Ephraim. In the Ezekiel list, Joseph is excluded and Ephraim and Manasseh are included. The Revelation list includes both Joseph and Manasseh. Any orthodox Israelite reading this list would say, "Who in the world made out this list?" I think the inclusion of both Joseph and his son, Manasseh, was done deliberately so that we would not try to hook it back specifically to the physical tribes of Israel. After much prayer, the Lord led me to conclude that this multitude represents all of the Christians from all over the world. The number, 144,000, would fit in beautifully because 12 times 12 equals 144. Twelve is a holy number associated with God and perfection. I would then interpret this that God is going to seal the *perfect number* of people.

In fact, I have come to believe that all believers, whether Jewish or not, are really Israelites! Let's look at Galatians 3:29:

> **29   And if you belong to Christ, then you are Abraham's offspring, heirs according to promise.**

Abraham, of course, was the father of all of the Israelites and the one to whom they directed their allegiance. Do you belong to Christ? If so, you are Abraham's offspring and you are heir to all of the promises made to Abraham. It does not matter if you are Chinese, Japanese, Latin, black or white—you are an offspring of Abraham if you belong to Christ. Outward appearance is not what counts. Let's read further:

> 28 For he is not a Jew who is one outwardly; neither is circumcision that which is outward in the flesh.
> 29 But he is a Jew who is one inwardly; and circumcision is that which is of the heart, by the Spirit, not by the letter; and his praise is not from men, but from God.
>
> —Romans 2

Probably the reason that Paul uses "Jew" here rather than "Israelite" is because all of the Israelites that were left were the Jews (and Benjamites). The Jewish people (those Israelites from the tribe of Judah) were still being circumcised. But Paul points out that those people were really not Jews. A true Jew is one who has had his heart circumcised by the Holy Spirit (a Christian). Our hearts have been circumcised by Jesus Christ; therefore, we are true Israelites!

Let's also look at Philippians 3:3:

> 3 for we are the *true* circumcision, who worship in the Spirit of God and glory in Christ Jesus and put no confidence in the flesh, . . .

Are we the true circumcised ones? Do we worship in the Spirit? Do we glory in Christ and put no confidence in the flesh? I do, and I hope that you all do too.

There are two other scriptures that we might look at, which point out the fact that there really is only one Israel. In the passage below we see that before the cross there were "two men" (Jews and Gentiles). After the cross, there was only one man, made from the two men, and this new man comprised all those who believe in Jesus Christ.

> 11 Therefore remember, that formerly you, the Gentiles in the flesh, who are called "Uncircumcision" by the so-called "Circumcision," *which is* performed in the flesh by human hands—
> 12 *remember* that you were at that time separate from Christ, excluded from the commonwealth of Israel, and strangers to the covenants of promise, having no hope and without God in the world.
> 13 But now in Christ Jesus you who formerly were far off have been brought near by the blood of Christ.
> 14 For He Himself is our peace, who made both *groups into* one, and broke down the barrier of the dividing wall,

15 by abolishing in His flesh the enmity, *which is* the Law of commandments *contained* in ordinances, that in Himself He might make the two into one new man, *thus* establishing peace,

16 and might reconcile them both in one body to God through the cross, by it having put to death the enmity.

—Ephesians 2

One of the most significant passages on this subject is the discussion of the olive tree, in Romans 11:

16 And if the first piece *of dough* be holy, the lump is also; and if the root be holy, the branches are too.

17 But if some of the branches were broken off, and you, being a wild olive, were grafted in among them and became partaker with them of the rich root of the olive tree,

18 do not be arrogant toward the branches; but if you are arrogant, *remember that* it is not you who supports the root, but the root *supports* you.

19 You will say then, "Branches were broken off so that I might be grafted in."

20 Quite right, they were broken off for their unbelief, and you stand *only* by your faith. Do not be conceited, but fear;

21 for if God did not spare the natural branches, neither will He spare you.

22 Behold then the kindness and severity of God; to those who fell, severity, but to you, God's kindness, if you continue in His kindness; otherwise you also will be cut off.

23 And they also, if they do not continue in their unbelief, will be grafted in; for God is able to graft them in again.

24 For if you were cut off from what is by nature a wild olive tree, and were grafted contrary to nature into a cultivated olive tree, how much more shall these who are the natural *branches* be grafted into their own olive tree?

The root of the olive tree is Christ, which makes the tree holy, and the olive tree is Israel. The individual Jews who did not believe in Christ were broken off. The Jews who did believe in Christ remained part of the olive tree (Israel). The Gentiles who believed were grafted in as branches into the olive tree of Israel.

Once a Jew who had been broken off of the tree of Israel received Christ, he was grafted back in. There is only one tree, there is only one Israel, and I believe that it has been a spiritual entity from the beginning. There are only four women mentioned in the genealogy of Christ, and two of these, Ruth and Rahab, were not part of "biological" Israel, but they were included as part of true Israel.

There are those who would make you think that a "completed Jew," a Jew who has received Christ as his Savior, is a superior citizen of the kingdom of God to anyone else. I think that this is a falsehood. We are all complete in Christ, lacking nothing (Colossians 2:10). There are no second-class citizens in the kingdom of God. I do praise God for every Jew that receives Christ, but just as much I also praise God for every Armenian, Chinese, and Colombian who receives Christ. I would in no way discourage those who have a burden to reach the Jews for Christ and I praise God for them. However, there should be no false pride in believing that a completed Jew is superior to a "completed Irishman," for example.

It is also interesting that all through the Old Testament the genealogies were meticulously preserved. The reason for this was so that people would know that Jesus was the son of David. After the crucifixion and the rending of the veil, all of the genealogies were destroyed. I think that God allowed this to happen so as to say that the physical lineage is not important anymore; it is the spiritual lineage that matters. His Son had come to make a new covenant.

Back to Revelation 7 and the 144,000 . . . If this is written to Israel, and we are part of true Israel, then we will be sealed. I believe that this means all true believers, of whatever lineage, will be sealed. It is inconceivable to me that God would seal only the "Jewish" Christians, as some teach, and not the rest of His sheep.

REVELATION 7:9-17
-THE VAST MULTITUDE

9 After these things I looked, and behold, a great multitude, which no one could count, from every nation and all tribes and peoples and tongues, standing before the throne and before the Lamb, clothed in white robes, and palm branches *were* in their hands;

10   and they cry out with a loud voice, saying,
"Salvation to our God who sits on the throne, and to the Lamb."

11   And all the angels were standing around the throne and *around* the elders and the four living creatures; and they fell on their faces before the throne and worshiped God,

12   saying,
"Amen, blessing and glory and wisdom and thanksgiving and honor and power and might, *be* to our God forever and ever. Amen."

13   And one of the elders answered, saying to me, "These who are clothed in the white robes, who are they, and from where have they come?"

14   And I said to him, "My lord, you know." And he said to me, "These are the ones who come out of the great tribulation, and they have washed their robes and made them white in the blood of the Lamb.

15   "For this reason, they are before the throne of God; and they serve Him day and night in His temple; and He who sits on the throne shall spread His tabernacle over them.

16   "They shall hunger no more, neither thirst any more; neither shall the sun beat down on them, nor any heat;

17   for the Lamb in the center of the throne shall be their shepherd, and shall guide them to springs of the water of life; and God shall wipe every tear from their eyes."

–Revelation 7

I do not believe that the book of Revelation is chronological in nature, although there are portions of it that are. This is the first evidence that we have of this lack of chronology. John is seeing a multitude here in a vision, and verse 14 says that they have "come out of the great tribulation," which means that this multitude is gathered after the Tribulation is over. Thus, if Revelation were in a chronological sequence, this would have to fall much later in the book, since the Tribulation does not end until Chapter 19.

Turning to John's vision specifically, we see that this multitude is so vast that no one could count it and that there are people from every nation. They are the Christians gathering around the throne praising God.

Since this vast multitude has come out of the great Tribulation and are in a special relationship to the Lamb, it could perhaps be the same multitude that is described at the beginning of the chapter, who were sealed with God's seal. We have no way of knowing if it is the same or not, but certainly the 144,000 who were sealed would be included in this vast multitude, because the 144,000 will certainly have come through the Tribulation victoriously because of God's protection.

God's ways have not changed. He did not take Daniel out of the lion's den, or Shadrack, Meshach, and Abed-nego out of the fiery furnace, or the children of Israel out of the plagues in Egypt. In each case, they went through the trial victoriously, because of the special protection of God. We are going to again see those kinds of miraculous occurrences during the Tribulation. Praise the Lord!

God's seal of protection on the foreheads of His bond–servants occurs before the really bad part of the Tribulation, which starts with the first six trumpets. Because of this seal, they will be here on the earth observing the events of the first six trumpets, but will not experience the full impact of the turmoil that will come. Just as God protected the three Hebrew men in the midst of the flames of a fiery furnace that should have consumed them, so He is well able to wrap a blanket of protection around His bond–servants in any of the events to come. What an assurance and joy it is to know that God wants to put His seal of protection on us.

6

THE FIRST SIX TRUMPETS
(Revelation 8 & 9)

REVELATION 8:1-6
—THE SEVENTH SEAL

1 And when He broke the seventh seal, there was silence in heaven for about half an hour.

2 And I saw the seven angels who stand before God; and seven trumpets were given to them.

3 And another angel came and stood at the altar, holding a golden censer; and much incense was given to him, that he might add it to the prayers of all the saints upon the golden altar which was before the throne.

4 And the smoke of the incense, with the prayers of the saints, went up before God out of the angel's hand.

5 And the angel took the censer; and he filled it with the fire of the altar and threw it to the earth; and there followed peals of thunder and sounds and flashes of lightning and and an earthquake.

6 And the seven angels who had the seven trumpets prepared themselves to sound them.

—Revelation 8

There was silence in heaven! Since the beginning of creation there has never been silence in heaven. Remember, the four creatures mentioned in Revelation 4 were praising, glorifying and magnifying God *day and night.* They had been doing this since they had been created, aeons ago. For there to be thirty minutes of silence, which will be the first time that this will have happened in billions of years, will be an incredible and suspenseful thing. You could look at that silence as the contents of the seventh seal. You could also look at the rest of Revelation as the contents of the seventh seal. I don't think that it really matters which way you view it. I would lean toward the explanation that most of the rest of Revelation deals with the seventh seal, rather than just the period of silence.

John saw seven angels standing before God with seven trumpets. Before they blew them, another angel came and stood at the altar, and much incense was added to the golden censer (bowl). Revelation 5:8 said that the bowls full of incense were the prayers of the saints. What the Lord showed me was that the incense being added to the prayers of the saints was the prayers of Jesus. He makes intercession for us, so His prayers are added to our prayers, and this goes up as a sweet smelling fragrance before the throne of God that is pleasant to God's nostrils. He is delighted by the prayers of His saints.

In Revelation thus far, we have seen a lot of terrible things happen to the earth—earthquakes, famine, world war, and such. In verses 3 and 4 of Revelation 8 we see Christians praying to God perhaps to warn their loved ones who do not know Christ that something worse is coming. In verse 5, God answers their prayers. The angel takes that same bowl and fills it with fire from the altar and throws it down to the earth. There are peals of thunder, flashes of lightning and earthquakes. We have seen in various scriptures that these are the signs that occurred when God was present on the earth or doing something on the earth. Here God seems to be giving those on earth a sign that there are bad things to come, and He wants them to turn to Him. Praise the Lord for answering prayers!

REVELATION 8:7
—THE FIRST TRUMPET

The silence in heaven is a prelude to the seven trumpets. We read about the first one as follows:

7 And the first sounded, and there came hail and fire, mixed with blood, and they were thrown to the earth; and a third of the earth was burnt up, and a third of the trees were burnt up, and all the green grass was burnt up.

—Revelation 8

Exodus 9 records a very similar event. It tells about one of the plagues in Egypt.

22 Now the LORD said to Moses, "Stretch out your hand toward the sky, that hail may fall on all the land of Egypt, on man and on beast and on every plant of the field, throughout the land of Egypt."

23 And Moses stretched out his staff toward the sky, and the LORD sent thunder and hail, and fire ran down to the earth. And the LORD rained hail on the land of Egypt.

24 So there was hail, and fire flashing continually in the midst of the hail, very severe, such as had not been in all the land of Egypt since it became a nation.

25 And the hail struck all that was in the field through all the land of Egypt, both man and beast; the hail also struck every plant of the field and shattered every tree of the field.

26 Only in the land of Goshen, where the sons of Israel *were*, there was no hail.

—Exodus 9

When God's judgment fell on Egypt, His people were spared. Praise God! I believe that those who have been sealed by God in their foreheads, His bond–slaves, will be spared the effects of this first trumpet.

Many interpreters feel that this first trumpet speaks of some sort of a nuclear fallout. This is possible. However, it couldn't have been nuclear fallout back in Egypt, yet the same thing happened in the incident we just quoted. I would lean a little more toward the theory of Immanuel Velikovsky. Without getting into it a great deal, one of the things the ancient people did, scientifically and very accurately, was to map the heavens—the stars and wandering planets. Before the crossing of the Red Sea, Venus did not appear in any of the star charts of the ancient people. That is the only visible planet that was absent. After the crossing of the Red Sea, Venus began to appear in its proper place.

Velikovsky feels that Venus was either a comet that was captured and went into orbit around the sun, or was a part of Jupiter that had broken off. Let's just say that it was a comet, as either would have acted very similarly. In the tail of a comet are millions of particles of rock (as we would think of them). Some of these are the size of a football, some the size of a baseball, and some the size of a pebble. These would all make a static electrical charge while traveling through space. Velikovsky feels that as this comet first passed close to the earth, the earth's gravity would have pulled a lot of these rocks down. Some may or may not have been coated by ice. We don't know whether this was an ice-type hail or not. But when they hit the earth, these rocks would have discharged the static electricity which, if it hit dry grass, would have caused it to burn.

Velikovsky also feels that the parting of the Red Sea did not happen the way that it was depicted in the movie, "The Ten Commandments," where there was a fifty yard gap in the Sea through which went 2 million Hebrew men, with their wives, children and cattle, while very fast chariots were charging after them. It would have taken them days to get through that little gap. He feels rather that as Venus, on one of its passes, came very close to the earth over the Red Sea, it would have pulled the Sea up like a giant inverted funnel, approximately six miles high. This would have emptied the entire Red Sea bed. They could then all go through en masse. Then as soon as Venus had passed, all of the water dropped back on top of the Egyptian army.

We have to differentiate two things here. One is *what* God does. We know that He turned the Red Sea into dry land (Exodus 14:20) and brought down hail mixed with fire (Exodus 9:23,24). The other is speculation on *how* He did these things. If God brought a wind or some other natural phenomenon to cause the Red Sea to temporarily dry up, praise God! To me it is even more miraculous (and fairly scientifically accurate) if God started a comet on its way a million years beforehand, knowing that it had to get to the Red Sea on a particular day at a certain hour. I do not think that this detracts from God, but rather shows us more clearly just how mighty He is. God is the one who did these remarkable things and the mechanisms that He chooses to use are up to Him.

Back to Revelation—I feel that we are probably going to be looking at another comet coming near the earth. We will see hail which, as it hits the earth, will give off static electrical charges causing fire. Trees are hard to ignite, which would account for only one-third of them being burned, while all of the grass will be burned. Whatever the cause—whether it be from nuclear fallout or rocks from the tail of a comet—it doesn't really matter.

The Bible does tell us some of the results, however. Wheat, oats, rice and such are considered grasses. What happens when all of the grass of the earth gets burned up? Again we would see more severe famine. This would also ruin the seed for the next year's crops. The food shortage that is coming is going to be incredible!

REVELATION 8:8-9
—THE SECOND TRUMPET

Now let's look at the results of the second trumpet in Revelation 8:

> 8 And the second angel sounded, and *something* like a great mountain burning with fire was thrown into the sea, and a third of the sea became blood;
>
> 9 and a third of the creatures, which were in the sea and had life, died; and a third of the ships were destroyed.

I look at this as the comet that we just spoke of actually crashing into the sea. Hal Lindsey says that it is a nuclear blast which looks like a mountain. It is not worth arguing about. It is up to God as to how He is going to cause this to occur. Some of you are likely familiar with the great meteor crater in New Mexico. It is a little better than three-quarters of a mile in diameter. They estimate that if that meteor hit in the Atlantic today, it would cause a tidal wave which would cover the Appalachian mountains.

The Pacific Ocean is roughly 63 million square miles, the

Atlantic 31 million, and the Indian Ocean about 28 million. If something like a burning comet fell into the northern Pacific or one of the other two oceans, this would be roughly one-third of the oceans. Certainly any ship that is in that ocean is going to be demolished. There would be tidal waves of 1,000 to 2,000 feet.

Revelation 8:9 says that this great burning "mountain" kills all of the fish which are in that third of the sea, which would also add to the food shortage. Some countries, such as Japan, depend heavily on fish as their main source of food. I don't know if any of you have ever seen the red tides in California, but when plankton dies, the water actually becomes red. With all of the plankton and the fish dead in one-third of the ocean, it would be conceivable that this part of the oceans would turn red like blood, which the Bible says will happen.

REVELATION 8:10-11
–THE THIRD TRUMPET

We read about the third trumpet as follows, in Revelation 8:

> 10   And the third angel sounded, and a great star fell from heaven, burning like a torch, and it fell on a third of the rivers and on the springs of waters;
> 11   and the name of the star is called Wormwood; and a third of the waters become wormwood; and many men died from the waters, because they were made bitter.

We have been reading about plagues coming against the *earth*. We have seen some against the vegetation, the sea and fish, and now we see one against the fresh water.

Before we look at the significance of "wormwood," let's consider the star that fell. In the second trumpet we saw that a great burning mountain fell down into the sea. A mountain has huge volume and mass, and this one was on fire. Apparently, the largeness and the mass were more significant than the fact that it was burning. On the other hand, we think of a star or a torch as primarily light and heat. So in this case we see that something primarily related to light and heat fell on a third of the fresh waters and turned them bitter.

A nuclear explosion could be thought of as creating primarily light and heat. Certainly the fallout from a nuclear explosion could make the waters bitter and people would die from the fallout radiation when they ingested it with the water. This seems to be the most reasonable interpretation of the star that fell from the heaven.

On the other hand it could be something to do with UFO's. That would not surprise me at all. I think Satan is probably using the UFO's very significantly. As I explain in my book, *Close Encounters of the Highest Kind,* UFO's have been spotted up to two miles in diameter. If a beautiful being arrived in a space ship two miles in diameter and said, "Give me your allegiance and I will solve your racial problems, your energy problems, your financial problems, and your food problems," the whole world would probably stand in line to give him allegiance. Thus, it is a possibility that the falling star could be something from a UFO.

Turning to the *results* of this fallen object, the Greek word for wormwood is *apsinthos,* which is a poisonous plant. When mixed with water, it could cause illness or death for people who drink it. Whether people feel that this could be ICBM's with radioactive fallout which contaminates the fresh water, UFO's or comet pollution, let me emphasize again—it doesn't matter *how* God does it. We *know* that a third of the fresh waters on the earth will become so bad they will be undrinkable. I would hope that it would be on some other third of the world than my own! However, if it is on our third of the world, it may be that a Christian could pray over his water and ask the Holy Spirit to purify it. I believe there will be a provision for Christians to survive through it, but we will have to be moving more in the realm of miracles than we are today.

Let's take a brief look at Jeremiah 9 in regard to wormwood:

> 13 And the LORD said, "Because they have forsaken My law which I set before them, and have not obeyed My voice nor walked according to it,

14 but have walked after the stubbornness of their heart and
after the Baals, as their fathers taught them,"
15 therefore thus says the LORD of hosts, the God of Israel,
"behold, I will feed them, this people, with wormwood and give
them poisoned water to drink. . . ."

It is hard for us to imagine God saying that He will give
anybody poisoned water to drink, because we think of every
good and perfect gift coming from God (which it does—James
1:17). However, if people rebel against God and are stubborn,
God can and does at times choose to give opposite things.

In Jeremiah 23 we read:

15 "Therefore thus says the Lord of hosts concerning the prophets,
'Behold, I am going to feed them wormwood
And make them drink poisonous water,
For from the prophets of Jerusalem
Pollution has gone forth into all the land.'"

Here God is speaking to prophets—spiritual men. This is
not speaking about air pollution, but spiritual pollution, which
is worse. So prophets of God can bring forth spiritual pollution
and God says that He will cause them to drink bitter and poisonous water. (This should be a word of warning to prophets. Take
care not to pollute the pure word of God.)

In Lamentations 3 we read:

15 He has filled me with bitterness.
He has made me drunk with wormwood.

Wormwood is something that God has used in times past,
as we have just seen, as punishment and an instrument of His
judgment. He is going to use it again. It may be something that
is foreign to us, but it is not foreign to the Lord.

REVELATION 8:12-13
—THE FOURTH TRUMPET

12 And the fourth angel sounded, and a third of the sun and a
third of the moon and a third of the stars were smitten, so that a
third of them might be darkened and the day might not shine for a
third of it, and the night in the same way.

13   And I looked, and I heard an eagle flying in midheaven, saying with a loud voice, "Woe, woe, woe, to those who dwell on the earth, because of the remaining blasts of the trumpet of the three angels who are about to sound!"

—Revelation 8

Here we see that the sun, moon and stars will give off 33–1/3 percent less light than they had previously given off. I think that this is likely because of the previous three trumpets. Have you any idea how much smoke would be created if all of the grass and one-third of the trees were burned? I have seen small forest fires and the smoke that they create, but that is just a drop in the bucket compared to the thick canopy of smoke that would be created. This light-reducing blanket of smoke could be further thickened from the results of comets crashing to the earth and nuclear explosions. One-third less light would also affect food production (if there were any left by that time).

I believe that just as there were seven fat years and seven lean years in the time of Joseph in Egypt (they had seven years of no food production), we will experience something similar.

God keeps warning people. Verse 13 of Revelation 8 says, "Woe, woe, woe, to those who dwell on the earth . . ." There are three woes yet to come at this point, and the Lord is trying to warn people to turn to Him. He holds out His hand and says, "Come to Me." If we are stubborn and refuse to do so, He has no choice in the end but to exercise His judgment on the unrepentant.

REVELATION 9:1–12
—THE FIFTH TRUMPET

Up until now, man has not been touched directly. It has been the sea, the vegetation, the water, the fish, and so forth. Man himself has not been touched, except indirectly. Some may have died on one of the ships that went down or may have starved to death. But man in general has not thus far been affected in his physical body.

The next two are plagues on the people themselves, but *only those who do not have the seal of God on their foreheads.*

So these plagues do not come against Christians who are "bond–slaves." We should be busy ministering spiritually and physically to all of those who are being attacked. Be ready for that call to minister.

Let's take a look at the fifth trumpet:

> 1   And the fifth angel sounded, and I saw a star from heaven which had fallen to the earth; and the key of the bottomless pit was given to him.
>
> 2   And he opened the bottomless pit; and smoke went up out of the pit, like the smoke of a great furnace; and the sun and the air were darkened by the smoke of the pit.
>
> 3   And out of the smoke came forth locusts upon the earth; and power was given them, as the scorpions of the earth have power.
>
> 4   And they were told that they should not hurt the grass of the earth, nor any green thing, nor any tree, but only the men who do not have the seal of God on their foreheads.
>
> 5   And they were not permitted to kill anyone, but to torment for five months; and their torment was like the torment of a scorpion when it stings a man.
>
> 6   And in those days men will seek death and will not find it; and they will long to die and death flees from them.
>
> 7   And the appearance of the locusts was like horses prepared for battle; and on their heads, as it were, crowns like gold, and their faces were like the faces of men.
>
> 8   And they had hair like the hair of women, and their teeth were like *the teeth* of lions.
>
> 9   And they had breastplates like breastplates of iron; and the sound of their wings was like the sound of chariots, of many horses rushing to battle.
>
> 10   And they have tails like scorpions, and stings; and in their tails is their power to hurt men for five months.
>
> 11   They have as king over them, the angel of the abyss; his name in Hebrew is Abaddon, and in the Greek he has the name Apollyon.
>
> 12   The first woe is past; behold, two woes are still coming after these things.
>
> —Revelation 9

By this plague men can be tortured but not killed. That is a little reminiscent of Job, isn't it? Satan could do anything to Job but kill him. It is *God* who is doing the restraining here. Back in verse 1, the star which had fallen from heaven is probably Satan (Isaiah 14 talks about Lucifer, the bright and morning star). The key to the bottomless pit is given to this being that fell, whom I think is Satan. I may be wrong, but let's assume that he is for now. Who had the keys of death and of the pit? . . . Jesus did. This is found in Revelation 1:

> 17 . . . "Do not be afraid; I am the first and the last,
> 18 and the living One; and I was dead, and behold, I am alive forevermore, and I have the keys of death and of Hades. . . ."

So who gives Satan the keys to the bottomless pit? Obviously Christ does. So Satan is not causing anything. He is not really in charge of anything. God is telling the angels to blow these trumpets, which cause these events to happen. Christ is handing Satan the keys to the bottomless pit and telling him that he can open it now, but *Christ* is the one in charge, *not* Satan.

Let's also look in Luke 8, where Christ went to the demoniac who was out among the tombstones. He was going to cast out the demons, and they responded in this manner:

> 31 And they were entreating Him not to command them to depart into the abyss.

> —Luke 8

Here were some demons deathly afraid of going to the pit. You might ask yourself why. It could be that there are some demons so bad that God has not allowed them to come upon the face of the earth, and the "regular" demons do not want to get thrown in with them.

Let's look further:

> 4 For if God did not spare angels when they sinned, but cast them into hell and committed them to pits of darkness, reserved for judgment; . . .

> —2 Peter 2

What judgment were they reserved for? It wasn't their judgment. It must have been for the judgment of the earth. Some of the angels—like Satan—became demons, and now roam about the earth harrassing and possessing non-Christians. (Christians cannot be demon-possessed.) We read above that some of the fallen angels God has put into this pit and has reserved them for judgment. There were some that He bound for the day of judgment (Jude 1:6). Maybe they were so bad that He didn't even want to put them in the pit.

Back in Revelation 9, we read that Satan opens up the bottomless pit and some locust–scorpion–type of creatures come out. In Revelation 9:11 we see that these creatures have a king over them, which is the angel of the abyss. In Proverbs 30, we read:

> 27 **The locusts have no king,**
> **Yet all of them go out in ranks; . . .**

This group of locusts, if you want to think of them that way, do have a king, which is the angel of the pit. So we know that they are not normal locusts. They could be special creatures that God has created for this purpose, which are small beings, part locust and part scorpion, or they could possibly be killer bees or something of that nature. Bees would not be interested in hurting the flowers or the trees. Can you imagine thousands of bees continually stinging you for five months? That is the kind of torment that is expressed here.

Locusts are really flying grasshoppers. (Real grasshoppers don't fly.) When they pass through a country, they strip away every leaf from every tree, every bush, every blade of grass—everything edible. This is why plagues of locusts were so feared. What they did to trees in the Old Testament, here they will do to human beings. When this plague comes, they will not touch the grass and the trees, but the human beings. Again, it is possible they could be something God creates uniquely for this time.

It is also possible that they could be instruments of war as we know them today. One Vietnam veteran read this and said that it described a Cobra helicopter. Can you imagine John trying to describe a helicopter? He was a first century man who had not even seen a car or anything else that is self–propelled.

Let's reread a few of those verses in Revelation 9:

> 7 **And the appearance of the locusts was like horses prepared for battle; and on their heads, as it were, crowns like gold, and their faces were like the faces of men.**
> 8 **And they had hair like the hair of women, and their teeth were like *the teeth* of lions.**

9 And they had breastplates like breastplates of iron; and the sound of their wings was like the sound of chariots, of many horses rushing to battle.

So here John may be describing something similar in nature to a helicopter. Out of the "helicopters" could come chemical warfare or a number of other things that would hit people's skin and cause it to burn as from a scorpion's sting, but it would not hurt the plants (and, miraculously, not hurt God's sealed bond–servants).

Now let me emphasize again: It does not matter if these are killer bees, something specially created by God for this time, or helicopters. God is going to use these entities to torment everybody that does not have the seal of God on his forehead. They will be tormented for five months. While they are being tormented and we are not, we should be able to minister to them. Praise the Lord! I think that people who get hung up on whether or not it has to be helicopters, killer bees, or whatever, are really making a mistake. They are presuming to tell God how it *should* be done. The main thing is that God *is* going to do it.

Again, the Christians will not be hurt by this plague. We need not have any fear, as perfect love casts out fear (1 John 4: 18), and God does love us. As believers in Christ, we are His children. He will not even allow anything from the pit to come against us; He will protect us because He loves us.

REVELATION 9:13–21
–THE SIXTH TRUMPET

13 And the sixth angel sounded, and I heard a voice from the four horns of the golden altar which is before God,

14 one saying to the sixth angel who had the trumpet, "Release the four angels who are bound at the great river Euphrates."

15 And the four angels, who had been prepared for the hour and day and month and year, were released, so that they might kill a third of mankind.

16 And the number of the armies of the horsemen was two hundred million; I heard the number of them.

17   And this is how I saw in the vision the horses and those who sat on them: *the riders* had breastplates *the color* of fire and of hyacinth and of brimstone; and the heads of the horses are like the heads of lions; and out of their mouths proceed fire and smoke and brimstone.

18   A third of mankind was killed by these three plagues, by the fire and the smoke and the brimstone, which proceeded out of their mouths.

19   For the power of the horses is in their mouths and in their tails; for their tails are like serpents and have heads; and with them they do harm.

20   And the rest of mankind, who were not killed by these plagues, did not repent of the works of their hands, so as not to worship demons, and the idols of gold and of silver and of brass and of stone and of wood, which can neither see nor hear nor walk;

21   and they did not repent of their murders nor of their sorceries nor of their immorality nor of their thefts.

—Revelation 9

In this passage we see four fallen angels. These were probably demon leaders. I believe that they were so bad that the Lord didn't even put them in the abyss with all the others. He actually bound these up. We read the following in Jude 1:

6 And angels who did not keep their own domain, but abandoned their proper abode, He has kept in eternal bonds under darkness for the judgment of the great day.

So God bound these fallen angels for the day of judgment. These four angel–demons, reserved for this time, are loosed at God's command. They raise an army of 200 million and use this army to kill one–third of humanity. One–fourth of humanity has already been killed (Revelation 6:8). There are on the earth today approaching 4 billion people. Using this figure, back in the fourth seal, 1 billion (25 percent) would have been killed. Out of the three–fourths (3 billion) that are left, one–third of those are killed as a result of this trumpet. This would mean that another billion people will die at this point.

Centuries ago people would read the book of Revelation—which speaks of this army of 200 million, and they would realize that there were hardly that many people on the earth. In

1965, it was estimated that China alone had a standing army of 200 million people. China has about as many military people as the United States has population. The book of Revelation does not specifically say that this is the Chinese army. However, later when we get into Revelation 16, which speaks of the armies from the east and the River Euphrates drying up, we will see that it is most likely an oriental army.

John emphasizes in Revelation 9:17 that this is a vision that he is trying to describe. The best thing I can come up with, and most commentators agree with this, is that he is most likely describing a tank. Tanks would have "breastplates" and out of their mouths would proceed fire and smoke (they would have a gun on the front and one on the rear). This may not be what God has in mind. He may have people on horses, but I don't feel that is what it will be, although it is not impossible. Whatever means God uses, an additional billion people are going to die.

When the fifth trumpet blew, the locusts that came forth upon the earth could only torture men, but men could not die even if they wanted to. People *will* die during this sixth trumpet. At this point, 50 percent of the people who began the Tribulation will be dead. We don't know if this is half the U.S. population, half of China, half of Russia, and so forth, or if it is all segregated in, say, the Orient or North or South America. But one way or another, the population of planet earth will have shrunk in half.

One interesting thing would be the task of burying 1 billion people. The stench and disease that comes with decaying bodies is going to make the earth a terribly undesirable place to live. But whatever we have to go through for the Lord is worth it, because He wants to use us as His tools on the earth.

NO REPENTANCE

Now you would think, after all of this, that people would turn and ask the Lord for mercy. But we read the following at the end of Revelation 9:

20 And the rest of mankind, who were not killed by these plagues, did not repent of the works of their hands, so as not to worship demons, and the idols of gold and of silver and of brass and of stone and of wood, which can neither see nor hear nor walk;

21 and they did not repent of their murders nor of their sorceries nor of their immorality nor of their thefts.

If one had talked of demon worship thirty years ago, it would have been so far out that no intelligent, thinking person would even have listened. But look at the rise in witchcraft and the number of people who worship Satan; these are the two fastest–growing religions in America today. Evidently this is going to continue and increase. In spite of all of the judgments of God, Revelation says that people will continue to worship the demons and idols of gold, silver, brass, stone and wood, which they themselves have created.

There are four things of which they did not repent:

1. Murders: In today's society, with the abolition of the death penalty, the number of murders has continued to increase. With the food shortages that people will be experiencing during the Tribulation, there will be those who will kill to get the food that someone else has.

2. Witchcraft: It says that people also will not repent of their witchcraft. Witches are referred to as sorcerers. Again, today we are seeing a dramatic rise in cult religions and witchcraft. Yet, even with all of the judgments of God, people are still not going to repent.

3. Immorality: I am sure that no one has to tell you that sexual immorality is steadily increasing today, whether it be homosexuality, living together, or whatever else. In spite of all of these judgments, it is going to continue. In addition, other forms of immorality, such as dishonesty, are rampant today and will continue to increase.

4. Thefts: You can see that there will be incredible shortages during the Tribulation. The theft spoken of here probably does not refer to someone stealing a comic book from the corner grocery store. I think that people will be stealing the necessities of life from others. As I said before, if they get caught, they will kill whomever catches them. This depicts a time of tremendous anarchy and lawlessness. And yet even then a Christian can have peace and victory, and can be a witness to others. If someone comes to steal your food and God says to give it to him, He will miraculously provide for you, and at the same time you could be a blessing to others. We may be living among people who will be desperate and will stop at nothing to get what they need and want; we could have the opportunity to show God's love to them.

BEFORE THE SEVENTH AND LAST TRUMPET

We have now finished a brief look at the results of God having the first six angels blow six of His trumpets. In the book of Revelation there are some significant things discussed before the results of the seventh trumpet are described. We will now take a look at those things.

7

THE LITTLE SCROLL,
THE TWO WITNESSES
AND THE SEVENTH TRUMPET
(Revelation 10 & 11)

REVELATION 10:1-7
—THE LITTLE SCROLL

In this chapter we will move into deeper water. I think that the Lord has made most things clear up until now. Again, we will trust the Holy Spirit to reveal what He has for us in this chapter.

We will be covering Chapters 10 and 11 of the book of Revelation. Let's now take a look at the first portion of Revelation 10:

> 1 And I saw another strong angel coming down out of heaven, clothed with a cloud; and the rainbow was upon his head, and his face was like the sun, and his feet like pillars of fire;
>
> 2 and he had in his hand a little book which was open. And he placed his right foot on the sea and his left on the land;
>
> 3 and he cried out with a loud voice, as when a lion roars; and when he had cried out, the seven peals of thunder uttered their voices.

4 And when the seven peals of thunder had spoken, I was about to write; and I heard a voice from heaven saying, "Seal up the things which the seven peals of thunder have spoken, and do not write them."

5 And the angel whom I saw standing on the sea and on the land LIFTED UP HIS RIGHT HAND TO HEAVEN,

6 AND SWORE BY HIM WHO LIVES FOREVER AND EVER, WHO CREATED HEAVEN AND THE THINGS IN IT, AND THE EARTH AND THE THINGS IN IT, AND THE SEA AND THE THINGS IN IT, that there shall be delay no longer,

7 but in the days of the voice of the seventh angel, when he is about to sound, then the mystery of God is finished, as He preached to His servants and prophets.

Even though this "strong angel" has some characteristics that sound similar to some of the characteristics of Christ as He was described in Revelation 1 (face shining like the sun, feet like pillars of fire and so forth), there is never any place where Christ is called an angel. Angels are created beings. Christ was with the Godhead at the beginning. He was not created.

What we are seeing in this passage is a glorious, strong angel. According to the Bible, degrees of strength and rank exist among the angels. This angel is a prominent one. I believe that the rainbow on the angel's head, reminiscent of God's post-Flood promise to Noah, is simply God's reminder that He keeps His word. He will never leave us, nor forsake us. Glory to God in the highest! We could look more extensively into angels but we will save that for a later chapter.

According to some translations, the angel was holding a small scroll in his hand. Today this would be the equivalent of a small booklet. Evidently this angel was large as well as strong because he had one foot on the sea and the other on the land. This gives the impression of an immense figure.

This angel cried out with a loud voice, and the seven peals of thunder spoke. We do not know what the peals of thunder said; God told John that their words were not to be revealed to us. This says to me that in all ages God still has some secrets. He still has some goodies that we don't know about. One of the reasons for this is that He wants us to walk day by day trusting

Him. If somebody had the entire book of Revelation figured out, except this part, this missing, unrevealed element might prove to be the key to the entire interpretation. The Lord wants us always to depend on *Him* and not on our own knowledge.

Before we get into the significance of this angel, let's look at one more thing in Revelation 5:

> 2 And I saw a strong angel proclaiming with a loud voice, "Who is worthy to open the book and to break its seals?"

This might possibly be referring to the same strong angel. Evidently this angel is a spokesman for God. He was a key figure in the drama that we dealt with when we discussed the fifth chapter of Revelation. He was making a critical announcement. Perhaps this isn't the same strong angel; we don't know for sure, but I would suspect that it is. In both instances, he is acting in an "announcing" capacity.

Let's also look at Luke 1:18–20. In this instance, the angel had appeared to Zacharias at the altar and had announced that Zacharias would have a son. This is what Zacharias said to the angel:

> 18 And Zacharias said to the angel, "How shall I know this is *for certain?* For I am an old man, and my wife is advanced in years."
> 19 And the angel answered and said to him, "I am Gabriel, who stands in the presence of God; and I have been sent to speak to you, and to bring you this good news.
> 20 "And behold, you shall be silent and unable to speak until the day when these things take place, because you did not believe my words, which shall be fulfilled in their proper time."
> —Luke 1

When these strong angels speak, we need to heed them. If Zacharias had believed Gabriel, he could have been singing and shouting praise to God during the next nine months rather than having to remain silent—the penalty for his unbelief.

In Revelation 10 we have a strong angel coming down and roaring like a lion. Let's review verses 5 through 7 to see what else occurs:

146   CHAPTER 7 . . .

> 5 And the angel whom I saw standing on the sea and on the land
> lifted up his right hand to heaven,
> 6 and swore by Him who lives forever and ever, WHO CREATED
> HEAVEN AND THE THINGS IN IT, AND THE EARTH AND THE
> THINGS IN IT, AND THE SEA AND THE THINGS IN IT, that
> there shall be delay no longer.
> 7 but in the days of the voice of the seventh angel, when he is
> about to sound, then the mystery of God is finished, as He preached
> to His servants the prophets.
>
> —Revelation 10

The angel is probably holding the scroll in his left hand as
he lifts his right hand to heaven. When you are sworn into court,
what do you do? You put your left hand on the Bible and raise
your right hand. You are taking an oath. This verse is possibly
where that tradition comes from.

Underscoring the importance of this long–awaited announcement by *swearing* to its truth, the angel delivers his message. He tells us that God will delay no longer. It is time to wrap
up this age and get on with God's plan. God went to a lot of
trouble to have an angel come down and tell us that, didn't He?
Praise the Lord!

Compare this to Revelation 6:11 where the souls of the
martyred saints under the altar were told to rest a little longer.
The time for patient anticipation is ended; it is now time for
their prayers to be answered. There will *no longer* be any delay.

This ties in with the mystery which we mentioned when
we discussed 1 Corinthians 15. Let's review what we read earlier:

> 50 Now I say this, brethren, that flesh and blood cannot inherit
> the kingdom of God; nor does the perishable inherit the imperish-
> able.
> 51 Behold, I tell you a mystery; we shall not all sleep, but we
> shall all be changed,
> 52 in a moment, in the twinkling of an eye, at the last trumpet;
> for the trumpet will sound, and the dead will be raised imperishable,
> and we shall be changed.
>
> —1 Corinthians 15

The mystery is going to be finished or completed during
the period of the seventh trumpet sounding (Revelation 10:7).

We don't know *when* during that period, but we do know that it will be completed then.

I might note that up until this point (from Chapter 4 through 9) John has been, at least spiritually, in heaven. But in Revelation 10:1, John says, ". . . I saw another strong angel coming down out of heaven . . ."; at this point he seems to be on earth in his visions.

Now let us proceed with the remainder of Revelation 10:

8 And the voice which I heard from heaven, *I heard* again speaking with me, and saying, "Go, take the book which is open in the hand of the angel who stands on the sea and on the land."

9 And I went to the angel, telling him to give me the little book. And he said to me, "Take it, and eat it; and it will make your stomach bitter, but in your mouth it will be sweet as honey."

10 And I took the little book out of the angel's hand and ate it, and it was in my mouth sweet as honey; and when I had eaten it, my stomach was made bitter.

11 And they said to me, "You must prophesy again concerning many peoples and nations and tongues and kings."

A similar episode is recorded in Ezekiel 2 and 3:

8 "Now you, son of man, listen to what I am speaking to you; do not be rebellious like that rebellious house. Open your mouth and eat what I am giving you."

9 Then I looked, behold, a hand was extended to me; and lo, a scroll *was* in it.

10 When He spread it out before me, it was written on the front and back; and written on it were lamentations, mourning and woe.

–Ezekiel 2

1 Then He said to me, "Son of man, eat what you find; eat this scroll, and go, speak to the house of Israel."

2 So I opened my mouth, and He fed me this scroll.

3 And He said to me, "Son of man, feed your stomach, and fill your body with this scroll which I am giving you." Then I ate it, and it was sweet as honey in my mouth.

–Ezekiel 3

So we see that Ezekiel was also asked to eat a scroll. Back in Revelation, shortly after the passage we just read, when the seventh trumpet is actually sounded, Christ returns to reign as Lord and King. The way that I would tend to interpret the eating of the scrolls is that John saw the sweetness of the return of the Lord, just as Ezekiel was looking forward to the coming of Christ the first time.

Yet Ezekiel really did not see the wrath of God poured out upon the earth. (The scroll that he ate did not turn bitter in his stomach.) John saw both the sweetness of the Lord's coming and the bitterness of the time of wrath and extreme tribulation that the world was about to experience. I think that he understood what was on the scroll and saw both aspects of it. The Lord symbolically is telling us that His return will be the sweetest thing that we can imagine. When we see Jesus we will be like Him (1 John 3:2). On the other hand, there is some bitterness that must take place also. Notice that John is instructed to *eat* the scroll. God does not want John simply to be an observer of the events he is witnessing. He wants him to *digest* them, making them a part of his being—heeding these great prophecies.

I believe that God meant this for all of us in a broader sense. When we learn things about Him, we must allow them to become a part of our being. In Matthew 4:4, God says that man shall not live by bread alone but by every word that proceeds out of the mouth of God. We can't just let the words of God go in one ear and out the other. That isn't spiritual food. Spiritual food, just like natural food, requires ingestion and digestion to be of value. God's word needs to be chewed and assimilated into our lives. If you aren't already doing this, I would certainly encourage you to begin today. We need to "heed" these lessons from God.

REVELATION 11:1–2
–MEASURE THE TEMPLE

Now, let's move on to the first couple of verses in Revelation 11:

1 And there was given me a measuring rod like a staff; and someone said, "Rise and measure the temple of God, and the altar, and those who worship in it.

2 "And leave out the court which is outside the temple, and do not measure it, for it has been given to the nations; and they will tread under foot the holy city for forty-two months. . . ."

This is referring to a temple on the earth. At this point, let me give you a little bit of background on the temple in Jerusalem. There were three temples altogether. The one that Solomon built was destroyed in 586 B.C. by Nebuchadnezzar. Ezra and Nehemiah rebuilt a temple, which was destroyed in 168 B.C. by Epiphanes. The third temple, the temple of Herod, was destroyed in 70 A.D. by Titus Vespasian.

The book of Revelation was written approximately sixty years after Christ died. It was written from about 90 to 95 A.D. This temple that John is told to measure could not be the temple that existed during Christ's time because the book of Revelation was written after that temple was destroyed in 70 A.D. There has not been a temple since then. Some people feel that the destruction of the temple spoken of in Revelation has already occurred because of the temple destroyed in 70 A.D., but when you place things in context, the destruction of the temple that we just read about is yet to come, sometime within the sixth and seventh trumpet era.

The Dome of the Rock was completed in about 1542 and stands, supposedly, on the sight of the Herodian temple. In the *New American Standard Bible,* an alternate reading for the *temple* of God is the *sanctuary.* The Greek word actually used there is "nads" which is translated as *sanctuary* in most versions. So the temple spoken of here in Revelation *could* be some other structure, such as the great Synagogue; it does not necessarily need to be a temple built on the place where the Dome of the Rock now stands and where the previous three Jewish temples stood. It is also possible that a temple could be built next to the Dome of the Rock, with the Dome of the Rock being in the outer court, which is yet to be "trampled underfoot" by the nations. There *will be* a temple, a sanctuary, or a place of worship someplace in Jerusalem that John is told here to (symbolically) measure.

There were a couple of courts in Solomon's and Herod's temples—one for the men and one for the women. There was also an outer court where anybody could go. When John is told to measure this temple, he is told to leave out the outside court, where the Gentiles or nonbelievers gather. (The Dome of the Rock could be located there, as I said before.) So this is talking about measuring just those devoted to Jehovah God.

You should also realize that when this passage refers to "measuring," it is not really talking about physical dimensions. Let's look at Zechariah 2:

> 1 Then I lifted up my eyes and looked, and behold, *there was* a man with a measuring line in his hand.
>
> . 2 So I said, "Where are you going?" And he said to me, "To measure Jerusalem, to see how wide it is and how long it is."
>
> 3 And behold, the angel who was speaking with me was going out, and another angel was coming out to meet him,
>
> 4 and said to him, "Run, speak to that young man, saying, 'Jerusalem will be inhabited without walls, because of the multitude of men and cattle within it.
>
> 5 'For I,' declares the LORD, 'will be a wall of fire around her, and I will be the glory in her midst.'"

It appears that when God "measures" a city, He is actually taking stock of it preparatory to either protecting it or destroying it. Here in Zechariah, God is sending an angel to measure the city so that He can place a ring of fire around it for protection.

In Revelation, God enlists John to measure the believers' part of the temple in the holy city (which would imply Jerusalem), so that He can protect those who are in the temple and are dedicated to God, while the outer court and the rest of the holy city suffer destruction.

The outer court and the holy city are going to be trampled underfoot for forty-two months, or three and one-half years. This is the first instance in which we are given a time factor. It may be that the Tribulation, up until this point, has lasted one year, three and one-half years, or twenty years; we honestly don't know. In a sense, we don't really have an accurate measure of just how long the Tribulation will be. We do, however, get the feeling that the time period from the measuring of the temple to the end of the Tribulation is three and one–half years.

Jerusalem is going to be trampled underfoot for three and one–half years. Only the believers will be protected. Some people would say that this happened in 70 A.D. or some other time, but in Luke 21 Jesus says this:

16 "But you will be delivered up even by parents and brothers and relatives and friends, and they will put *some* of you to death.

17 and you will be hated by all on account of My name.

18 "Yet not a hair of your head will perish.

19 "By your endurance you will gain your lives.

20 "But when you see Jerusalem surrounded by armies, then recognize that her desolation is at hand.

21 "Then let those who are in Judea flee to the mountains, and let those who are in the midst of the city depart, and let not those who are in the country enter the city;

22 because these are days of vengeance, in order that all things which are written may be fulfilled.

23 "Woe to those who are with child and to those who nurse babes in those days; for there will be great distress upon the land, and wrath to this people,

24 and they will fall by the edge of the sword, and will be led captive into all the nations; and Jerusalem will be trampled underfoot by the Gentiles until the times of the Gentiles be fulfilled. . . ."

–Luke 21

This is not referring to Jerusalem being trampled by the Romans in 70 A.D. because that did not last until the time of the Gentiles was fulfilled. Christ says that there is a time coming when Jerusalem will be trampled underfoot that will continue until the time of the Gentiles has ended (or rather, this age has ended).

REVELATION 11:3–13
–THE TWO WITNESSES

Now let's proceed with the next portion of Revelation 11:

3   "And I will grant *authority* to my two witnesses, and they will prophesy for twelve hundred and sixty days, clothed in sackcloth."

4   These are the two olive trees and the two lampstands that stand before the Lord of the earth.

5   And if anyone desires to harm them, fire proceeds out of their mouth and devours their enemies; and if anyone would desire to harm them, in this manner he must be killed.

6   These have the power to shut up the sky, in order that rain may not fall during the days of their prophesying; and they have power over the waters to turn them into blood, and to smite the earth with every plague, as often as they desire.

7   And when they have finished their testimony, the beast that comes up out of the abyss will make war with them, and overcome them and kill them.

8   And their dead bodies *will lie* in the street of the great city which mystically is called Sodom and Egypt, where also their Lord was crucified.

9   And those from the peoples and tribes and tongues and nations *will* look at their dead bodies for three days and a half, and will not permit their dead bodies to be laid in a tomb.

10   And those who dwell on the earth *will* rejoice over them and make merry; and they will send gifts to one another, because these two prophets tormented those who dwell on the earth.

11   And after the three and a half days the breath of life from God came into them, and they stood on their feet; and great fear fell upon those who were beholding them.

12   And they heard a loud voice from heaven saying to them, "Come up here." And they went up into heaven in the cloud, and their enemies beheld them.

13   And in that hour there was a great earthquake, and a tenth of the city fell; and seven thousand people were killed in the earthquake, and the rest were terrified and gave glory to the God of heaven.

–Revelation 11

Let's see if we can digest this bite by bite. There are many rich things here. First, we see that God never abandons his people without a witness. God is leaving a witness for Himself in this instance.

Hal Lindsey, author of *The Late Great Planet Earth,* and a number of other commentators, say that the two witnesses are undoubtedly Moses and Elijah. I definitely disagree with that. I will give you their reasoning and then explain why I don't believe this interpretation is possible.

These people say that neither Moses nor Elijah finished their ministries, so they are coming back to complete their work. One of Moses' greatest miracles was turning water into blood, and one of Elijah's was shutting up the sky. These are the same miracles that are mentioned in this passage of scripture in Revelation. Because of the common elements, it is presumed that the two witnesses must be Moses and Elijah.

However, it is not possible for Moses to be one of these two. Let's see what Hebrews 9 has to say on this:

> 27 . . . it is appointed for men to die once and after this *comes* judgment . . .

Moses has already died once, and he would be dying again if he were killed as one of the two witnesses. That would be inconsistent with what the Bible says. There is no reincarnation because a man only dies once. Enoch and Elijah are the only two men who have been taken by the Lord directly without dying. In Malachi 4 we read:

> 5 "Behold, I am going to send you Elijah the prophet before the coming of the great and terrible day of the LORD.
> 6 "And he will restore the hearts of the fathers to *their* children, and the hearts of the children to their fathers, lest I come and smite the land with a curse."

Thus, it was prophesied in the Old Testament that Elijah would return. Now let's look at Mark 9:

> 11 And they *began* questioning Him, saying, *"Why is it* that the scribes say that Elijah must come first?"
> 12 And He said to them, "Elijah does first come and restore everything. And *yet* how is it written of the Son of Man that He should suffer many things and be treated with contempt?
> 13 "But I say to you, that Elijah has indeed come, and they did to him whatever they wished, just as it is written of him."

Here Christ tells His disciples that Elijah *has* returned. We know that he returned as John the Baptist (Matthew 11:11–15).

Elijah did not die when he was taken up into the fiery chariot; however, he did die as John the Baptist, for John the Baptist was beheaded by Herod. So both Moses and Elijah have already died once. This is why I cannot agree with those who take the standpoint that Moses and Elijah are the two witnesses.

Now who are the two witnesses? We do not know whether they are going to be two individuals, who will live in the future, or two "companies" of witnesses. Probably, half of all commentators on the book of Revelation would say that this refers to two individuals, and the other half would say that it is two witness companies. Personally, I tend to think that it will be two companies of witnesses.

These two witnesses—whoever they may be—will prophesy for 1260 days. The Jewish year is 360 days, not 365. This is why the Jewish months keep catching up with us once every few thousand years. By the Jewish calendar, 1260 days is exactly three and one-half years.

The two witnesses, who are going to witness for three and a half years, are said in Revelation 11:4 to be the two olive trees and the two lampstands that stand before the Lord of the earth. This description is something which can be found in the Old Testament as well. Let's look at Zechariah 4:

> 1 Then the angel who was speaking with me returned, and roused me as a man who is awakened from his sleep.
>
> 2 And he said to me, "What do you see?" And I said, "I see, and behold, a lampstand all of gold with its bowl on the top of it, and its seven lamps on it with seven spouts belonging to each of the lamps which are on the top of it;
>
> 3 also two olive trees by it, one on the right side of the bowl and the other on its left side." . . .
>
> 11 Then I answered and said to him, "What are these two olive trees on the right of the lampstand and on its left?"
>
> 12 And I answered the second time and said to him, "What are the two olive branches which are beside the two golden pipes, which empty the golden *oil* from themselves?"
>
> 13 So he answered me saying, "Do you not know what these are?" And I said, "No, my lord."
>
> 14 Then he said, "These are the two anointed ones, who are standing by the Lord of the whole earth."
>
> —Zechariah 4

These two olive trees are the two anointed witnesses of God. They will be empowered in a special way by God.

If the two witnesses are actually two companies of Christians, there is the possibility that we may be a part of that group. If so, God will want us to be like the two witnesses described in Revelation 11. He will want us to be anointed witnesses for Him during the end days of this age. That not only means that He will give us the words that He wants us to speak, but also (reviewing Revelation 11) that He will give us power over nature "to shut up the sky, in order that rain may not fall, to have power over the waters to turn them into blood, and to smite the earth with every plague." Most Christians are not even aware of this possibility and, therefore, might never exercise authority over nature, even if God wanted them to. God's initial command to Adam and Eve was to take dominion over the earth and subdue it. That command has never been revoked; we are still under that command. I believe that God wants to anoint us and give us the power to do that very thing in the days that lie ahead. Those Christians who do not believe in miracles will be in for some rude awakenings.

When the two witnesses are attacked (Revelation 11:5), fire proceeds out of their mouths, and their enemies are killed. Almost universally, Christians perceive that killing is, in all instances, wrong. Even if God were to call upon them to do so, I think that it would be extremely hard for some Christians to say, "In the name of Christ, be consumed with fire," or something of that sort. But I do believe that someday we will *need* to know how to move in supernatural power. A special sensitivity to the Holy Spirit will be necessary in order to be a part of this two witness company that the Lord is going to raise up during this time period.

Lest you think that the ability to call down fire and destroy one's enemies is something unique to the book of Revelation, let's examine a situation recorded in 2 Kings, wherein Elijah exhibited this ability:

9 Then *the king* sent to him a captain of fifty with his fifty. And he went up to him, and behold, he was sitting on the top of the hill. And he said to him, "O man of God, the king says, 'Come down.'"

10   And Elijah answered and said to the captain of fifty, "If I am a man of God, let fire come down from heaven and consume you and your fifty." Then fire came down from heaven and consumed him and his fifty.

11   So he again sent to him another captain of fifty with his fifty. And he answered and said to him "O man of God, thus says the king, 'Come down quickly.'"

12   And Elijah answered and said to them, "If I am a man of God, let fire come down from heaven and consume you and your fifty." Then the fire of God came down from heaven and consumed him and his fifty.

13   So he again sent the captain of a third fifty with his fifty. When the third captain of fifty went up, he came and bowed down on his knees before Elijah, and begged him and said to him, "O man of God, please let my life and the lives of these fifty servants of yours be precious in your sight.

14   "Behold fire came down from heaven, and consumed the first two captains of fifty with their fifties; but now let my life be precious in your sight."

15   And the angel of the LORD said to Elijah, "Go down with him; do not be afraid of him." So he arose and went down with him to the king.

–2 Kings 1

As you can see from these verses, under the direction of God Elijah called down fire and destroyed the first two captains and their companies of fifty. However, God apparently did not direct him to do that in the third case. (Just as an aside, if God leads us a certain way two times in a row, it would be easy to make the mistake of assuming that on a third occasion God would want us to do the same thing. Perhaps because we do not listen moment by moment to God's direction, He cannot entrust us with this kind of power as of yet. Also, we have to be leading a holy and righteous life to be able to have this type of power, so that God can be confident that we would not use it selfishly. I believe that God wants us to live holy and righteous lives, walking very sensitive to the Holy Spirit so that He *can* give us additional power.)

Returning to Revelation 11 and the two witnesses, in verse 7 we read that nobody can touch them until they finish their testimony and have completed what God gave them to do. I believe that we too can boldly move out for Christ, knowing that nobody will be able to kill us until we have completed what God wants us to do. When our service for God is finished, we will doubtless be anxious to go and join Him.

Verses 7-10 of Revelation 11 say that the two witnesses will be killed by the beast from the abyss. (We will be dealing more with the beast a little later.) Their bodies are going to lie in Jerusalem, which is also called Sodom and Egypt. It will probably come as a shock to you to hear Jerusalem spoken of in this way. Sodom and Egypt were two places that were really hostile toward God. They enslaved God's people, and in Sodom they tried to rape God's angel messengers (Genesis 19:1-11). Jerusalem, too, was malevolent toward Jesus. This indicates that Jerusalem is still going to be antagonistic toward God's people (just like Egypt and Sodom used to be) at the time when the bodies of the two witnesses lie in Jerusalem.

Many people think that after the Rapture, the Jewish people are going to turn to the Lord, and Jerusalem is going to be the glorious center of the witness of God. This belief is not in accordance with the Bible. Revelation 11 tells us that the inhabitants of Jerusalem are still going to be in rebellion toward God. They are still going to kill God's witnesses. In fact, if God did not place a ring of protection around His people in the temple, no one would live through this.

Some people use verse 9 of Revelation 11 to try to prove that the Bible isn't true. Let's review what that verse says:

9 And those from the peoples and tribes and tongues and nations *will* look at their dead bodies for three and a half days, and will not permit their dead bodies to be laid in a tomb.

–Revelation 11

Critics have said that it would be impossible for the entire world to view the bodies at the same time. However, with the advent of television and communication satellites, it is now certainly within the realm of possibility for all the people in the world to view the bodies at the same time. We can now begin to see *how* some of these prophecies could conceivably be fulfilled.

After the two witnesses are killed, the people of the earth will have a gigantic party. They will give gifts to each other and there will be rejoicing and merrymaking because God's prophets are dead. That is a sad commentary on what the state of the world (and Jerusalem) will be at that point in time. This means that people will have really turned against God.

Verse 11 says that after three and a half days, the two witnesses come back to life. I don't think that this has anything to do with the three days that Christ was in the grave. Three and a half in the Bible, as we have seen, tends to be related to a time of turmoil. The time of celebration here is a temporary victory for the sources of evil, but God ends that celebration quickly.

In verse 12, a voice from heaven says to "come up into heaven." Some people would say that this is the Rapture and is symbolic of all the Christians going up into heaven. That may be. Two verses later the seventh trumpet sounds at the time when the Scriptures indicate that the Rapture *does* occur. It is unclear as to whether these are two different descriptions of the same event, or possibly some minute time difference between the voice and the trumpet. It could be that these two witnesses are representing all Christians, and that they go up at this time, and a few verses later, when the seventh trumpet is sounded, the rest of the Christians are taken up. This is a possibility we should not necessarily exclude. What we know of a certainty is that the time for the Rapture is near and, according to Revelation 10:6, the delay is over. Praise God! He will bring His people to Himself at the right time!

In Revelation 11:13 an earthquake comes and part of Jerusalem falls. The people who are not killed give glory to God. I think this is saying that they give *praise* to God. Any part of God's creation can praise Him—non–Christians, rocks, mountains, oceans, dragons of the deep, and so forth (see Psalm 148). I don't think their giving glory to God is talking about repentance to a born-again experience.

REVELATION 11:15-19
—THE SEVENTH TRUMPET

We will now read from Revelation 11:15 to the end of the chapter:

15   And the seventh angel sounded; and there arose loud voices in heaven, saying,

"The kingdom of the world has become *the kingdom* of our Lord, of His Christ; and He will reign forever and ever."

16   And the twenty-four elders, who sit on their thrones before God, fell on their faces and worshiped God,

17   saying,

"We give Thee thanks, O Lord God, the Almighty, who art and who wast, because Thou has taken Thy great power and hast begun to reign.

18   "And the nations were enraged, and Thy wrath came, and the time *came* for the dead to be judged, and *the time* to give their reward to Thy bond-servants the prophets and to the saints and to those who fear Thy name, the small and the great, and to destroy those who destroy the earth."

19   And the temple of God which is in heaven was opened; and the ark of His covenant appeared in His temple, and there were flashes of lightning and sounds and peals of thunder and an earthquake and a great hailstorm.

—Revelation 11

Christ has now begun to reign (verse 17)! The kingdom of the world *has* become the kingdom of God (verse 15)! These kingdoms had formerly belonged to Satan. Now they have been taken over by God. This alone implies that the Tribulation is over because obviously Satan still rules the world during the Tribulation.

Not only does the Rapture occur at the seventh trumpet (see Chapter 4 of this book), but in verse 18, which is also part of the seventh trumpet, we see that the battle of Armageddon occurs, too. Christ will "destroy those who destroy the earth." Not all human beings on the earth will be killed at the battle of Armageddon. The significance of the battle is that Christ will destroy all of the armies gathered against Him. Those people who are overtly hostile toward God, and those who destroy the earth are going to be destroyed. God is *righteous,* which means *He will always do the right thing.* As we will see later in this book, only those who receive the mark of the beast *and* worship the beast will be destroyed. This implies that all those who do not fit into this category are spared. These are the ones over whom we (either the overcomers or all Christians) will reign for one thousand years.

I believe this seventh trumpet is right at the end of the Tribulation. This is when the Rapture and the battle of Armageddon occur. Some think that this seventh trumpet sounds in the middle of the Tribulation and that that is when the Rapture occurs. I am convinced that the Rapture occurs whenever the seventh trumpet blows. But remember Christ begins to reign on the earth at the seventh trumpet, so I would have to place it at the very end of the great Tribulation.

We have covered a lot of ground in this chapter. The main thing we see is that God has everything under control. He is going to protect His people. He will have anointed witnesses who will exhibit supernatural power to the extent that nobody will be able to kill them (until God decides it is time for them to be martyred). If we are in this category of being witnesses for Him, it will be both bitter and sweet. We will rejoice that God is using us, but we will be sad because of some of the judgments coming upon the earth. At this point in time, God is going to wrap up this current age and start the millennium age, wherein Christ will rule and reign here on the earth. That will be glorious. I think it will be a wonderful time to be alive. Let us all look forward to being used as mighty witnesses for God!

8

THE WOMAN,
THE MAN CHILD
AND THE TWO BEASTS
(Revelation 12 & 13)

As we said earlier, the events of Revelation are not in chronological order. Even if there is a rough chronology, it would end with Revelation 11. We have seen the seven seals and the seven trumpets. Now we are going to be looking at what the Lord has shown me to be seven "snapshots." These seven snapshots can be thought of as seven film clips of different parts of the Tribulation, at times covering a spectrum even broader than the Tribulation. The seven snapshots are as follows:

Snapshot	Scriptures	Title
1	Revelation 12:1 – 13:18	The Woman, The Man Child and The Two Beasts
2	Revelation 14:1-5	The Second 144,000
3	Revelation 14:6-13	The Three Angels
4	Revelation 14:14-20	The Two Harvests
5	Revelation 15:1 – 16:21	The Seven Angels and The Seven Bowls of Wrath
6	Revelation 17:1 – 18:24	Mystery Babylon
7	Revelation 19:1-10	The Marriage Feast

With a little prayerful examination of the Scriptures, one would have to conclude that these portions of scripture are miniature scenes of various portions of the Tribulation, not necessarily in chronological order. For example, we see the fall of Babylon twice during this sequence. In Revelation 14:8, one of the angels says that Babylon has fallen. Later, in Revelation 18, we find that Babylon falls again. It is obvious that Babylon is not destroyed twice during the Tribulation; therefore, we must be viewing snapshots of overlapping events, not arranged in actual time sequence.

Another way to look at Revelation 12–19 is that these are seven different visions. If you have never had a vision, think of it as similar to dreaming while you are awake. If you had seven different dreams about a particular period of time, it is possible that the dreams might overlap; you might see the same event occurring at the end of one dream and perhaps in the middle of a later dream.

You can usually tell when John is relating a new vision that he had because he will frequently use a phrase like, "And then I saw . . . ."

Now, let us turn our attention specifically to the first of these seven exciting snapshots.

SNAPSHOT 1
–THE WOMAN, THE MAN CHILD
AND THE TWO BEASTS

This snapshot covers Revelation 12 and 13. We will begin with the first portion which deals with the woman and the man child:

1 And a great sign appeared in heaven; a woman clothed with the sun, and the moon under her feet, and on her head a crown of twelve stars;

2 and she was with child; and she cried out, being in labor and in pain to give birth.

3 And another sign appeared in heaven: and behold, a great red dragon having seven heads and ten horns, and on his heads were seven diadems.

4 And his tail swept away a third of the stars of heaven, and threw them to the earth. And the dragon stood before the woman who was about to give birth, so that when she gave birth he might devour her child.

5 And she gave birth to a son, a male child, who is to rule all the nations with a rod of iron; and her child was caught up to God and to His throne.

6 And the woman fled into the wilderness where she had a place prepared by God, so that there she might be nourished for one thousand two hundred and sixty days.

7 And there was war in heaven, Michael and his angels waging war with the dragon. And the dragon and his angels waged war,

8 and they were not strong enough, and there was no longer a place found for them in heaven.

9 And the great dragon was thrown down, the serpent of old who is called the devil and Satan, who deceives the whole world; he was thrown down to the earth, and his angels were thrown down with him.

10 And I heard a loud voice in heaven, saying, "Now the salvation, and the power, and the kingdom of our God and the authority of His Christ have come, for the accuser of our brethren has been thrown down, who accuses them before our God day and night.

11 "And they overcame him because of the blood of the Lamb and because of the word of their testimony, and they did not love their life even to death.

12 "For this reason, rejoice, O heavens and you who dwell in them. Woe to the earth and the sea, because the devil has come down to you, having great wrath, knowing that he has *only* a short time."

13 And when the dragon saw that he was thrown down to the earth, he persecuted the woman who gave birth to the male child.

14 And the two wings of the great eagle were given to the woman, in order that she might fly into the wilderness to her place, where she was nourished for a time and times and half a time, from the presence of the serpent.

15 And the serpent poured water like a river out of his mouth after the woman, so that he might cause her to be swept away with the flood.

16 And the earth helped the woman, and the earth opened its mouth and drank up the river which the dragon poured out of his mouth.

17   And the dragon was enraged with the woman, and went off to make war with the rest of her offspring, who keep the commandments of God and hold to the testimony of Jesus.

—Revelation 12

1   And he stood on the sand of the seashore.
And I saw a beast coming up out of the sea, having ten horns and seven heads, and on his horns *were* ten diadems, and on his heads *were* blasphemous names.

—Revelation 13

Before going through Chapter 12 verse by verse, we need to cast it in a broad reference frame. First, verse 1 says that "a great sign appeared in heaven." A modern translation might be "a miraculous signpost." Something is going to happen in heaven that will be an incredible sign, announcing the "birthing" of this man child by the woman. What occurs in this snapshot is going to be of major significance, so we need to try to understand it as best we can.

This is probably one of the most confusing chapters in Revelation and in the Bible as a whole. There are two basic interpretations of Revelation 12 of which I am aware.

The classical interpretation, which we will go through first, is that the woman described is Israel (physical Israel), and the man child is Christ. Some scholars believe that the birth of the man child represents the actual physical birth of Christ on earth; others feel this refers to the arrival of His kingdom.

Now, let's examine the point of view that the woman represents Israel and the man child represents Christ.

Some commentators maintain that the woman clothed with the sun, with the moon under her feet, and a crown of 12 stars on her head, refers back to Joseph's dream (Genesis 37:9–11). He had a dream in which the sun, the moon and the 11 stars bowed down to him (his star). His father interpreted this as Joseph's mother and himself being the sun and the moon, and the 11 stars being Joseph's 11 brothers. (This, of course, won him no popularity awards with his brothers.)

You could then go on to say that Joseph is a type of Israel. He was carried away into captivity and God raised him up and restored him. Many of the things that happened to the nation of

Israel are reminiscent of things which happened to Joseph. If the woman is Israel, the stars on the woman's head would be the 12 patriarchs (Joseph and his brothers, who were the heads of the 12 tribes). The people who hold this view of the woman base this on: (1) the dream of Joseph where the 12 stars represented the 12 patriarchs, and (2) the fact that Joseph represents Israel.

Another thing that the proponents of this position point out is that this woman is expecting; therefore, she is not a virgin. All the way through the Old Testament, the nation of Israel is frequently referred to as a wife or an unfaithful wife. Let's read one example:

15 Thou hast increased the nation, O LORD,
   Thou hast increased the nation, Thou art glorified;
   Thou hast extended all the borders of the land.
16 O LORD, they sought Thee in distress;
   They could only whisper a prayer,
   Your chastening was upon them.
17 As the pregnant woman approaches *the time* to give birth,
   She writhes *and* cries out in her labor pains,
   Thus were we before Thee, O LORD.
18 We were pregnant, we writhed *in labor*,
   We gave birth, as it were, *only* to the wind.
   We could not accomplish deliverance for the earth
   Nor were inhabitants of the world born.

–Isaiah 26

Here is a picture of Israel referred to as a pregnant woman. Conversely, the church is frequently referred to as a virgin. So the woman could not be the church, the theory goes, for she was no longer a virgin. In 2 Corinthians 11 we read this:

2 For I am jealous for you with a godly jealousy; for I betrothed you to one husband, that to Christ I might present you *as* a pure virgin.

Further in Revelation 12, the dragon tries to kill the man child. This is said to represent Herod trying to kill Jesus. Verse 5, where it speaks of the man child being caught up to God and His throne, is compared to Christ's ascension. Revelation 12:5 says that the man child will rule the nations with a rod of iron.

This is prophesied of Christ in the Old Testament (Psalm 2:8–9) and also in Revelation 19; hence the belief that the man child is Christ:

> **15   And from His mouth comes a sharp sword, so that with it He may smite the nations; and He will rule them with a rod of iron; and He treads the wine press of the fierce wrath of God, the Almighty.**
>
> **—Revelation 19**

Those who hold to this interpretation would also claim that the persecution of the woman corresponds with the persecution of the Jews through the ages. (They tend to get Jews and Israelites confused. Remember only one–twelfth, or 8 percent, of Israel is made up of Jews. Too often Israel is viewed as being all Jews.)

There can be no doubt that the book of Revelation is extremely difficult to interpret, and I would not argue with someone who holds to the interpretation I have outlined above. However, this interpretation does present a lot of problems for me, which we will now discuss.

First, in Revelation the man child ascends so the dragon will not kill Him. To me, Christ's ascension was not to escape Satan because He had won the victory over Satan in death. There was a totally different reason for Christ to ascend.

Another problem that I have with this interpretation is that the woman is seen both in heaven in verse 1 and on earth in verse 13. Physical Israel does not deal in the heavenlies, like Christians do. Their involvement is exclusively with things on the earth. So for Israel to be in the heavens presents a problem.

In Revelation 12:17, we learn that the woman has other offspring besides the man child; I believe that these are Christians because they are said to "keep the commandments of God and hold to the testimony of Jesus." So if the nation of Israel is the woman, this means that the "other offspring" (who are Christians) must all be biological descendants of Israel. This is a problem since it is obvious that this group of Christians can and does contain Gentiles.

Another problem is that twice it says that the woman is being persecuted for three and a half years. Three and a half is repeated many times because God wants to emphasize it. If He just said it once, it might be taken as a symbolic number, but he emphasizes it repeatedly and also breaks the three and one–half years into days for added emphasis. Certainly, the Jewish part of Israel has lasted more than three and one–half years.

Still another difficulty is that, at this point, Satan has access to both the throne of God and the earth. In the book of Job he talks with God, yet you see him on the earth in Genesis talking with Eve. So he does have free access to both places. Right now, he is standing before God accusing Christians day and night. If you wake up in the middle of the night and feel a spiritual struggle going on, Satan is conversing with God trying to convince Him of how bad you are. Therefore, if in this passage the woman *does* represent Israel and the man child represents Christ, Satan would no longer be accusing us because the accuser of the brethren is thrown down from the presence of God in this chapter, and that would already have occurred. I see Satan still in that accusing role, which is a further snag in this theory.

Also, the Revelation 12–13 snapshot includes the appearance of the Antichrist. Again, if the woman is Israel, the Antichrist's appearing as part of this whole scene doesn't make sense because he has not yet appeared.

I am not saying that considering the woman as Israel and the man child as Christ is not a legitimate interpretation, but I do have some major difficulties with it.

THE WOMAN IS THE CHURCH AND THE MAN CHILD IS THE OVERCOMERS?

An interpretation which I lean toward is that the woman is the church and the man child represents the overcomers. Let me say a few words about this.

If an individual believes in the pre–Tribulation Rapture of the church, he has to exclude as a possibility the woman being the church because in his mind the church will not be on the earth during the Tribulation period. When we approach the Scriptures with a preconceived idea, we may exclude from consideration things that God would have us to consider. What I like to do when I study a passage is to tell God that I know nothing and to ask Him to tell me what it says. If it conflicts with something else that I know, I can dig back through the Scriptures and let the Holy Spirit resolve those conflicts in my heart. This is one possible error that the pre–Tribulation–Rapture advocates might make, because they would automatically exclude from consideration any possibility that the church might be the woman.

Hopefully, you will be open enough to at least consider the possibility that the woman might be the church and that the church is giving birth to some "overcomers." The overcomers, again, would be a subset of all Christians, as we discussed when we looked at Christ's letters to the churches. I believe these overcomers are going to have a unique roll in the Tribulation. Now, let's talk about some other concepts held today that may be misconceptions.

First, let's consider the "manifest sons of God." A significant number of believers today maintain that some Christians will become the "manifest sons of God," who will "bring in the kingdom of God" (or something of this nature). It is based on this scripture from Romans:

> 18 For I consider that the sufferings of this present time are not worthy to be compared with the glory that is to be revealed to us.
>
> 19 For the anxious longing of the creation waits eagerly for the revealing of the sons of God.
>
> 20 For the creation was subjected to futility, not of its own will, but because of Him who subjected it, in hope
>
> 21 that the creation itself also will be set free from its slavery to corruption into the freedom of the glory of the children of God.
>
> 22 For we know that the whole creation groans and suffers the pains of childbirth together until now.
>
> 23 And not only this, but also we ourselves, having the first fruits of the Spirit, even we ourselves groan within ourselves, waiting eagerly for *our* adoption as sons, the redemption of our body.
>
> –Romans 8

When we come into full adoption our bodies will be redeemed, according to verse 23. We will be made like Jesus! Let's look at all of the characteristics of this event: (1) our bodies will be redeemed, (2) we will come into full adoption, and (3) creation will be set free. I cannot see that creation is set free during the Tribulation. If anything, it is in chaos and turmoil with gigantic upheaval occurring. So I would have to put the manifestation of the sons of God at the end of the Tribulation, when our bodies will be redeemed, creation will be set free, and Christ will begin to reign for a thousand years over a perfectly liberated earth.

Those who believe that the manifestation of the sons of God will occur prior to the time when Christ returns to reign refer to this special group as the "first fruits company," the "manifest sons of God company," and by some other names. From what I can see here, the Scriptures clearly point out that it is at the end of the Tribulation that the sons of God will be made manifest. This is when we will come into our *full* right and role as sons of God. Our bodies will be redeemed, and we will rule and reign with Christ over a perfect nature. We are to live holy and righteous lives, but we are not going to "bring in the kingdom." *Christ* is going to do that.

Now I'm going to step out into some deep water. If Christ's life is a pattern for us, we can look at His life to help us understand the passage in Revelation 12. At one point He was born, just as we are born spiritually. At His baptism the Holy Spirit descended upon Him. This happens to us when we are baptized or filled with the Holy Spirit. He died and had a resurrected body, and at some point we too will die and have a resurrected body.

There is one major event in the life of Christ, though, that we tend to skip over: that is His experience on the Mount of Transfiguration. The glory and power of God came upon Him so mightily that He radiated. His face was like the sun. When this happened to Moses, his face shone so brightly that Aaron actually had to put a veil over it. It is possible that if we are living in the end times of this age, we could experience something like Christ did on the Mount of Transfiguration. The overcomers might have such an encounter with God, transfiguring them in the way that Jesus was. They would have the glory and power of God glowing on their faces.

It is possible, then, that the birth of the man child could be referring to a transfiguration experience wherein God will give us a special power that we will need to go through the remainder of the Tribulation. I must state clearly that I cannot find any scripture to back up this concept; I am just sharing what is on my heart. (I always like to label my opinion as distinct from what the Scriptures clearly say.)

If the woman is the church and the man child is the overcomers who have been transfigured, does this solve any of the problems we discussed concerning the more traditional interpretation of this passage of scripture? The problem of this occurring in the future and the appearance of the Antichrist has disappeared. The three and a half years of persecution you would expect, so that isn't a problem.

As Christians, who have not yet tasted death, we both live on the earth and battle in the heavenlies; so that problem is solved.

Let's examine a couple of scriptures with which you may not be familiar. There is a heaven where today's spiritual warfare is going on (Ephesians 6:12), and that is not where God is. God cannot tolerate any evil in His presence. There is also a heaven where God is:

> 6 Then God said, "Let there be an expanse in the midst of the waters, and let it separate the waters from the waters."
>
> 7 And God made the expanse, and separated the waters which were below the expanse from the waters which were above the expanse; and it was so;
>
> 8 And God called the expanse heaven. And there was evening and there was morning, a second day.
>
> —Genesis 1

I like to think of the "waters below" as the ocean and the "waters above" as the clouds. God created an expanse in between. In verse 8, He calls this expanse *heaven.* So the heaven that is referred to here is the concentric gaseous sphere surrounding the earth. Our feet are on the earth, and our heads are in the heaven, as described here. This is where the spiritual battle is going on.

We know that there is at least a third heaven, spoken of in 2 Corinthians. Most people believe that Paul was actually talking about himself and not somebody else:

> 2 I know a man in Christ who fourteen years ago—whether in the body I do not know, or out of the body I do not know, God knows—such a man was caught up to the third heaven.
> 3 And I know how such a man—whether in the body or apart from the body I do not know, God knows—
> 4 was caught up into Paradise, and heard inexpressible words, which a man is not permitted to speak.
>
> —2 Corinthians 12

So Paul was caught up into the third heaven, where he saw some incredibly marvelous things, which he was not permitted to reveal to us. Whether he was caught up in body or in spirit, he really did not know. Since we are involved in spiritual warfare, Christians are in the "heavens" as well as on the earth. So, again, the problem with Israel being earth–bound and not able to enter into the heavenly warfare sphere is no longer problematic.

Also, if the woman is the church, and she has other offspring, who are Christians but not overcomers (the man child), this doesn't present a problem either.

REVELATION 12
—A CLOSER LOOK

Let's now go back and examine Revelation 12 verse by verse:

> 1 And a great sign appeared in heaven: a woman clothed with the sun, and the moon under her feet, and on her head a crown of twelve stars; . . .
>
> —Revelation 12

What are these stars? Very often in the Scriptures angels are referred to as stars. I think we can interpret this verse in that way. I used to think that when all of this was being written, the writers looked at the fine dots up in the sky and thought that they were a host of angels. They didn't realize that each of those dots was a giant, flaming mass of hydrogen and helium, being converted so powerfully that it would be the equivalent of millions of hydrogen bombs exploding per second. Had they really known what the stars were, I did not think that John would have mistaken such a powerful heavenly body for a simple angel. But then the Lord showed me that the spiritual power that He gives to an angel is infinitely greater than the physical power of a sun. I think we often underestimate the power involved in spiritual warfare.

If the woman is the church, as we have discussed, and she wears a crown of twelve stars, this says that the church is greater than a whole host of suns; she just wears them like a wreath. The woman is clothed with the sun, which is one of the stars. The moon, which reflects the light of a star, is under her feet. This is looking at it from the physical side, but if the woman is the church and if you call these stars *angels* (and the angels are ministering spirits sent out to serve the elect—Hebrews 1:14), you get the same picture. I think this is really beautiful! God is saying that the church is a magnificent creature packed with power, if we would just turn on the valve and let it loose! Praise the Lord!

Now the woman was with child. Something wanted to come out—*needed* to come out—and the time was right for it. I sense in my spirit that the church is about "eight month's pregnant." Soon the Lord is going to bring forth something out of the church which will be glorious!

In verse 3 of Revelation 12 a dragon with seven heads and ten horns appears in the heavens (expanse). On each head is a crown (diadem). The beast, once the dragon gives power to it (Revelation 13), is described in the same way. The only difference is the number of crowns. So this must be the same system, being, or source that is bringing forth these events. The beast is also found in Daniel 7:

> 23   "Thus he said: 'The fourth beast will be a fourth kingdom on the earth, which will be different from all the *other* kingdoms, and it will devour the whole earth and tread it down and crush it.
>
> 24   'As for the ten horns, out of this kingdom ten kings will arise after them, and he will be different from the previous ones and will subdue three kings.

25   'And he will speak out against the Most High and wear down the saints of the Highest One, and he will intend to make alteration in times and in law; and they will be given into his hand for a time, times, and half a time....'"

This fourth beast in Daniel has ten horns. There are some reasons why people connect these prophecies with Rome. The first beast is interpreted as being the Babylonian kingdom; the second beast as the Medo–Persian kingdom; the third beast as the Grecian Empire; and the fourth as the Roman Empire. Some commentators think that the kingdom out of which the ten kings (ten horns in verse 24) will arise is the ancient Roman Empire in a revived or re–born form.

This is why you see so much interest in the European Economic Community and its ten nations. It covers roughly the same geographic area as the Roman Empire, so some people believe that this ten–nation confederacy may be the fulfillment of this prophecy. These nations may be the ten horns of which Daniel is speaking. Let's also take a look at Daniel 8:

5   While I was observing, behold, a male goat was coming from the west over the surface of the whole earth without touching the ground, and the goat *had* a conspicuous horn between his eyes.

6   And he came up to the ram that had the two horns, which I had seen standing in front of the canal, and rushed at him in his mighty wrath.

7   And I saw him come beside the ram, and he was enraged at him; and he struck the ram and shattered his two horns, and the ram had no strength to withstand him. So he hurled him to the ground and trampled on him, and there was none to rescue the ram from his power.

8   Then the male goat magnified *himself* exceedingly. But as soon as he was mighty, the large horn was broken; and in its place there came up four conspicuous *horns* toward the four winds of heaven.

9   And out of one of them came forth a rather small horn which grew exceedingly great toward the south, toward the east, and toward the Beautiful *Land.*

10   And it grew up to the host of heaven and caused some of the host and some of the stars to fall to the earth, and it trampled them down.

—Daniel 8

Here we have a description of Satan. In this last verse, it says that he caused some of the stars to fall to the earth—again stars being angels. Back in Revelation 12 we read:

> **4 And his tail swept away a third of the stars of heaven, and threw them to the earth. And the dragon stood before the woman who was about to give birth, so that when she gave birth he might devour her child.**

So Satan's influence caused a third of the angels (stars) to fall down to the earth. This is consistent with the prophecies of the Old Testament.

Verse 5 of Revelation 12 says that the man child is going to rule the nations with a rod of iron, yet Christ was the one who was prophesied to do this. However, in Revelation 2:26, 27, Christ promises "to him who overcomes" that he will rule the nations with a rod of iron. So the overcomers will rule the nations with Christ, which further substantiates the possibility that the man child is the overcomers.

Now comes the real problem in Revelation 12. It says that the man child was caught up to God and to His throne. Some people feel this is talking about Christ's ascension or about the Rapture. These are the easiest ways to interpret it. On the other hand, Paul was caught up to the third heaven, and John witnessed some things in heaven, but both returned and remained on the earth. It doesn't say that they were permanently taken to heaven (or even physically).

Looking at this prophecy in the same light as the experiences of John and Paul, and assuming that the man child does not *remain* in heaven, is the only way I can make sense out of this. It might be similar to the transfiguration process—a form of being caught up to God and His throne and endowed with His glory and power, before returning to the earth to do the work of the Lord (like Paul and John). I have not met anybody who interprets this passage that way, but after praying and thinking about it, this is what the Lord has shown me. I am just passing it on for whatever it might be worth.

By verse 6 of Revelation 12, I begin to get excited. Glorious things start to happen! It says that the woman flees into the wilderness. When we speak of fleeing into the wilderness, it is easy to develop a mental image of something like a herd of elk scattering at the sound of a rifle shot, or frightened people wandering about, shivering in caves or wilderness areas. This passage implies that God is not going to let His church experience that. It also says in verse 6 that the woman flees *to* something—to a place *prepared by God* to nourish her. So when the believers flee to the wilderness, it is going to be to a place which God has prepared, and there will be food.

Verses 7 through 9 describe the war in heaven which Satan lost. He and his angels were thrown down to the earth. Then in verses 10 and 11 Satan again loses to the overcomers here on earth.

> **10** And I heard a loud voice in heaven, saying,
> "Now the salvation, and the power, and the kingdom of our God and the authority of His Christ have come, for the accuser of our brethren has been thrown down, who accuses them before our God day and night.
> **11** "And they overcame him because of the blood of the Lamb and because of the word of their testimony, and they did not love their life even to death. . . ."
>
> —Revelation 12

How do we overcome the evil one? Verse 11 tells us the three things necessary to defeat him. The first is "the blood of the Lamb." As a Christian you must use the blood of the Lamb in your spiritual warfare. I have often seen people come against demons rebuking them in the name of Jesus. However, they sometimes forget to use the *blood* of Christ.

It is necessary to use both the name of Jesus and His blood. We need to plead the blood of Jesus to cover us and prevent us from being overcome by Satan. The blood of Jesus can "wash" a demon right out of a person. It is His blood that will cleanse and make whole. This is one of the three things we must do in order to defeat Satan and demons.

The second key to overcoming is the word of our testimony. Again, I don't think this refers simply to witnessing as we have been doing for years, but rather to an anointed speaking under God's control, having real power and authority. When the two witnesses speak, fire comes out of their mouths and consumes their enemies. They obviously speak with authority.

The third thing we must do to defeat Satan is to not love our lives even unto death. We must be perfectly willing to lay down our lives for Jesus.

Right after the first atomic bomb exploded, I heard Red Harper, the converted cowboy singer, talk at a youth conference. He said: "You know, this here *a*-tomic bomb don't bother me *a*-tall; it'll just be: *BOOM!* . . . 'Hello Lord'." If we are going to lose our lives for the Lord, praise God! We will instantly be in His presence! Will be stepping through a doorway into something more magnificent than what we know now. Paul wanted to die to be with the Lord but realized that it was better for those to whom he was writing and witnessing that he remain on the earth. I don't want any tears and sad faces at my funeral. Praise God, I'm going to be with the Lord! I want rejoicing instead!

Now let's take another look at verses 12 through 17 of Revelation 12:

12 "For this reason, rejoice, O heavens and you who dwell in them. Woe to the earth and the sea, because the devil has come down to you, having great wrath, knowing that he has *only* a short time."

13 And when the dragon saw that he was thrown down to the earth, he persecuted the woman who gave birth to the male *child.*

14 And the two wings of the great eagle were given to the woman, in order that she might fly into the wilderness to her place, where she was nourished for a time and times and half a time, from the presence of the serpent.

15 And the serpent poured water like a river out of his mouth after the woman, so that he might cause her to be swept away with the flood.

16 And the earth helped the woman, and the earth opened its mouth and drank up the river which the dragon poured out of his mouth.

17 And the dragon was enraged with the woman, and went off to make war with the rest of her offspring, who keep the commandments of God and hold to the testimony of Jesus.

Satan has been defeated in heaven and is being defeated by the overcomers on earth. In verse 12 we see that he begins to really get angry and starts to persecute with new vehemence because he doesn't have much time left. At that time there are going to be spiritual battles, warfare, and persecution like we have never known.

We have seen that God will provide a place and nourishment for the woman in the wilderness. Now He provides the transportation to that place (verse 14), and food and protection after she gets there. So is there anything to fear? No! When we have to flee from where we are, God is going to provide a place for us to go, the transportation to get there, and the protection and sustenance once we arrive. Praise God! (This does not mean that we do not need to make any preparations because we might need to endure quite a bit before He tells us to flee.)

Verse 15 says that the serpent pours water out of his mouth after the woman. We don't know if this is going to be physical water (or something else physical, like radioactive dust) or if it will be something spiritual in nature. It may even be both. Wherever the attack is, the earth will open up and swallow it, and God's people will again be protected. Whatever Satan throws at us, physical or spiritual, God will protect us. Praise the Lord!

It is difficult to know the identities of the other offspring referred to in verse 17. I believe that this is simply another reference to the overcomers. It appears here that not all Christians will be taken to the wilderness. Some will be left behind to fight Satan. It would seem reasonable that these would be the overcomers.

REVELATION 13:1-10
—THE DICTATOR BEAST

The first half of Revelation 13 describes the first of two beasts—the dictator beast:

1 **And he stood on the sand of the seashore.**
And I saw a beast coming up out of the sea, having ten horns and seven heads, and on his horns *were* ten diadems, and on his heads *were* blasphemous names.

2 And the beast which I saw was like a leopard, and his feet were *like those* of a bear, and his mouth like the mouth of a lion. And the dragon gave him his power and his throne and great authority.

3 And *I saw* one of his heads as if it had been slain, and his fatal wound was healed. And the whole earth was amazed *and followed* after the beast;

4 and they worshiped the dragon, because he gave his authority to the beast; and they worshiped the beast, saying, "Who is like the beast, and who is able to wage war with him?"

5 And there was given to him a mouth speaking arrogant words and blasphemies; and authority to act for forty-two months was given to him.

6 And he opened his mouth in blasphemies against God, to blaspheme His name and His tabernacle, *that is,* those who dwell in heaven.

7 And it was given to him to make war with the saints and to overcome them; and authority over every tribe and people and tongue and nation was given to him.

8 And all who dwell on the earth will worship him, *everyone* whose name has not been written from the foundation of the world in the book of life of the Lamb who has been slain.

9 If any one has an ear, let him hear.

10 If any one *is destined* for captivity, to captivity he goes; if any one kills with the sword, with the sword he must be killed. Here is the perseverance and the faith of the saints.

—Revelation 13

There are two beasts in the book of Revelation. There is the dictator beast and the prophet beast. The dictator beast is, in a sense, a false Christ, and the prophet beast is, as we will see later, a false Holy Spirit. The dictator beast arises out of the sea. This does not mean the ocean, as can be seen in Revelation 17:

15 And he said to me, "The waters which you saw where the harlot sits, are peoples and multitudes and nations and tongues. . . ."

The Bible is the best commentary on itself. Here it explains that the sea described is the sea of humanity. Thus, we know that the dictator beast will be a human.

In verse 2 of Revelation 13, the dictator beast is described as being like a leopard with the feet of a bear and a mouth like a lion. Satan gives him his power. To help us understand the symbology, let's refer to some verses in Daniel 7:

> 3 "And four great beasts were coming up from the sea, different from one another.
>
> 4 "The first *was* like a lion and had *the* wings of an eagle. I kept looking until its wings were plucked, and it was lifted up from the ground and made to stand on two feet like a man; a human mind also was given to it.
>
> 5 "And behold, another beast, a second one, resembling a bear. And it was raised up on one side, and three ribs *were* in its mouth between its teeth; and thus they said to it, 'Arise, devour much meat!'
>
> 6 "After this I kept looking, and behold, another one, like a leopard, which had on its back four wings of a bird; the beast also had four heads, and dominion was given to it. . . ."

Here we see the first beast is like a lion with eagles' wings. The second is like a bear, and the third, like a leopard. These are beasts that are unmerciful when they devour. In Revelation they are in reverse order to the way they are sequenced in Daniel. Daniel was looking forward to something about to happen. He saw the lion, the bear and the leopard, in that order. John, having a different perspective, sees a leopard, a bear and a lion, in that order.

England for many years, was referred to as a lion. The U.S. has, of course, the eagle as a symbol, and Russia's symbol is the bear. (The leopard may be China or the European Economic Community.) I don't know if these will be the countries involved with the dictator beast, but it will be worth watching.

The beast, to whom the dragon gives great power, has a fatal wound, which is healed. The whole earth is amazed and follows this beast. I do not believe that Satan can actually bring somebody back to life, so this "fatal wound" spoken of is probably a deception. It will be as though this leader were stabbed or wounded in the head and pronounced dead, only to reappear a few days later, very much alive. It would be like John Kennedy coming back to life after being shot in the head before a multitude of witnesses. If he said, "Follow me," I suspect that the whole world would eagerly obey.

In verse 4 we see that Satan finally receives the worship he has sought through the centuries. At this point, the dragon and the beast both receive the worship of the masses. The dictator beast must have tremendous power because nobody can wage war against him.

For forty-two months the dictator beast blasphemes the Lord. In verse 7 of Revelation 13 God gives him permission to overcome the saints and, as we will read later (Revelation 13:15), to kill them. Everyone on earth will worship him, except those whose names are written in the Lamb's book of life. It may even be that there are some unbelievers who will not worship the dictator beast. If their names are written in the Lamb's book of life, and God knows they will eventually receive Christ, they will not worship the beast.

I believe God is talking to Christians in verse 9: "If anyone has an ear, let him hear." Verse 10 goes on to say:

> **10   If anyone *is destined* for captivity, to captivity he goes; if anyone kills with the sword, with the sword he must be killed. Here is the perseverance and the faith of the saints.**
>
> **–Revelation 13**

If you are going to be put in prison for the sake of Christ, go to prison. That's the way I read this. The latter part of verse 10 may mean that those Christians who take up arms to defend themselves will wind up dying. We must be obedient to do whatever God tells us to do, no matter what the consequences may be. For in so doing "is the perseverance and the faith of the saints." Christ may need to build perseverance and faith in us by our captivity.

The Lord is bringing forth or birthing a "man child." If we are to be a part of this man child, I believe we are going to overcome Satan by the word of our testimony, by the blood of the Lamb, and by not loving our lives even unto death. A time will come when God will *allow* Satan to overcome the saints for a period; perhaps at that point we will be able to glorify Him more by our death than in life. Whatever occurs, *He is in control!* I can just see God's loving hand protecting the saints. No matter what comes, we are going to abide in the love of the Lord to the glory of Christ.

REVELATION 13:11-18
–THE PROPHET BEAST

In this section we will be discussing the prophet beast—the false Holy Spirit. The Holy Spirit does not glorify himself; He glorifies Christ. This prophet beast does not glorify himself, but, rather, he glorifies the dictator beast. Let's begin by reading the ramainder of this chapter in Revelation:

11   And I saw another beast coming up out of the earth; and he had two horns like a lamb, and he spoke as a dragon.

12   And he exercises all the authority of the first beast in his presence. And he makes the earth and those who dwell in it to worship the first beast, whose fatal wound was healed.

13   And he performs great signs, so that he even makes fire come down out of heaven to the earth in the presence of men.

14   And he deceives those who dwell on the earth because of the signs which it was given him to perform in the presence of the beast, telling those who dwell on the earth to make an image to the beast who had the wound of the sword and has come to life.

15   And there was given to him to give breath to the image of the beast, that the image of the beast might even speak and cause as many as do not worship the image of the beast to be killed.

16   And he causes all, the small and the great, and the rich and the poor, and the free men and the slaves, to be given a mark on their right hand, or on their forehead,

17   and *he provides* that no one should be able to buy or to sell, except the one who has the mark, *either* the name of the beast or the number of his name.

18   Here is wisdom. Let him who has understanding calculate the number of the beast, for the number is that of a man; and his number is six hundred and sixty-six.

–Revelation 13

Unlike the authoritative dictator beast (symbolized by powerful animal images), the prophet beast is like a lamb—sweet and gentle. He causes people to glorify or worship the dictator beast, just as the sweet, comforting Holy Spirit causes us to glorify Christ.

In verses 13–14, we see that the prophet beast is able to perform miracles, and he even makes fire come down from heaven. (As we know, Elijah also caused fire to come down out of heaven.) Satan is the great deceiver, and he can and does duplicate many of God's miracles in order to deceive. For example, Pharoah's magicians could perform many of the same miracles that Moses did. Satan can also "heal" people. I have talked to converted Christian Science people, who have told me that they received miraculous healings before they were born again. They did not feel that the healings were of God. If someone performs great miracles and healings, this does not necessarily mean that that person is of God. We need to rely on the discernment of the Holy Spirit to know whether or not a person is of God. Many people, fooled by such a miracle worker, would as easily be fooled by the prophet beast, but if we ask God to show us the truth, He will give us discernment so that we will not be deceived.

In Revelation 13:14–15, an image of the beast is created, and it speaks. This could be an idol. Some people feel it might be a computer. With the technical sophistication in our world today, this image will not be anything crude or clumsy. Perhaps some of you have seen Lincoln give his address at Disneyland. This shows that the technology exists to create such a speaking, lifelife image. If such an approach were used, the image would have to be preprogrammed as to what to say. It might even be able to answer questions. But I think that this "image" is probably something even more sophisticated than that. The whole world will be worshiping it. It is hard for me to imagine the whole world worshiping something similar to the Lincoln exhibit at Disneyland. I think that it will be much more impressive and powerful.

Reviewing verses 16 through the end of Revelation 13, we find that the prophet beast causes everyone to take the mark of the dictator beast on his forehead or right hand. Anyone who refuses becomes an outlaw. It says that the mark is the beast's name or number and that the number is 666. The footnotes in some of the manuscripts tell us the number is 616. Let's first discuss the number itself. Seven is the number associated with

God and completeness. Six is the number of man (man was created on the sixth day). I do not think that the number of the beast is a numeral (666) but rather (looking at it mathematically) that it is 6x6x6 or 6^3. This seems to represent man to the ultimate height of rebellion. It could be an actual number, but I really don't think it is. I believe the people looking for that number will be surprised. This is primarily saying that the number of the beast is the epitomy of humanity and its rebellion against God. Only time will tell whether or not it is an actual number.

Concerning the mark on the hand and forehead, I would like to dispel a fear that people have concerning this. First we should not exclude the possibility that it may be spiritual and not physical. Our forehead represents what we think and our hand represents what we do. This could be interpreted to mean: as we think like the world, and as we do like the world, we are in the process of taking on the mark of the beast. I think this is a valid interpretation. We need to guard our minds and deeds so that we are in God's will and under His control. However, I do believe that the mark of the beast will likely be something physical as well as spiritual. Sometimes when the Lord gives someone a spiritual interpretation of a passage of scripture, he or she discards the physical or literal interpretation. That is unfortunate because both may be applicable; God may just be revealing something additional, not invalidating the physical or literal.

I would now like to leave the mark of the beast (we will return to it later in this chapter) and discuss a related subject. When I worked for IBM, I was one of the top computer experts and writers in the United States. We experimented with a "paperless city"—that is, having financial transactions made without all the paper floating around. For example: somebody gets paid, deposits his check, buys a belt on his credit card, gets billed, and then pays for it. That one transaction generates something like 17 pieces of paper, handled approximately 30 times. The papers would include a paycheck, a deposit slip, an envelope to mail the deposit slips, a stamp, the sales slip at the department store, the customer's ledger card, his monthly statement, the envelope for the monthly statement, the customer's check, the return stub of the department store invoice, the envelope which the customer uses to mail his check, the stamp, the department store's deposit slip, and so on.

You can see that there is an incredible amount of paper involved in just that simple transaction. As the population explodes, the number of transactions of this type increases, and the amount of paper that must be handled increases geometrically. If this were to continue, pretty soon we would be buried under paper.

Before the advent of dial telephones, the telephone company did some projections and realized that, at the rate they were growing, in a number of years they would need more operators than there were employable people. Of necessity, they had to develop dial telephones.

IBM has done a similar projection concerning paper. At the current rate of growth, there will be so much paper to move that it will become unmovable. However, computers could manage that problem for us. If there were a central computer, you could type in a person's wages, and immediately the computer would remove the funds from the employer's account and deposit the money in the employee's account. When an individual went to a store to buy a belt, that amount could be entered into a computer, which would remove the funds from the purchaser's account and place that amount into the store's account. At the end of the month, the computer would print out all of the individual's transactions, the company's transactions, the store's transactions, and so forth. This could be done in virtually a paperless mode.

The difficulty with such a system arises in that one might lose the single card that identifies him and enables him to make all of these transactions with the computer. Thus, that card must be made unlosable. Initially, the answer to that problem seemed to be the use of people's thumbprints. However, the optical scanning and character recognition of this was too horrendous to work. Another approach that was considered, which I shared on the radio in 1963, was that an identification number could be tattooed on an individual's right hand in ultraviolet ink—an ink which only shows up under ultraviolet light. When a person wanted to make a transaction, he could just hold his hand under an ultraviolet light. If someone did not have a right hand, his forehead would be an alternative. I don't know if this means of making economic transactions will evolve or not, but it is certainly a possibility.

Today, your credit cards can act in a similar way. All of the information on the front of a credit card is also recorded magnetically on the back. Computers can read any of these credit cards today. You could make almost all of your financial transactions with your VISA card and write only one check at the end of the month. It is a simple step from that point to letting the computer write that check for you.

What about small cash transactions? In the BART system in San Francisco, they have little paper cards which you can buy for $5 or $10, and change can be taken from them. The amount of purchasing power remaining after each transaction is also printed on the front of the card. Something like this could be used for all small change purchases.

I am not talking about the mark of the beast now; I'm just talking about an economic credit system that could be installed in the United States or anywhere else. The technology is there and, like dial telephones, is inevitable if the Lord tarries.

You have possibly heard people talk about the three–story computer in Brussels and heard rumors that it might be "the beast." I have installed three–story computers before and have called many computers "beasts." The problem with computers is that the speed of electricity becomes a limiting factor. In stringing out computers horizontally, you must have long horizontal cables connecting components. However, if you put the components on floors above or below one another, you can use much shorter cables. Things can then be processed faster. Once you understand this, a three–story computer ceases to conjure up the image of a monster.

Some Christians are worried about the computer markings on almost all the items available today in grocery stores. Others are worried about the magnetic ink characters across the bottom of checks. These are simply mechanical devices for speeding up the reading and processing of data. Some people feel they should get rid of their credit cards. Many of them probably should for economic reasons (they don't know how to use them correctly) but not for spiritual reasons. Using credit cards, or having special characters on your checks or cans of beans, does not mean that you are adopting the mark of the beast. The mark of the beast involves *worship.*

It is possible that Christ is not going to come back for another thousand years. We have no concept of the intricate computer and economic system that people might be experiencing five hundred years from now. Until someone is called on to denounce Christ and to worship the beast, there is nothing wrong with using the mechanical devices which are a part of our economy. Satan loves to churn up Christians over these things and rob them of their peace. I think there will come a time when, in order to participate in the economy, a person is going to have to acknowledge and worship someone other than Jesus Christ.

In Chapter 5 of this book, I pointed out that the bond–slaves of God are already sealed on their foreheads with the seal of God, and thus they will have no room on their foreheads for the mark of the beast. I think that Satan would like to use unknowing Christians to generate fear and anxiety among other Christians over these kinds of things. When the time comes, God will clearly show us what the mark of the beast is. But there should be no fear or anxiety between now and that point in time.

Perfect love casts out fear, and God loves you perfectly. If you are fully aware of His tremendous love for you, you will never be afraid.

9

THE SECOND 144,000,
THE THREE ANGELS,
AND THE TWO HARVESTS
(Revelation 14)

In this chapter, we will cover snapshots 2, 3 and 4. The second snapshot deals with 144,000 individuals who have a unique relationship to Christ. The third snapshot tells us about three angels, who have important messages. The fourth snapshot describes the two harvests that occur at the end of the age.

SNAPSHOT 2
—THE SECOND 144,000

The second snapshot is recorded in the first five verses of Revelation 14:

1 And I looked, and behold, the Lamb *was* standing on Mount Zion, and with Him one hundred and forty-four thousand, having His name and the name of His Father written on their foreheads.

2 And I heard a voice from heaven, like the sound of many waters and like the sound of loud thunder, and the voice which I heard *was* like *the sound* of harpists playing on their harps.

3 And they sang a new song before the throne and before the four living creatures and the elders; and no one could learn the song

> except the one hundred and forty-four thousand who had been pur-
> chased from the earth.
>
> 4 These are the ones who have not been defiled with women,
> for they have kept themselves chaste. These *are* the ones who follow
> the Lamb wherever He goes. These have been purchased from among
> men as first fruits to God and to the Lamb.
>
> 5 And no lie was found in their mouth; they are blameless.

In verse 1, the Lamb is standing on Mount Zion with
144,000 individuals. Many of us have often sung, "We are
marching to Zion." I always like to ask people *why* they are so
happy about going to Zion. Many of them aren't really sure; they
are just happy about it because everyone else is happy. I think
the Lord wants us to understand the relevance and importance
of Mount Zion, so our excitement can have a solid basis.

Zion is a mountain area outside the walled city of Jerusalem. During the thousand-year millennium, Christ is going to
rule and reign from Mount Zion, outside of Jerusalem. Psalm
132 tells us why Mount Zion is the place from which He will
rule:

> 13 For the LORD has chosen Zion;
>   He has desired it for His habitation.
> 14 "This is My resting place forever;
>   Here I will dwell, for I have desired it. . . ."

God chose Zion *because He wanted it.* He doesn't give us
any real clues as to *why* He wanted it, but out of the entire
earth that is the place that He chose.

Now let's look at Isaiah 2:

> 2 Now it will come about that
>   In the last days,
>   The mountain of the house of the LORD
>   Will be established as the chief of the mountains,
>   And will be raised above the hills;
>   And all the nations will stream to it.
> 3 And many peoples will come and say,
>   "Come, let us go up to the mountain of the LORD,
>   To the house of the God of Jacob;
>   That He may teach us concerning His ways.
>   And that we may walk in His paths."

> For the law will go forth from Zion,
> And the word of the LORD from Jerusalem.
> 4 And He will judge between the nations,
> And will render decisions for many peoples;
> And they will hammer their swords into plowshares,
>   and their spears into pruning hooks.
> Nations will not lift up sword against nations,
> And never again will they learn war.

Here we see the foretelling of the reign of Christ. The law will go forth from Zion and the word of the Lord from Jerusalem. Christ will be reigning there. This is also found in Isaiah 24:

> 23 Then the moon will be abashed and the sun ashamed,
> For the LORD of hosts will reign on Mount Zion and in Jerusalem,
> And *His* glory will be before His elders.

If you want to learn more about why Zion is called "the city of David," you can read 2 Samuel 5:5–10. The ark of the covenant was brought to Zion and was then moved from Zion to the temple. This is recorded in 1 Kings 8:

> 1 Then Solomon assembled the elders of Israel and all the heads of the tribes, and leaders of the fathers' *households* of the sons of Israel, to King Solomon in Jerusalem, to bring up the ark of the covenant of the LORD from the city of David, which is Zion.

Mount Zion is where we are going to rule and reign with Christ during the millennium. Since in this snapshot Christ is seen standing on Mount Zion, this must be taking place *after* the Tribulation and *after* Christ has returned in power and glory to rule.

Let's now take a look at the 144,000 spoken of in the first five verses of Revelation 14. As in Revelation 7, I do not think this is a literal number. Some people feel that this is the same 144,000 that we encountered in Revelation 7. This is possible, but I doubt it. Even if you consider the 144,000 in Revelation 7 as physical Israel, you cannot equate them to the Jews. (Remember that we pointed out that Judah was just one of the 12 tribes; so at best, the Jews were 8 percent of physical Israel, since they were from only one of the 12 tribes.) There is a more signifi-

cant problem here with trying to consider this 144,000 as physical Israel, because that says that exactly 12,000 males out of
each tribe had taken a vow of celibacy of some kind and had
never told a lie. I'm sure the physical Israelites are no more perfect than the non–Israelites. I doubt if you could find 12,000
virgins, who had never lied, out of *each* tribe, including the 10
lost tribes. Thus, I have some difficulty with this interpretation.

As we discussed in Chapter 5, I believe the 144,000 in Revelation 7 to be spiritual Israel, the church, and I doubt if you
could find 144,000 males with these qualifications in the church
either. Thus, we are forced to conclude that these 144,000 are
not the same as the ones in Revelation 7.

Verse 4 says that the 144,000 have not been "defiled with
women" but rather have kept themselves chaste. Another thing
that makes me a little uncomfortable with a physical interpretation of this passage is that it almost implies that sex is bad and
that people who have never had sex are better than people who
have had godly, ordained (marital) sex. God created sex, and it
is a very beautiful thing within God's will. I don't think God
looks at sex within a marriage as unholy or undesirable.

Another interpretation might be that these 144,000 are
spiritual virgins. In 2 Corinthians 11:2 Paul talks about wanting
to present the church to Christ as an unblemished virgin. James
4:4 says that people who are friends of the world have committed adultery against God. So this 144,000 could be a group of
spiritually pure Christians, who have been true and faithful to
the Lord. I would be comfortable with this approach.

There is a third interpretation concerning the 144,000 that
I would like to share with you, although I do not have a solid
scriptural basis for it. This is something that I believe the Holy
Spirit has shown me. These people are in such a special category
that they get to sing a song that we don't get to sing, and they
get to follow Christ around. This so intrigued me that I prayed
for the Lord to show me just what this group is.

I have always thought of "heaven" as basically being popu-
lated exclusively by adults; I never used to think about there
being children in heaven. There are some precious little children, who have come to know the Lord and have died. As I was

praying about this, I caught a glimpse of these children who knew Christ as their Savior and were pure and undefiled; their skin was unblemished and their cheeks rosy, and they were following Jesus around and praising Him. They were skipping, dancing and leaping at His feet, singing a song of simplicity and joy to the Lord—one that our minds couldn't handle. That may or may not be the way it will be, but it was a very beautiful thought to me.

In Revelation 5, the elders in heaven began to sing a new song just as Christ was ready to break the first seal and open the scroll. Now, in Revelation 14 we have another new song as He begins His reign.

SNAPSHOT 3
—THE THREE ANGELS

Whereas the second snapshot took place after the Tribulation was completed, the third one puts us back into the Tribulation. Thus, we know that the snapshots are not sequential or chronological. Let's read the scriptures on the third snapshot:

6 And I saw another angel flying in midheaven, having an eternal gospel to preach to those who live on the earth, and to every nation and tribe and tongue and people;

7 and he said with a loud voice, "Fear God, and give Him glory, because the hour of His judgment has come; and worship Him who made the heaven and the earth and sea and springs of waters."

8 And another angel, a second one, followed, saying, "Fallen, fallen is Babylon the great, she who has made all the nations drink of the wine of the passion of her immorality."

9 And another angel, a third one, followed them, saying with a loud voice, "If anyone worships the beast and his image, and receives a mark on his forehead or upon his hand,

10 he also will drink of the wine of the wrath of God, which is mixed in full strength in the cup of His anger; and he will be tormented with fire and brimstone in the presence of the holy angels and in the presence of the Lamb.

11 "And the smoke of their torment goes up forever and ever, and they have no rest day and night, those who worship the beast and his image, and whoever receives the mark of his name."

12 Here is the perseverance of the saints who keep the commandments of God and their faith in Jesus.

13 And I heard a voice from heaven, saying, "Write, 'Blessed are the dead who die in the Lord from now on!'" "Yes," says the Spirit, "that they may rest from their labors, for their deeds follow with them."

—Revelation 14

This snapshot appears to cover a long period of time. It concerns three angels, and since angels are messengers, you could say it concerns messages.

The first angel is giving a message of salvation—the eternal gospel. He is preaching to those who live on the earth. If the mark of the beast has not occurred at this point, then this angel is speaking in the early part of the Tribulation or before it starts. On the other hand, if the mark of the beast has already occurred, it must still be possible for people to become Christians, or the angel wouldn't be giving out this message. I doubt if all of the non–Christians will have the mark of the beast. Even with the most sophisticated computers, people down in Fiji, for example, aren't going to be hooked into the world's massive computer system. It appears as though it will still be possible for these people to be saved. The gospel will continue to go out and will not return void (Isaiah 55:11).

The angel then urges the people to repent, to fear God, and to give Him glory.

In verse 8, the second angel says that Babylon has fallen. We are not going to deal with that here since we have the details of Babylon's fall later in Revelation 17 and 18. This angel says that Babylon *has* fallen. Thus, this third snapshot overlaps in time with snapshot number six, which covers the entire chapters of Revelation 17 and 18 and deals with the actual fall of Babylon. Here we get just a little glimpse of that fall, which we will discuss in more detail later.

The third angel, in verses 9–11, says that anyone who receives the mark of the beast and worships him is going to drink the full wrath of God and will be tormented with fire and brimstone in the presence of the holy angels and in the presence of the Lamb. Notice that this torment does not take place a great distance away from the presence of Christ. It occurs "in the presence of the Lamb."

Incidentally, this also points out why Christians will not take the mark of the beast and worship him. Romans 5:9 tells us that "we shall be saved from the wrath of God through Him." Praise God! No Christian is going to experience the *wrath* of God. Thus, no Christian will both take the mark of the beast *and* worship him. Let me reemphasize that. One must do both before he is condemned to suffer the wrath of God.

One thing I might point out here is that no one is going to spend eternity in either heaven or hell. Everyone is going to spend eternity either on the new earth (home of the believers in Christ) or in the lake of fire (destination of the unbelievers). (See Revelation 20:13–21:4.) *God* is in charge of the lake of fire, not Satan. He casts death, hell, Satan and all of the non-Christians into the lake of fire. The smoke of their torment goes up forever and ever and there will be no rest day or night. There is no way of escape from this place, and Christ has the only set of keys.

In a loving way, I would like to use Hal Lindsey as an example to make a point. I know and love Hal, and he knows and loves Jesus Christ. In one of his books he says that verses 10 and 11 of Revelation 14 *are* talking about hell. Yet, as I pointed out, nobody is going to be in hell forever and ever. He says Babylon *is* Rome and that the 144,000 *are* redeemed Jewish evangelists. People who take such an absolute stand on these issues leave little room for the Holy Spirit to deal with them. They seem to have made up their minds and are no longer open to other possibilities.

Do not take anything that I am saying as "absolute." I am just sharing with you what the Lord has shown me up to this point. I have taught classes on the book of Revelation about four times at about five–year intervals. Each time I teach through

the book, the Lord shows me something new. I hope the Lord
continues to teach me and that we all can keep open hearts and
minds.

In contrast to those who receive the mark of the beast, in
Revelation 14:12 the angel commends the perseverance of the
saints and encourages them to keep their faith in Jesus. The
people with the mark of the beast are going to persecute us, but
we *know* what their fate is going to be and also what ours will
be. Thus, the Lord wants us to have patience and to persevere.

Verse 13 of Revelation 14 is one of the beatitudes (discussed in Chapter 1): ". . . 'Blessed are the dead who die in the
Lord from now on!' . . . that they may rest from their labors,
for their deeds follow with them." This is just as much a beatitude from Jesus as the beatitudes recorded in the Gospels. Just
as Jesus said that meekness and purity of heart are "blessed"
character qualities, He also says here that those who die for him
are "blessed."

Summarizing the third snapshot, we see three angels bringing important messages: (1) Babylon is going to fall, probably
at the battle of Armegeddon or near that time, (2) the evangelism of the people still on the earth will probably continue
throughout this period, and (3) the result of taking the mark of
the beast and worshiping him is going to be torment in front of
Christ and the angels. That torment is going to go on forever
and ever, even after the millennium. It is obvious, then, that this
snapshot covers a long period of time.

SNAPSHOT 4
—THE TWO HARVESTS

Now let's read the remainder of Revelation 14, which discusses the fourth snapshot:

14 And I looked, and behold, a white cloud, and sitting on the
cloud *was* one like a son of man, having a golden crown on His head,
and a sharp sickle in His hand.

15 And another angel came out of the temple, crying out with a
loud voice to Him who sat on the cloud, "Put in your sickle and
reap, because the hour to reap has come, because the harvest of the
earth is ripe."

16   And He who sat on the cloud swung His sickle over the earth; and the earth was reaped.

17   And another angel came out of the temple which is in heaven, and he also had a sharp sickle.

18   And another angel, the one who has power over fire, came out from the altar; and he called with a loud voice to him who had the sharp sickle, saying, "Put in your sharp sickle, and gather the clusters from the vine of the earth, because her grapes are ripe."

19   And the angel swung his sickle to the earth, and gathered *the clusters from* the vine of the earth, and threw them into the great wine press of the wrath of God.

20   And the wine press was trodden outside the city, and blood came out from the wine press, up to the horses' bridles, for a distance of two hundred miles.

There are two harvests outlined here. In verses 14–16 God harvests those things which are pleasing in His sight. The second harvest is described in verses 17–20, wherein those things which displease God are harvested for wrath.

Concerning the first harvest, there is a lot of discussion about who the person on the cloud is. Some say it is obviously Jesus. They point out that he is like a son of man, he has a golden crown, and he comes on a white cloud. However, verse 15 says "another angel" came out, which implies that the first one was also an angel. This second angel gives commands to the one on the clouds. An angel would not give commands to Christ. Thus, we must conclude that we are looking at two angels in the first harvest. My feeling is that it is not really important. Christ is in charge of this harvest, and whether He Himself or one of His representatives performs the act is not significant.

Let's see what Matthew 24 has to say about this first harvest:

29   "But immediately after the tribulation of those days THE SUN WILL BE DARKENED, AND THE MOON WILL NOT GIVE ITS LIGHT, AND THE STARS WILL FALL from the sky, and the powers of the heavens will be shaken,

> 30   and then the sign of the Son of Man will appear in the sky,
> and then all the tribes of the earth will mourn, and they will see the
> SON OF MAN COMING ON THE CLOUDS OF THE SKY with
> power and great glory.
>
> 31   "And He will send forth His angels with A GREAT TRUM-
> PET AND THEY WILL GATHER TOGETHER His elect from the
> four winds from one end of the sky to the other.
>
> —Matthew 24

Verses 29–30 say that *after the Tribulation* the sun will be
darkened and then the Son of Man will come. Christ will then
send out the angels, who will gather together the elect (the
Christians).

I would like to digress for a moment to talk about the difference between bearing fruit and gathering fruit. John 4 talks
about gathering fruit.

> 35   "Do you not say, 'There are yet four months, and *then* comes
> the harvest'? Behold, I say to you, lift up your eyes, and look on the
> fields, that they are white for harvest.
>
> 36   "Already he who reaps is receiving wages, and is gathering
> fruit for life eternal; that he who sows and he who reaps may rejoice
> together. . . ."

It is important to remember that as we go out into the harvest, it is the *Lord's* harvest and we are *gathering* His fruit; we
are not *bearing* fruit. When you lead a person to Christ, you are
not *bearing* fruit; the fruit is Christ's, not yours. We are simply
gathering fruit when we have the privilege of helping someone
find Christ as his Savior.

On the other hand, in John 15:8 we read that the Father
is glorified if we bear much fruit. Christ says: "I am the vine,
you are the branches . . ." (John 15:5). A grape vine bears
grapes. So if Jesus is the vine to which I am attached, I am going
to *bear* "Jesus fruit," which is the fruit of the Spirit (see Galatians 5:22, 23). But I *gather* people (fruit) into His kingdom.

The second harvest in Revelation 14 is found in verses 17–
20. Two more angels appear, one with a sharp sickle and one
who commands the one with the sickle to harvest the grapes
from the vine of the earth and to throw them into the wine
press of God's wrath.

I agree with most commentators that this harvest is referring to the battle of Armegeddon. Verse 20 talks about blood rising up to the horses' bridles. Some people think this is actually a 4–foot deep lake of blood, and this could be. Yet, consider this: frequently someone standing near a wine press gets splattered with some of the juice as it is pressed out. In like manner, I don't think there is necessarily going to be a lake of blood, but rather blood splattering up to the height of the horses' bridles for 200 miles. However it happens, the war will be terrible, and the people who battle against the Lamb will be slaughtered by the word of Christ as He declares the wrath of the Lord with His mouth.

Let's also look at the two harvests as Christ talked about them in the Gospels:

> 24 He presented another parable to them, saying, "The kingdom of heaven may be compared to a man who sowed good seed in his field.
>
> 25 "But while men were sleeping, his enemy came and sowed tares also among the wheat, and went away.
>
> 26 "But when the wheat sprang up and bore grain, then the tares became evident also.
>
> 27 "And the slaves of the landowner came and said to him, 'Sir, did you not sow good seed in your field? How then does it have tares?'
>
> 28 "And he said to them, 'An enemy has done this!' And the slaves said to him, 'Do you want us, then to go and gather them up?'
>
> 29 "But he said, 'No; lest while you are gathering up the tares, you may root up the wheat with them.
>
> 30 'Allow both to grow together until the harvest; and in the time of the harvest I will say to the reapers, "First gather up the tares and bind them in bundles to burn them up; but gather the wheat into my barn."'"

—Matthew 13

Tares are weeds that are almost indistinguishable from wheat until they ripen. In their early growth stages you can hardly tell the difference between them. Many times here on the earth we cannot really tell those who know Jesus from those who don't. But in the final harvest, those who are against the

Lord are going to be gathered and burned, but the elect will be gathered into His "barn."

Further in Matthew 13, we read:

37   And He answered and said, "The one who sows the good seed is the Son of Man,

38   and the field is the world; and *as for* the good seed, these are the sons of the kingdom; and the tares are the sons of the evil *one;*

39   and the enemy who sowed them is the devil, and the harvest is the end of the age; and the reapers are angels.

40   "Therefore just as the tares are gathered up and burned with fire, so shall it be at the end of the age.

41   "The Son of Man will send forth His angels, and they will gather out of His kingdom all stumbling blocks, and those who commit lawlessness,

42   and will cast them into the furnace of fire; in that place there shall be weeping and gnashing of teeth. . . ."

Matthew 24 and Luke 17 tell us that two men will be working in a field and two women will be grinding at the same place; in both instances one will be taken and the other will be left behind. Luke 17:37 informs us that the ones taken will be taken to a place of death where the vultures will be gathered. Again, in the passage we just read from Matthew 13, we see that God's angels are going to gather *out* of His kingdom all of the stumbling blocks and those who commit lawlessness. They will be cast into the lake of fire.

Now let's skip down to verse 45:

45   "Again, the kingdom of heaven is like a merchant seeking fine pearls,

46   and upon finding one pearl of great value, he went and sold all that he had, and bought it.

47   "Again, the kingdom of heaven is like a dragnet cast into the sea, and gathering *fish* of every kind;

48   and when it was filled, they drew it up on the beach; and they sat down, and gathered the good *fish* into containers, but the bad they threw away.

49   "So it will be at the end of the age; the angels shall come forth, and take out the wicked from among the righteous,

50   and will cast them into the furnace of fire; there shall be weeping and gnashing of teeth. . . ."

—Matthew 13

Repeatedly, we see the *wicked being removed* with the angels doing the separating and harvesting. The Christians will be taken into the barn of the Lord, and those who are against Christ will be cast into the lake of fire.

Let's also look at Joel 3, which ties it all together.

12   **Let the nations be aroused
And come up to the valley of Jehoshaphat,
For there I will sit to judge
All the surrounding nations.**

13   **Put in the sickle, for the harvest is ripe.
Come, tread, for the wine press is full;
The vats overflow, for their wickedness is great.**

14   **Multitudes, multitudes in the valley of decision!
For the day of the LORD is near in the valley of decision.**

15   **The sun and moon grow dark.
And the stars lose their brightness.**

16   **And the LORD roars from Zion
And utters His voice from Jerusalem,
And the heavens and the earth tremble.
But the LORD is a refuge for His people
And a stronghold to the sons of Israel.**

17   **Then you will know that I am the LORD your God,
Dwelling in Zion my Holy mountain.
So Jerusalem will be holy,
And strangers will pass through it no more.**

—Joel 3

The valley of Jehoshaphat is the valley of decision. Jehoshaphat really means *Jehovah judges*. After the harvests, the millennium will start, and the believers will flow in and out of Jerusalem in a loving, peaceful, harmonious relationship with Christ as King. Praise God!

SUMMARY AND REVIEW

We have now completed our survey of the first four snapshots. In the first snapshot, we saw the woman and the man child, the fall of Satan, and the victory of the overcomers in Christ. We also saw the two beasts arise: the dictator beast, who is going to rule the world, and the prophet beast, who causes everyone to worship the dictator beast. Part of worshiping him involves taking on the mark of the beast. Taking this mark implies that one is going to worship the beast and acknowledge him as king. Receiving the mark of the beast is not simply being involved in the world system. It will be a specific, unmistakable action, and, I believe, it will be very clear to Christians when they are offered this mark. We should not live in any fear between now and then.

In the second snapshot, we saw Christ with 144,000 individuals (possibly children) standing on Mount Zion. It seems that this event takes place right after Christ returns and sets up His kingdom on the earth.

In the third snapshot we saw three angels with three messages. One of the angels was still evangelizing and spreading the word of the Lord. Evidently people will still be able to become Christians at that time. Another angel declared that Babylon (which we will deal with later) had fallen, while the third angel announced the disastrous end that will befall those who take on the mark of the beast and worship him. This angel also encouraged the saints to persevere.

In the fourth snapshot we discussed the two harvests, which are consistent with everything that Jesus taught. There will be a harvest of the righteous, who will come into the fold of God, and a harvest of the non–Christians, who will be *taken out* to taste of God's wrath.

We need to go out into the present harvest to *gather* fruit. We know that there is fruit to be gathered because Christ said that it was ripe (John 4:34–38). The people that we help to come to a saving knowledge of Jesus Christ will enjoy God forever and will be spared from experiencing His wrath. If you have a friend or a relative who does not know Christ as Savior, I hope this provides a tremendous incentive to share the good news with him or her.

10

THE SEVEN ANGELS
AND THE SEVEN
BOWLS OF WRATH
(Revelation 15 & 16)

SNAPSHOT 5
—THE SEVEN BOWLS OF WRATH

The fifth snapshot covers Chapters 15 and 16 of the book of Revelation and deals with the seven bowls of God's wrath. We will begin by reading Revelation 15:

1 And I saw another sign in heaven, great and marvelous, seven angels who had seven plagues, *which are* the last, because in them the wrath of God is finished.

2 And I saw, as it were, a sea of glass mixed with fire, and those who had come off victorious from the beast and from his image and from the number of his name, standing on the sea of glass, holding harps of God.

3 And they sang the song of Moses the bond-servant of God and the song of the Lamb, saying,

> "Great and marvelous are Thy works,
> O Lord God, the Almighty;
> Righteous and true are Thy ways,
> Thou King of the nations.

4   "Who will not fear, O Lord, and glorify Thy name?
For Thou alone art holy;
For ALL THE NATIONS WILL COME AND WORSHIP
BEFORE THEE,
For Thy righteous acts have been revealed."

5 After these things I looked, and the temple of the tabernacle of testimony in heaven was opened,

6 and the seven angels who had the seven plagues came out of the temple, clothed in linen, clean *and* bright, and girded around their breasts with golden girdles.

7 And one of the four living creatures gave to the seven angels seven golden bowls full of the wrath of God, who lives forever and ever.

8 And the temple was filled with smoke from the glory of God and from His power; and no one was able to enter the temple until the seven plagues of the seven angels were finished.

–Revelation 15

Verse 1 says that with the plagues of these seven angels, the wrath of God will be finished. Yet in Chapters 17, 18, and 19, we will see more of the wrath of God, so again this tells us that the events described in Revelation are not arranged in chronological order. With the seven bowls, God's wrath is still being poured out, and later it falls upon Babylon and on the army at Armageddon. The pouring out of God's wrath is not completed until the end of the Tribulation.

In verse 2 of Revelation 15, John again sees a sea of glass. In Revelation 4:6, we also saw a "sea of glass like crystal," said to be before the throne of God. Here in Revelation 15 we find those who have been victorious (overcomers) over the beast and his image and the mark of the beast standing on the sea of glass. They are holding harps of God and are singing a song of Moses and of the Lamb (verse 3).

I love harp music. Imagine a concert with several million harps. It would set your entire being vibrating! This will be the most beautiful music we have ever heard because it will glorify God in a perfect way.

The harp music provides accompaniment for the singing of the song of Moses, most of which is taken from bits and pieces of Deuteronomy 32. By the way, Moses must have had a terrible voice because he had to *speak* the words of this song:

> **30   Then Moses spoke in the hearing of all the assembly of Israel the words of this song, until they were complete:**
>
> **—Deuteronomy 31**

This is repeated in Chapter 32:

> **44   Then Moses came and spoke all the words of this song in the hearing of the people, . . .**
>
> **—Deuteronomy 32**

He got the message across, even without singing, and it continues to communicate to us thousands of years later. It doesn't matter how pretty one's voice is; God looks on the heart!

Let's reread the song of Moses as recorded in Revelation 15:

> 3   . . . **"Great and marvelous are Thy works,**
> **O Lord God, the Almighty;**
> **Righteous and true are Thy ways,**
> **Thou King of the nations.**
> 4   **"Who will not fear, O Lord, and glorify Thy name?**
> **For Thou alone art holy;**
> **For ALL THE NATIONS WILL COME AND WORSHIP BEFORE THEE,**
> **For Thy righteous acts have been revealed."**

In the next verse we read:

> **5   After these things I looked, and the temple of the tabernacle of testimony in heaven was opened, . . .**

After reading this, the Spirit directed my thoughts back to the temple and the tabernacle. An important common element for both the temple and the tabernacle is that they each housed the ark of the covenant inside the holy of holies. On top of the ark were two golden cherubim and the mercy seat. There were three items in the ark of the covenant. These were the Ten Commandments, some manna from heaven, and Aaron's rod. God set this up in an interesting way. All the items contained within the ark represented some aspect of the Hebrew people's rejection of God's will. For example, the Ten Commandments represented their *rejection of God's holy law and order.* While He was feeding the Israelites in the wilderness with manna, they grumbled. So the manna in the ark represented the *rejection of God's provision.* Aaron's rod (the one that budded) was representative of their *rejection of God's chosen leadership.* If you will remember, there was a contest concerning who was to be their leader. God said that He would indicate His chosen leader by making branches grow on his staff. The fact that the mercy seat sits on top of all this rejection is very beautiful. In spite of it all, God was showing mercy to this stubborn, willful people.

I get the feeling (although the Scriptures do not explicitly say this) that in Revelation 15:5, when the temple of the tabernacle in heaven is opened, God is saying that rejection of Him by His people has come to an end, at least for one thousand years.

In verses 6 and 7 the seven angels who had the seven plagues come out of the temple, and one of the four living creatures gives them seven golden bowls full of the wrath of God. These four living creatures obey God the Father only, so, despite the fact that the four living creatures hand the bowls to the seven angels, we know that the source of the wrath we are about to witness is God Himself.

The next verse is really interesting:

> **8 And the temple was filled with smoke from the glory of God and from His power; and no one was able to enter the temple until the seven plagues of the seven angels were finished.**
>
> **—Revelation 15**

There are verses in the New Testament which speak of coming "boldly" before the throne of God. However, it seems that during this period of the seven plagues that privilege is no longer available. God's glory is too powerful to be approachable. I get the feeling from this verse that at this point, people will not be able to repent and receive forgiveness. The day of God's mercy and patience with man's rebellion and rejection will be over. Let's look at 1 Kings 8:

> **10** And it came about when the priests came from the holy place, that the cloud filled the house of the LORD,
>
> **11** so that the priests could not stand to minister because of the cloud, for the glory of the LORD filled the house of the LORD.

In this instance, the Lord filled His house with a glory so powerful that the priests could not go in. This is an incredible thing to comprehend. Here in Revelation, we see the Lord manifesting this same power. Let's also look at Exodus 19:

> **18** Now Mount Sinai *was* all in smoke because the LORD descended upon it in fire; and its smoke ascended like the smoke of a furnace, and the whole mountain quaked, violently.
>
> **19** When the sound of the trumpet grew louder and louder, Moses spoke and God answered him with thunder.

Here we see that Mount Sinai was also engulfed in smoke as God displayed His glory and power. So, in Revelation 15, it is no surprise to see the temple in heaven filled with smoke as God prepares to manifest His power in a mighty way. This glory is so overwhelming that no one is able to enter the temple, and it remains that way until the seven bowls of wrath are completed.

Someday, when we are transformed and become like Jesus, we can receive and enjoy the full impact of the glory of God. Then, we will be able to really understand what a mighty Creator we have. If we were to try to look at the sun directly, it would burn our eyes. This must be how it is with God's brilliant glory. We see Him now as through a smoked glass. Someday that glass will drop, and we will be able to enjoy His glory face to face!

THE RESULTS OF THE SEVEN BOWLS OF WRATH

Now let's look at Revelation 16 and what actually occurs when the seven angels pour out the seven bowls:

> **1** And I heard a loud voice from the temple, saying to the seven angels, "Go and pour out the seven bowls of the wrath of God into the earth."
>
> **2** And the first *angel* went and poured out his bowl into the earth; and it became a loathsome and malignant sore upon the men who had the mark of the beast and who worshiped his image.

3 And the second *angel* poured out his bowl into the sea, and it became blood like *that* of a dead man; and every living thing in the sea died.

4 And the third *angel* poured out his bowl into the rivers and the springs of waters; and they became blood.

5 And I heard the angel of the waters saying, "Righteous art Thou, who art and who wast, O Holy One, because Thou didst judge these things;

6 for they poured out the blood of saints and prophets, and Thou has given them blood to drink. They deserve it."

7 And I heard the altar saying, "Yes, O Lord God, the Almighty, true and righteous are Thy judgments."

8 And the fourth *angel* poured out his bowl upon the sun; and it was given to it to scorch men with fire.

9 And men were scorched with fierce heat; and they blasphemed the name of God who has the power over these plagues; and they did not repent, so as to give Him glory.

10 And the fifth *angel* poured out his bowl upon the throne of the beast; and his kingdom became darkened; and they gnawed their tongues because of pain,

11 and they blasphemed the God of heaven because of their pains and their sores; and they did not repent of their deeds.

12 And the sixth *angel* poured out his bowl upon the great river, the Euphrates; and its water was dried up, that the way might be prepared for the kings from the east.

13 And I saw *coming* out of the mouth of the dragon and out of the mouth of the beast and out of the mouth of the false prophet, three unclean spirits like frogs;

14 for they are spirits of demons, performing signs, which go out to the kings of the whole world, to gather them together for the war of the great day of God, the Almighty.

15 ("Behold, I am coming like a thief. Blessed is the one who stays awake and keeps his garments, lest he walk about naked and men see his shame.")

16 And they gathered them together to the place which in Hebrew is called Har-Magedon.

17 And the seventh *angel* poured out his bowl upon the air; and a loud voice came out of the temple from the throne, saying, "It is done."

18 And there were flashes of lightning and sounds and peals of thunder; and there was a great earthquake, such as there had not been since man came to be upon the earth, so great an earthquake *was it*, and so mighty.

19 And the great city was split into three parts, and the cities of the nations fell. And Babylon the great was remembered before God, to give her the cup of the wine of His fierce wrath.

20 And every island fled away, and the mountains were not found.

21 And huge hailstones, about one hundred pounds each, came down from heaven upon men; and men blasphemed God because of the plague of the hail, because its plague was extremely severe.

—Revelation 16

These seven bowls (or vials as the *King James Version* calls them) are very similar to Revelation's seven trumpets and to some of the plagues God sent against Egypt. If you would like to compare them, the following table might be helpful:

Plague	Bowl	Trumpet	Egypt
Sores	#1 – Rev. 16:1–2	#5 – Rev. 9:1–5	Ex. 9:10–11
Sea is blood	#2 – Rev. 16:3	#2 – Rev. 8:8–9	-----------
Water is blood	#3 – Rev. 16:4–7	#3 – Rev. 8:10–11	Ex. 7:17–21
Extreme heat	#4 – Rev. 16:8–9	----------------	-----------
Darkness	#5 – Rev. 16:10–11	#4 – Rev. 8:12–13	Ex. 10:21–23
Preparation for battle	#6 – Rev. 16:12–16	#6 – Rev. 9:13–16	-----------
Earth upheaval and hail	#7 – Rev. 16:17–21	#7 – Rev. 11:19	-----------

There are three basic ways one could view the time relationships between the seals, the trumpets, and the bowls. The first way would be an actual sequence of events. The second way would be a complete overlap with seal seven, trumpet seven, and bowl seven, all ending at the same point in time. The third way would be a partial overlap. These three different ways of viewing John's three visions are shown in Figure 3, on the next page.

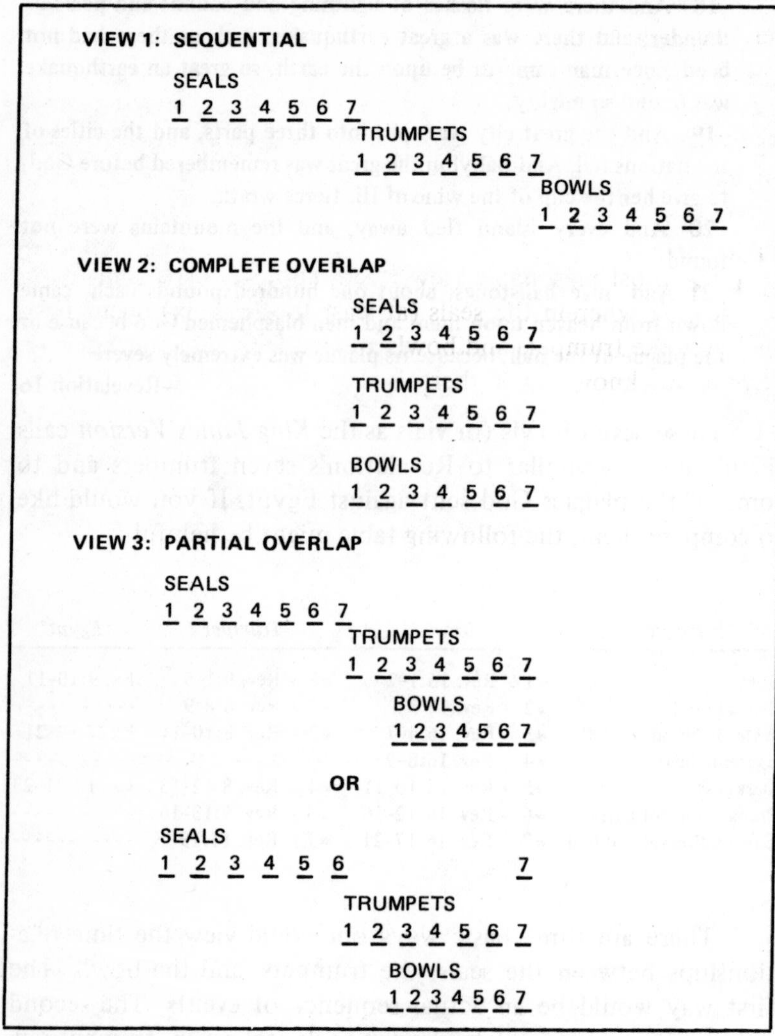

VIEW 1: SEQUENTIAL

SEALS
1 2 3 4 5 6 7

TRUMPETS
1 2 3 4 5 6 7

BOWLS
1 2 3 4 5 6 7

VIEW 2: COMPLETE OVERLAP

SEALS
1 2 3 4 5 6 7

TRUMPETS
1 2 3 4 5 6 7

BOWLS
1 2 3 4 5 6 7

VIEW 3: PARTIAL OVERLAP

SEALS
1 2 3 4 5 6 7

TRUMPETS
1 2 3 4 5 6 7

BOWLS
1 2 3 4 5 6 7

OR

SEALS
1 2 3 4 5 6   7

TRUMPETS
1 2 3 4 5 6 7

BOWLS
1 2 3 4 5 6 7

Figure 3

View 1 is difficult to accept because, as we have seen earlier, trumpet seven occurs at the end of the Tribulation when Christ begins to reign. View 2, a complete overlap, is also difficult to accept because God's bond–servants aren't sealed in their foreheads until after seal six, yet we know that the seals were on God's bond–servants during the plagues of the trumpets and bowls because it specifically says that they were protected in many cases.

The most reasonable view, then, appears to be some form of View 3, wherein the seals (at least the first six) occur first, and then the trumpets and bowls are overlapped to some degree. We do not know (1) if there is a complete overlap, (2) if the bowls might occur between trumpet six and seven, or (3) if a trumpet brings a partial plague on the earth, followed by a bowl, completing that plague around the world, then the next trumpet and the next bowl, and so forth. We do not know exactly how these trumpets and bowls overlap, but they appear to be very similar in nature and to occur in roughly the same time frame. Since the degree of overlap of the trumpets and bowls is certainly subject to wide speculation and interpretation, please do not take *either* of the *possibilities* shown in View 3 of Figure 3 as being a precise description of the overlaps, but simply an attempt to help you to get a feeling for the possible time relationships between the seals, the trumpets, and the bowls.

The First Bowl – Sores

Remember, these are *God's* bowls of wrath. *He* is in charge of the Tribulation and the timing of all of these events. In verse 2, the bowl is poured out (at God's command), and the men who had the mark of the beast and worshiped his image are covered with malignant sores. Notice that this does not affect the Christians. It may be that some of the people who take the mark of the beast become Christians later and refuse to *worship* the image of the beast. The people who both take the mark of the beast *and* worship his image are definitely affected by these sores.

This plague is very similar to one of the plagues in Egypt, as noted in the previous table:

> 8 Then the LORD said to Moses and Aaron, "Take for your-selves handfuls of soot from a kiln, and let Moses throw it toward the sky in the sight of Pharaoh.
> 9 "And it will become fine dust over all the land of Egypt, and will become boils breaking out with sores on man and beast through all the land of Egypt."
> 10 So they took soot from a kiln, and stood before Pharoah; and Moses threw it toward the sky, and it became boils breaking out with sores on man and beast.
> 11 And the magicians could not stand before Moses because of the boils, for the boils were on the magicians as well as on all the Egyptians.
> 12 And the LORD hardened Pharoah's heart, and he did not listen to them, just as the LORD had spoken to Moses.
>
> —Exodus 9

While it is impossible to know exactly *how* God will bring this plague about, some people have speculated that the mark of the beast will be tattooed on with an ink, which will in some way produce a rapidly–spreading cancer.

Others have recalled that after the atomic explosion at Hiroshima, the survivors had what are called skin ulcers because of the radiation. Many of the phenomena that we will be looking at in this chapter could be caused by a nuclear holocaust.

The Second Bowl – Sea Like Blood

In verse 3 of Revelation 16, the second angel pours out his bowl into the sea, and the sea becomes like blood, causing every living thing in the sea to die. Back in the second trumpet, we find a close parallel:

> 8 And the second angel sounded, and *something* like a great mountain burning with fire was thrown into the sea; and a third of the sea became blood;
> 9 and a third of the creatures, which were in the sea and had life, died; and a third of the ships were destroyed.
>
> —Revelation 8

When the second angel pours out his bowl in Revelation 16:3, *all* of the sea turns to blood and *every* living thing in it dies. This differs somewhat from Revelation 8:8–9 where we find that one–third of the creatures died. This might be something that occurs within the same time frame as the second trumpet. However, I believe that what God is really saying is that something is going to happen at the second bowl that is much worse than what happens at the second trumpet.

All of the events of these bowls are probably happening within a short period of time, and some of them are happening simultaneously.

The Third Bowl – Fresh Water Like Blood

In verses 4–7 of Revelation 16, the events of the third bowl are recorded:

4 And the third *angel* poured out his bowl into the rivers and the springs of waters; and they became blood.

5 And I heard the angel of the waters saying, "Righteous art Thou, who art and who wast, O Holy One, because Thou didst judge these things;

6 for they poured out the blood of saints and prophets, and Thou has given them blood to drink. They deserve it."

7 And I heard the altar saying, "Yes, O Lord God, the Almighty, true and righteous are Thy judgements."

Here we see that the fresh water becomes blood. Back in Revelation 8:10–11 (the third trumpet), one–third of the fresh water became blood, causing the deaths of multitudes of people. Also, in Exodus 7:17–21, it is recorded that Moses turned the water into blood in Egypt.

At this point in time, the ocean will have become blood, and all of the fish will be dead. The ocean contains a great supply of food. If all of the water—100 percent of it—were undrinkable, everyone would have to drink something other than water: apple juice, orange juice, wine, Coca Cola, or whatever they had stored.

The Fourth Bowl — A Scorching Heat

The next bowl compounds the problems. Let's look at the next couple of verses in Revelation 16:

> **8 And the fourth *angel* poured out his bowl upon the sun; and it was given to it to scorch men with fire.**
>
> **9 And men were scorched with fierce heat; and they blasphemed the name of God who has the power over these plagues; and they did not repent, so as to give Him glory.**

I don't know if any of you have ever experienced the extreme heat of the sun. If you were to try walking across Death Valley, or any other desert of your choice, during the summer, you would get literally fried and dehydrated. You probably wouldn't last a day. It says here that the sun will give out just such a torturous heat, and that there will be no water. The pain and the agony of the non–Christians—those who will be worshiping the beast—is going to be incredible. People will be running into caves and basements—any place that is cool. There will be blackouts and brownouts because there will not be enough air conditioning to take care of the situation.

Again, this incredible heat could be caused by a nuclear holocaust, which could upset the ionosphere that protects us from the sun. The atomic fireballs going off could heat up the atmosphere incredibly, and this could be amplified by the sun's increased intensity.

Any of a number of phenomena could easily bring about an increased intensity of the sun. The main thing to remember here, though, is that it is *God's* wrath, *His* bowl, and *His* angels; *He* is the one saying, "Now is the time to pour it out." We know that He will protect us *if* we follow and obey Him, whatever the cost.

The Fifth Bowl — Darkness

The next event in Revelation 16 is this:

> **10 And the fifth *angel* poured out his bowl upon the throne of the beast; and his kingdom became darkened; and they gnawed their tongues because of pain.**

11   and they blasphemed the God of heaven because of their pains and their sores; and they did not repent of their deeds.

The fifth plague is a total darkness. The darkness brought about by the fifth bowl is so terrifying that it is physically pain-ful. The people, of course, are still suffering from the plagues of the previous bowls, such as the sores of bowl one. Again, bowl five is reminiscent of one of the trumpets. The fourth trumpet (Revelation 8:12) brought partial darkness on the earth, when a third of the sun, a third of the moon, and a third of the stars were smitten.

Also, one of the plagues in Egypt was darkness, as recorded in Exodus 10:

21   Then the LORD said to Moses, "Stretch out your hand toward the sky, that there may be darkness over the land of Egypt, even a darkness which may be felt."

22   So Moses stretched out his hand toward the sky, and there was thick darkness in all the land of Egypt for three days.

23   They did not see one another, nor did anyone rise from his place for three days, but all the sons of Israel had light in their dwellings.

Notice in verse 23 above that, in spite of this all–encom-passing darkness, the sons of Israel had light in their homes. God's people will be taken care of again in the end times. He will not fail!

Why is absolute, pitch–black darkness a plague? Most peo-ple are afraid of the dark. Darkness has always been a symbol of evil and malevolence; it is contrary to light and life. Psycholog-ically, long–term darkness does something to people which causes them to go crazy. In other words, if a total darkness set in some Friday morning and lasted through the next Sunday—absolutely *zero* light . . . no stars or moon—there would be an incredible awe, and likely a terror among the people. Everyone would wonder what was happening and, again, there would be pervasive brownouts and blackouts because people would over-load electrical circuits. I have a feeling that God will not allow artificial light at this time. People are going to be forced to grope in the darkness. This plague is not new; He has used it be-fore in Egypt, and He will use it again to punish and pour out His wrath on those who refuse to repent.

The Sixth Bowl — Preparation for the Final Battle

The final two bowls are more significant, so we will spend more time on each of them. To refresh your memory, we will repeat verses 12-16 of Revelation 16:

12 And the sixth *angel* poured out his bowl upon the great river, the Euphrates; and its water was dried up, that the way might be prepared for the kings from the east.

13 And I saw *coming* out of the mouth of the dragon and out of the mouth of the beast and out of the mouth of the false prophet, three unclean spirits like frogs;

14 for they are spirits of demons, performing signs, which go out to the kings of the whole world, to gather them together for the war of the great day of God, the Almighty.

15 ("Behold, I am coming like a thief. Blessed is the one who stays awake and keeps his garments, lest he walk about naked and men see his shame.")

16 And they gathered them together to the place which in Hebrew is called Har-Magedon.

Before covering Har-Magedon (Armageddon), let's discuss the "*un*holy trinity." The biblical Trinity consists of God the Father, the Son, and the Holy Spirit. In verse 13 of the above passage we see an "unholy" trinity: the dragon, which is Satan; the beast, which is the dictator beast; and the false prophet, which is the prophet beast. Satan (the dragon) is a false counterpart to our heavenly Father; the dictator beast is a false Christ; and the false prophet is a false Holy Spirit. Out of this unholy trinity come three unclean spirits. While they are referred to as being "like frogs," I doubt that they will actually look like frogs any more than Christ, who is called a "lamb," looks like a lamb. These unclean spirits go all over the world performing signs and wonders so that all the presidents, kings, and rulers will be willing to send their armies to Har-Magedon.

In the Hebrew language, Har-Magedon means "mount of Megiddo." Megiddo is actually not a mountain; it is a hill. The Jezreel Valley lies at its base. Many significant battles have taken place in this valley: this is where Deborah and Barak overthrew Jabin and the Canaanites (Judges 4:15), where Gideon was victorious over the Midianites (Judges 7), and where Saul died in battle with the Philistines (1 Samuel 31:8). But this valley has not yet seen its last battle. This is also where the final encounter will occur between Christ and armies that the Antichrist has gathered. This event is described in Revelation 19, which we will be discussing in a later chapter.

Juxtaposing the sixth bowl and the sixth trumpet, we find that they are set on similar stages. Each contains the Euphrates River, the Valley of Megiddo, and the armies "from the east." Let's look back at Revelation 9, where the sixth trumpet is recorded. I believe that this is the same event as what we have in the sixth bowl. The sixth bowl and the sixth trumpet are probably happening at the same time.

> 13 And the sixth angel sounded, and I heard a voice from the four horns of the golden altar which is before God,
>
> 14 one saying to the sixth angel who had the trumpet, "Release the four angels who are bound at the great river Euphrates."
>
> 15 And the four angels, who had been prepared for the hour and day and month and year, were released, so that they might kill a third of mankind.
>
> 16 And the number of armies of the horsemen was two hundred million; I heard the number of them.
>
> —Revelation 9

So an army of 200 million horsemen, instigated by these four satanic angels at the river Euphrates, enters the scene. In verse 12 of Revelation 16 we read:

> 12 And the sixth *angel* poured out his bowl upon the great river, the Euphrates; and its water was dried up, that the way might be prepared for the kings from the east."

No plagues have occurred on the earth during this sixth bowl. However, it is significant that the Euphrates River dries up, providing a means whereby the armies of the east can reach this final battle.

The Seventh Bowl — Earth Upheaval and Hail

Let's now read what happens when the final bowl is poured out:

> **17** And the seventh *angel* poured out his bowl upon the air; and a loud voice came out of the temple from the throne, saying, "It is done."
>
> **18** And there were flashes of lightning and sounds and peals of thunder; and there was a great earthquake, such as there had not been since man came to be upon the earth, so great an earthquake *was it, and* so mighty.
>
> **19** And the great city was split into three parts, and the cities of the nations fell. And Babylon the great was remembered before God, to give her the cup of the wine of His fierce wrath.
>
> **20** And every island fled away, and the mountains were not found.
>
> **21** And huge hailstones, about one hundred pounds each, came down from heaven upon men; and men blasphemed God because of the plague of the hail, because its plague was extremely severe.
>
> —Revelation 16

In case you are using the *King James Version* of the Bible for this study, you will find that rather than the word "pounds" in verse 21, the term "talents" is used. A talent is equivalent to approximately 100 pounds, so these hailstones will actually be boulders falling out of the heavens.

There are several interesting items in this passage; let's take the difficult one first. Verse 19 says that the "great city" is split into three parts, all of the cities of the nations are flattened, and Babylon the great is remembered by God because He is going to give her His fierce wrath. This "great city" could be either Jerusalem or Babylon. Let's look at both possibilities from the Scriptures. Revelation 11 says that the great city was split, and it tells us which city the great city was:

> **8** And their dead bodies *will lie* in the street of the great city which mystically is called Sodom and Egypt, where also their Lord was crucified. . . .

> 13   And in that hour there was a great earthquake, and a tenth of the city fell; and seven thousand people were killed in the earthquake, and the rest were terrified and gave glory to the God in heaven.
>
> —Revelation 11

We know where the Lord was crucified, so we know that the "great city" spoken of here is Jerusalem. Since this passage also says that the "great city" is split by an earthquake, it could well be that the "great city" of both Revelation 11:13 and Revelation 16:19 are the same city—Jerusalem.

On the other hand, consider for a moment that Babylon might be the great city:

> 9   "And the kings of the earth, who committed *acts of* immorality and lived sensuously with her, will weep and lament over her when they see the smoke of her burning,
>
> 10   standing at a distance because of the fear of her torment, saying, 'Woe, woe, the great city, Babylon, the strong city! For in one hour your judgment has come.' . . .
>
> 17   . . . And every shipmaster and every passenger and sailor, and as many as make their living by the sea, stood at a distance,
>
> 18   and were crying out as they saw the smoke of her burning, saying, 'What *city* is like the great city?' . . ."
>
> —Revelation 18

In these verses, *Babylon* is called the great city. So both Babylon and Jerusalem are called by this name.

Let's now reread verse 19 of Revelation 16:

> 19   And the great city was split into three parts, and the cities of the nations fell. And Babylon the great was remembered before God, . . .

There are a number of possibilities here. First, this passage could be referring to Jerusalem in the first half of the verse and Babylon in the second half. Or it could be referring to Babylon in both parts of the verse. Another possibility is that "Babylon" and "Jerusalem" are being used as interchangeable terms, referring to the same city (more on that in Chapter 11).

Some biblical scholars say that Babylon is Rome and that the Babylonian church system is the Catholic church. However,

Rome is not really referred to as the great city in this context. (We will be discussing Babylon and Rome further in the next chapter.) We do know that one of these cities (Jerusalem or Babylon) will be split into three parts and that Babylon will suffer under the great wrath of God.

Revelation 16:18–20 says that there will be a great earthquake, so gigantic that there will be no more mountains. The islands will be moved out of their places. The earth will be plowed up to become a garden of God again. This is going to be an incredible thing to experience and observe. This gigantic earthquake should really be called an earth upheaval. An earthquake refers to a shaking of the earth. This event will be much more than a mere shaking. Do we as Christians need to fear what will happen to us when all of this occurs? *No!* Through every one of these events, God will protect His children, just as He did in Egypt, if we have the seal of God on our foreheads.

We will never experience God's wrath. We will experience Tribulation, suffering, and difficult times, but we will never experience His wrath. For that I am very, very thankful.

Consider one more thing here. What would happen if someone flew to 30,000 feet and dropped something weighing 100 pounds on your house? Verse 21 of Revelation 16 says that hailstones weighing 100 pounds will rain down. Only God's all–powerful umbrella can protect us. Some Christians speak in terms of building a structure that will withstand multiple impacts of 100–pound hailstones. God may lead them to do something of that sort, but in the final analysis, it will be God's protection that counts.

The seventh bowl ends God's wrath. Let's turn back to Revelation 11, which deals with the seventh trumpet:

> 19 And the temple of God which is in heaven was opened; and the ark of His covenant appeared in His temple, and there were flashes of lightning and sounds and peals of thunder and an earthquake and a great hailstorm.
>
> —Revelation 11

Again, with the seventh bowl in Revelation 16:18, we have lightning, thunder, an earthquake, and a great hail storm. It is very possible that the seventh bowl and the seventh trumpet are occurring at the same time, since they record similar events. Remember, we saw that trumpet seven occurs at the end of the Tribulation because when it sounds Christ begins to reign on the earth. We also know that bowl seven occurs at the end of the Tribulation since with it God's wrath is finished. Therefore, the most reasonable conclusion is that the seventh trumpet and the seventh bowl are occurring concurrently.

What we have looked at in this chapter is the fifth snapshot, which probably takes place at the very end of the seven trumpets. There is solid scriptural evidence that both trumpet seven and bowl seven occur right at the end of the Tribulation. This snapshot of the seven bowls is another vision that John had, amplifying and providing more detail concerning God's plans for showing His wrath to those who have rejected Him.

11

MYSTERY BABYLON
(Revelation 17 & 18)

SNAPSHOT 6
—BABYLON

Revelation 14:8 introduced the city of Babylon as one focal point of the third snapshot. As we have pointed out, between Chapters 11 and 20 of Revelation, we have seven snapshots that can be thought of as short subjects or flashbacks in a movie about the Tribulation. In the third snapshot, an angel says: "Fallen, fallen is Babylon the great." Revelation 16:19, which describes the seventh bowl, said that "Babylon the great was remembered before God, to give her the cup of wine of His fierce wrath." Thus, we know that the sixth snapshot does not follow the first five snapshots in time because twice already Revelation has said that Babylon has fallen. Yet Revelation 17 and 18 deal with the fall of Babylon in detail.

Before exploring this "mystery Babylon" of Revelation, I think it would be good to provide a little background on the original Babylon, which may or may not be on the same geographic location as mystery Babylon. Let's begin by looking at Genesis 10:

8 Now Cush became the father of Nimrod; he became a mighty one on the earth.

9 He was a mighty hunter before the LORD; therefore it is said, "Like Nimrod a mighty hunter before the LORD."

10 And the beginning of his kingdom was Babel and Erech and Accad and Calneh, in the land of Shinar.

Verse 10 lists four cities that were in the land of Shinar.
Remember that word *Shinar* because it will come up again.
Nimrod established four cities, and the Euphrates River ran
through ancient Babylon. All of this was in the land of Shinar,
which we know today as Iraq.

Now, let's look at Genesis 11:

   1 Now the whole earth used the same language and the same
words.

   2 And it came about as they journeyed east, that they found a
plain in the land of Shinar and settled there.

   3 And they said to one another, "Come, let us make bricks and
burn *them* thoroughly." And they used brick for stone, and they
used tar for mortar.

   4 And they said, "Come, let us build for ourselves a city, and a
tower whose top *will reach* into heaven, and let us make for ourselves a name; lest we be scattered abroad over the face of the whole
earth."

This was the tower of Babel in Babylon. Incidentally, next
to Jerusalem, there is more written about Babylon in the Bible
(Old and New Testaments) than about any other city.

In Isaiah 47 we read about the religion of ancient Babylon:

   12   "Stand *fast* now in your spells
         And in your many sorceries
         With which you have labored from your youth,
         Perhaps you will be able to profit,
         Perhaps you may cause trembling.
   13   "You are wearied with your many counsels,
         Let now the astrologers,
         Those who prophesy by the stars,
         Those who predict by the new moons,
         Stand up and save you from what will come upon you.
   14   "Behold, they have become like stubble,
         Fire burns them;
         They cannot deliver themselves from the power of the flame;
         There will be no coal to warm by,
         Nor a fire to sit before!
   15   "So have those become to you with whom you have labored,
         Who have trafficked with you from your youth,
         Each has wandered in his own way.
         There is none to save you. . . ."

Now let's look at Isaiah 13, where an oracle about Babylon is introduced:

> 1 The oracle concerning Babylon which Isaiah the son of Amoz saw. . . .

> 9 Behold, the day of the LORD is coming,
> Cruel, with fury and burning anger.
> To make the land a desolation;
> And He will exterminate its sinners from it.

Back then God knew that He was going to judge Babylon. Let's read further:

> 19 And Babylon, the beauty of kingdoms, the glory of Chaldeans' pride,
> Will be as when God overthrew Sodom and Gomorrah.
> 20 It will never be inhabited or lived in from generation to generation;
> Nor will the Arab pitch *his* tent there,
> Nor will shepherds make *their flocks* lie down there.
> 21 But desert creatures will lie down there,
> And their houses will be full of owls,
> Ostriches also will live there, and shaggy goats will frolic there.
> 22 And hyenas will howl in their fortified towers
> And jackals in their luxurious palaces.
> Her *fateful* time also will soon come
> And her days will not be prolonged.

—Isaiah 13

The Chaldeans spoken of in verse 19 were a priestly class of astronomers. They had a priestly inheritance but actually served as astronomers.

Once God destroys Babylon, it will never be inhabited again. I do not think that God has destroyed Babylon yet. Ancient Babylon was destroyed by armies, but I don't think that the full and final destruction of Babylon has 'yet come. Babylon has been continuously inhabited through the centuries and is inhabited today. When *God* destroys it, it will never be inhabited again.

Let's look in Jeremiah for another prophecy concerning Babylon.

6 Flee from the midst of Babylon,
   And each of you save his life!
   Do not be destroyed in her punishment,
   For this is the LORD's time of vengeance;
   He is going to render recompense to her.

7 Babylon has been a golden cup in the hand of the LORD,
   Intoxicating all the earth.
   The nations have drunk of her wine;
   Therefore the nations are going mad.

8 Suddenly Babylon has fallen and been broken,
   Wail over her!
   Bring balm for her pain;
   Perhaps she may be healed.

9 We applied healing to Babylon, but she was not healed;
   Forsake her and let us each go to his own country,
   For her judgment has reached to heaven
   And towers up to the very skies.

10 The LORD has brought about our vindication;
   Come and let us recount in Zion
   The work of the LORD our God!

—Jeremiah 51

Let's also look at Zechariah 5 (to make this reading easier, keep in mind that an *ephah* is a dry measure, roughly equivalent to a bushel).

5 Then the angel who was speaking with me went out, and said to me, "Lift up now your eyes, and see what this is, going forth."

6 And I said, "What is it?" And he said, "This is the ephah going forth." Again he said, "This is their appearance in all the land

7 (and behold, a lead cover was lifted up); and this is a woman sitting inside the ephah."

8 Then he said, "This is Wickedness!" And he threw her down into the middle of the ephah and cast the lead weight on its opening.

9 Then I lifted up my eyes and looked, and there two women were coming out with the wind in their wings; and they had wings like the wings of a stork and they lifted up the ephah between the earth and the heavens.

10 And I said to the angel who was speaking with me, "Where are they taking the ephah?"

11 Then he said to me, "To build a temple for her in the land of Shinar; and when it is prepared, she will be set there on her own pedestal."

—Zechariah 5

So, according to verse 11, there is going to be a temple built in the land of Shinar, probably in the city of Babylon. The person we see here will be displayed on a pedestal. This gives you some background concerning the old Babylon and the biblical prophecies associated with it.

REVELATION 17:1–18
—THE WOMAN AND THE DICTATOR BEAST

Now let's explore Revelation 17 and 18 to see what factual information there is concerning Babylon. Revelation 17 says this:

1 And one of the seven angels who had the seven bowls came and spoke with me, saying, "Come here, I shall show you the judgment of the great harlot who sits on many waters,

2 with whom the kings of the earth committed *acts of* immorality, and those who dwell on the earth were made drunk with the wine of her immorality."

3 And he carried me away in the Spirit into a wilderness; and I saw a woman sitting on a scarlet beast full of blasphemous names, having seven heads and ten horns.

4 And the woman was clothed in purple and scarlet, and adorned with gold and precious stones and pearls, having in her hand a gold cup full of abominations and of the unclean things of her immorality,

5 and upon her forehead a name *was* written, a mystery, "BABYLON THE GREAT, THE MOTHER OF HARLOTS AND OF THE ABOMINATIONS OF THE EARTH."

6 And I saw the woman drunk with the blood of the saints, and with the blood of the witnesses of Jesus. And when I saw her, I wondered greatly.

7 And the angel said to me, "Why do you wonder? I shall tell you the mystery of the woman and of the beast that carries her, which has the seven heads and the ten horns.

8   "The beast that you saw was and is not, and is about to come up out of the abyss and to go to destruction. And those who dwell on the earth will wonder, whose name has not been written in the book of life from the foundation of the world, when they see the beast, that he was and is not and will come.

9   "Here is the mind which has wisdom. The seven heads are seven mountains on which the woman sits,

10   and they are seven kings; five have fallen, one is, the other has not yet come; and when he comes, he must remain a little while.

11   "And the beast which was and is not, is himself also an eighth, and is *one* of the seven, and he goes to destruction.

12   "And the ten horns which you saw are ten kings, who have not yet received a kingdom, but they receive authority as kings with the beast for one hour.

13   "These have one purpose and they give their power and authority to the beast.

14   "These will wage war against the Lamb, and the Lamb will overcome them, because He is Lord of lords and King of kings, and those who are with Him *are the* called and chosen and faithful."

15   And he said to me, "The waters which you saw where the harlot sits, are peoples and multitudes and nations and tongues.

16   "And the ten horns which you saw, and the beast, these will hate the harlot and will make her desolate and naked, and will eat her flesh and will burn her up with fire.

17   "For God has put it in their hearts to execute His purpose by having a common purpose, and by giving their kingdom to the beast, until the words of God should be fulfilled.

18   "And the woman whom you saw is the great city, which reigns over the kings of the earth."

—Revelation 17

There is a great deal in this passage and even more in the next chapter of Revelation, but with the help of the Holy Spirit we should be able to go through it fairly easily. First, we find that John saw a harlot sitting on a scarlet beast. The beast had seven heads and ten horns and was full of blasphemous names. Let's review a verse in Revelation 13:

1   . . . And I saw a beast coming up out of the sea, having ten horns and seven heads, and on his horns *were* ten diadems, and on his heads *were* blasphemous names.

Revelation 13:1 is describing the dictator beast. (Remember, there is also a prophet beast.) Since the descriptions are the same, we conclude that John is probably describing the dictator beast again in Revelation 17:3. In Revelation 17 we read further about the woman who rides this beast:

> 4 And the woman was clothed in purple and scarlet, and adorned with gold and precious stones and pearls, having in her hand a gold cup full of abominations and of the unclean things of her immorality,
>
> 5 and upon her forehead a name *was* written, a mystery, "BABYLON THE GREAT, THE MOTHER OF HARLOTS AND OF THE ABOMINATIONS OF THE EARTH."

In verse 5 this woman is called "Babylon" and "the mother of harlots." This indicates that she has daughters who are called "harlots." Verse 6 goes on to say that she is drunk with the blood of the saints.

One thing that we need to understand is the difference between a harlot and an adulteress. An adulteress commits adultery for some reason other than pay. A harlot is an adulteress for commercial purposes. What we are seeing here is not someone who is simply unfaithful on a spiritual level but someone who has abandoned the things of God for financial gain. There is a significant difference, as we shall see later. What we are probably looking at then is a commercial system that rebels against God and controls the dictator beast. Babylon appears to control the beast because in Revelation 17:3 we find that she is the beast's rider.

Next, the angel reveals to John the meanings of some of these symbols.

> 7 And the angel said to me, "Why did you wonder? I shall tell you the mystery of the woman and of the beast that carries her, which has the seven heads and the ten horns.
>
> 8 "The beast that you saw was and is not, and is about to come up out of the abyss and to go to destruction. And those who dwell on the earth will wonder, whose name has not been written in the book of life from the foundation of the world, when they see the beast, that he was and is not and will come.
>
> 9 "Here is the mind which has wisdom. The seven heads are seven mountains on which the woman sits,

10   and they are seven kings, five have fallen, one is, the other has not yet come; and when he comes, he must remain a little while.

11   "And the beast which was and is not, is himself also an eighth, and is one of the seven, and he goes to destruction. . . ."

—Revelation 17

So, in verse 8 we learn that the beast is about to come out of the sbyss, only to go "to destruction"—the lake of fire. This individual, who is the Antichrist and the dictator beast, is empowered by Satan.

In verses 8 and 11 of Revelation 17, we encounter what at first sounds like double-talk: "The beast . . . was and is not, and is about to come. . . ." In Revelation 13 we read a similar thing about this beast:

3   And I *saw* one of his heads as if it had been slain, and his fatal wound was healed. . . .

Earlier, we illustrated the drama of this event by comparing it to a Jack Kennedy resurrection. Suppose President Kennedy reappeared after hundreds of thousands of people had seen him dead on worldwide television. If he claimed that God had returned him to the earth in order to lead the world in a certain direction, I believe the masses would follow him down just about any path.

The dictator beast will be *pronounced* dead—not necessarily truly killed—and then will be "brought back to life." Obviously, this will startle the entire world. In every way the beast will be trying to imitate Christ, and this "resurrection" will be one act in his charade. This explains the apparent double-talk of the beast that "was, is not, and is going to be again." It really isn't double-talk; it is just a way of describing an apparent death and return to life.

Revelation 17:9 tells us that the seven heads are seven mountains. The seven mountains are really seven kings, not actual geological mountains. Five of these seven kings have already fallen from power at the time John is writing this. Concerning the two remaining kings, the angel tells John that "one is" and "the other" has not yet come. The one that "is" would be the Roman Empire that reigned during John's life. The "other" would be a kingdom that still is to come some time in the future. When this seventh one comes, it says that it must remain a little while. Out of the seventh will come an eighth (the beast) which will still have its roots in the seventh kingdom.

I don't totally understand all of this, but it is apparent that there is a world kingdom coming and that it will involve the dictator beast. He will be the dictator of the whole world and will rule from the seventh and eighth kingdoms.

Verses 12 through 17 talk about the "ten horns." Horns are powerful and smooth. Perhaps you are familiar with the term, "a ten–horn gambler." This refers to a smooth, powerful, ruthless kind of gambler. These ten horns are going to be ten kings without kingdoms. These are evidently rich, smooth, powerful men, who will not have a piece of geography over which they are already ruling. It might be someone like the Rothschilds or Rockefellers. They do not have their own "kingdoms" but they do have extreme power and wealth. Let's reread these verses:

> 12   "And the ten horns which you saw are ten kings, who have not yet received a kingdom, but they receive authority as kings with the beast for one hour.
> 13   "These have one purpose and they give their power and authority to the beast.
> 14   "These will wage war against the Lamb, and the Lamb will overcome them, because He is Lord of lords and King of kings, and those who are with Him *are the* called and chosen and faithful."
> 15   And he said to me, "The waters which you saw where the harlot sits, are peoples and multitudes and nations and tongues.
> 16   "And the ten horns which you saw, and the beast, these will hate the harlot and will make her desolate and naked, and will eat her flesh and will burn her up with fire.
> 17   "For God has put it in their hearts to execute His purpose by having a common purpose, and by giving their kingdom to the beast, until the words of God should be fulfilled. . . ."

> –Revelation 17

Verse 12 says that these ten "kings" will receive authority from the beast. In verse 13 they give their power and authority to the beast. So they turn over to the beast the wealth and power which belongs to them.

Verse 14 says that these ten kings (not the beast, nor the woman) will wage war against the Lamb, and the Lamb will overcome them. If I were a John Bircher and believed in an international conspiracy to take over the world, it would appear that this passage is describing such a conspiracy or the much-publicized Illuminati. I don't know whether or not I believe in such a conspiracy, so I'm going to remain neutral. However, if I held that view, I could find a basis for it in this passage, where all the people are giving their allegiance to one man. They are controlled by the beast, and they are really waging war against the Lamb.

In verse 16, the ten horns (ten kings) begin to hate the harlot. Verse 18 says that the woman is ". . . the great city, which reigns over the kings of the earth." For now, let's assume that the harlot is a city. The ten kings will make her naked and desolate and will eat her flesh and burn her up. The source of this punishment will be God, but He will use these powerful men (kings) as His instruments. Verse 17 tells us that God puts it into the hearts of these kings to execute His will in this instance.

To recapitulate, we see Babylon involved with the dictator beast. The dictator beast has, as part of his staff, ten kings who do not have a kingdom. Verse 18 says that the great city rules over all of the kings of the earth (hence, over all of the people). Thus, we know a one-world government is coming. Verse 15 says that the waters that the harlot sits upon are the peoples and multitudes and nations and tongues. In my thinking, the dictator beast and the kings would like to have charge over all of the people of the world. In order to do that, Babylon, the controlling rider of the beast (see Revelation 17:3) has to be eliminated. By destroying her, they çan take over the people of the world. The "organization chart" of this structure can be seen in Figure 4.

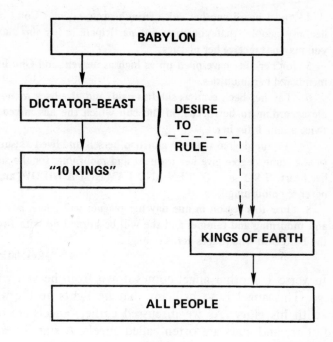

Figure 4

REVELATION 18:1-8
–THE DESTRUCTION OF BABYLON

The destruction of the woman, Babylon, is recorded in detail in Revelation 18:

1 **After these things I saw another angel coming down from heaven, having great authority, and the earth was illumined with his glory.**

2 **And he cried out with a mighty voice, saying, "Fallen, fallen is Babylon the great! And she has become a dwelling place of demons and a prison of every unclean spirit, and a prison of every unclean and hateful bird.**

3 **"For all the nations have drunk of the wine of the passion of her immorality, and the kings of the earth have committed *acts of* immorality with her, and the merchants of the earth have become rich by the wealth of her sensuality."**

4 And I heard another voice from heaven, saying, "Come out of her, my people, that you may not participate in her sins and that you may not receive her plagues;

5 for her sins have piled up as high as heaven, and God has remembered her iniquities.

6 "Pay her back even as she has paid, and give back *to her* double according to her deeds; in the cup which she has mixed, mix twice as much for her.

7 "To the degree that she glorified herself and lived sensuously, to the same degree give her torment and mourning; for she says in her heart, 'I SIT *as* A QUEEN AND I AM NOT A WIDOW, and will never see mourning.'

8 "For this reason in one day her plagues will come, pestilence and mourning and famine, and she will be burned up with fire; for the Lord God who judges her is strong. . . ."

—Revelation 18

In verse 1 another angel comes down from heaven with a message. This angel is so brilliant that he lights up the whole earth with his glory. As we discussed earlier, angels are often called stars, and stars are often called angels. A star is really a sun, so when this angel comes down, it will be like a sun descending to the earth!

Verse 2 tells us that Babylon is full of demons, witchcraft, astrology, sorcery, and all the unclean spirits of the world. These are the central focus of Babylon's religion.

The nations of the earth have become drunk with the wine of Babylon's immorality, and the merchants have become rich in their dealings with her (verse 3). Since Babylon seems to be quite wealthy, we could possibly draw a parallel to the Middle East situation with Saudi Arabia, Iraq and Iran. We used to think of this area as just miles and miles of sand. But today, the wealth of the world is pouring into that little area in exchange for its oil, and very soon it will control the vast majority of the wealth in the world.

Concerning our relationship to Babylon, in verses 4 and 5 we see a warning to God's people to "come out of her." Let's look closely at what it means to "come out of her." We are told that if we don't come out, we will receive the same punishment that she will receive. What does coming out of Babylon really mean? It means having nothing to do with immorality, the occult, a lust for riches, or an ungodly sensuality.

In verses 6 and 7, we see that God is going to punish Babylon doubly because she has set herself against God. She has glorified herself and lived luxuriously, proclaiming that she is a queen.

In verse 8 we see that in one day Babylon is going to be totally destroyed. Before nuclear and atomic bombs, it would have been difficult to conceive of a city being destroyed in one day. There were a couple of cases, one in 96 A.D. when the volcano Vesuvius blew up and covered two cities within a three–day period, and Sodom and Gomorrah were also destroyed quickly. Today it would be easy to imagine the one–day destruction of Babylon from a nuclear blast. Or, God may simply wipe it out as He did Sodom and Gomorrah. At any rate, we know from both Revelation and Isaiah 13:19 that Babylon's destruction will be sudden and complete.

REVELATION 18:9–19
–KINGS AND MERCHANTS WEEP

Let's now read the next portion of Revelation 18. This describes a lamentation for Babylon.

9 "And the kings of the earth, who committed *acts of* immorality and lived sensuously with her, will weep and lament over her when they see the smoke of her burning,

10 standing at a distance because of the fear of her torment, saying, 'Woe, woe, the great city, Babylon, the strong city! For in one hour your judgment has come.'

11 "And the merchants of the earth weep and mourn over her, because no one buys their cargoes any more;

12 cargoes of gold and silver and precious stones and pearls and fine linen and purple and silk and scarlet, and every *kind* citron wood and every article of ivory and every article *made* from very costly wood and bronze and iron and marble,

13   and cinnamon and spice and incense and perfume and frankincense and wine and olive oil and fine flour and wheat and cattle and sheep, and *cargoes* of horses and chariots and slaves and human lives.

14   "And the fruit you long for has gone from you, and all things that were luxurious and splendid have passed away from you and *men* will no longer find them.

15   "The merchants of these things, who became rich from her, will stand at a distance because of the fear of her torment, weeping and mourning,

16   saying, 'Woe, woe, the great city, she who was clothed in fine linen and purple and scarlet, and adorned with gold and precious stones and pearls;

17   for in one hour such great wealth has been laid waste!' And every shipmaster and every passenger and sailor, and as many as make their living by the sea, stood at a distance,

18   and were crying out as they saw the smoke of her burning, saying, 'What *city* is like the great city?'

19   "And they threw dust on their heads and were crying out, weeping and mourning, saying, 'Woe, woe, the great city, in which all who had ships at sea became rich by her wealth, for in one hour she had been laid waste!' . . ."

—Revelation 18

When I was a new Christian, I was told that adultery was sex between a married person and someone other than his spouse, and that fornication was sex between two single people. That was not correct information. Fornication is a broad term for immorality, and it usually involves prostitution. Adultery is simply one form of fornication. Homosexuality is another form of fornication. All of these forms of sexual immorality are considered fornication.

In this passage of Revelation, we see the kings of the earth who had participated in Babylon's immorality (committed fornication with her), the merchants who sold to her, and the ships that carried supplies to her. They were all getting rich in their dealings with her, and now they are weeping and mourning because their source of income and pleasure is gone.

Listed in this passage of scripture are seven categories of goods which the merchants were selling to her. The gold, silver, precious stones and pearls represent *wealth*. The fine linen, purple silk and scarlet, represent *clothes*. The citron wood, ivory, bronze, iron, and marble articles are *decorative things*. The spices, incense, cinnamon, perfume, and frankincense are *luxurious fragrances*. Then *food* is listed: wine, olive oil, fine flour, wheat, cattle, and sheep. The horses and chariots are *war machines*. And we also see that they were selling *slaves*.

These are things that the merchants were selling to Babylon, but she has now been destroyed and cannot take delivery. To help you understand the emotion involved here, imagine that you are a manufacturer who receives an order for a million trinkets from a prominent store. You fill 18 trucks with these trinkets and send them to the store, only to find when you arrive that the store has been wiped out. What would you do with 18 truckloads of trinkets with no one to buy them? You can see why the merchants in this passage are crying!

What was Babylon using to pay for all of these things that she was buying? We really don't know, but a good conjecture would be that since Babylon is in present–day Iraq, and Iraq is the world's second largest oil producer, the payments may well have been made in oil.

REVELATION 18:20
—THE SAINTS REJOICE

In verse 20 of Revelation 18, we see rejoicing rather than weeping or mourning.

> **20** "**Rejoice over her, O heaven, and you saints and apostles and prophets, because God has pronounced judgment for you against her.**"
>
> —**Revelation 18**

Evidently Babylon has also been persecuting the Christians because, according to Revelation 17:6, she is drunk with "the blood of the saints." God will take out His wrath on her because of her actions against the saints. We will rejoice because the terrible, immoral city that was persecuting us will have been destroyed!

There is no way that we can know exactly how this Babylonian persecution and blood spilling will occur. However, it is interesting to observe the rejuvenation of the Muslim religion in conjunction with the economic power they hold. With their control of the Mideast oil and the religious fervor they incite in their followers, this is certainly emerging as a major force in the world.

It is possible then, that this persecution could be the work of the rejuvenated Muslims. Frequently, in times past, they have had holy wars with both the Christians and the Jews. They have a history of expanding their religion by the use of the sword. When capturing a town or a city, their pattern is to kill anyone who will not convert to Islam. Just as today they will cut off the hand of a thief, so they have cut off the heads of those who refused to accept Islam.

Since the original city of Babylon was located in present-day Iraq, this locates it right in the heart of the Muslim world. We should watch this area carefully, for it is very possbile that the persecution of Christians by "Babylon" will emerge from it.

REVELATION 18:21–24
–BABYLON'S ULTIMATE DEMISE

Now let's read the remaining verses in Revelation 18:

21   And a strong angel took up a stone like a great millstone and threw it into the sea, saying, "Thus will Babylon, the great city, be thrown down with violence, and will not be found any longer.

22   "And the sound of harpists and musicians and fluteplayers and trumpeters will not be heard in you any longer; and no craftsman of any craft will be found in you any longer; and the sound of a mill will not be heard in you any longer;

23   and the light of a lamp will not shine in you any longer; and the voice of the bridegroom and bride will not be heard in you any longer; for your merchants were the great men of the earth, because all the nations were deceived by your sorcery.

24   "And in her was found the blood of prophets and of saints and of all who have been slain on the earth."

These are the last recorded characteristics of this city. So we see that Babylon "the great" is violently cast down, never to rise again.

WHO OR WHAT IS BABYLON?

Let's assume that Babylon is a city, a country, or a system. What are some of the characteristics of this entity? We know that she is "a whore," who has forsaken the things of God for financial gain. We know that she has shed the blood of martyrs, Christians, and prophets. We know that sorcery, astrology, and demons are heavily involved in the religion of this entity. She is a center of commerce, providing the merchants and ships of the world with wealth in exchange for their goods. She rules all of the people of the earth. The great men of the earth are her merchants. Eventually, she will be destroyed by the dictator beast. These are the characteristics of Babylon as depicted in Revelation 17 and 18.

No city, country, or system today fulfills all of those characteristics. Nobody rules the whole earth. No one ever has fulfilled all of those characteristics. Even Rome didn't rule the entire earth. The best we can do is to project who the most likely candidates to *become* this entity are, since this is something yet in the future. Let's look at some of the possibilities.

Some biblical scholars feel that "mystery Babylon" is the present-day city of Rome, and that a new Roman Empire will arise out of the old one. Rome, of course, is the central governing city of the Catholic Church, which some feel is a false religion. Those holding this opinion say that the Catholic Church is quite wealthy and has abandoned the true things of God in order to gain wealth. One of the bases on which they support this theory is that Rome is geographically located on seven hills (see Revelation 17:9–10). This is a possibility, and I certainly would not discount it, but the seven hills (actually seven mountains) spoken of in Revelation 17:9–10 are said to be seven kings. So, using the hills of Rome as a basis for a Babylon–Rome correlation certainly presents some difficulties.

Even though Catholicism may have added many unbiblical facets to what Protestants call "pure Christianity," I personally know many Catholics who know Jesus Christ as their Savior. Their basic religion isn't sorcery, demons, witchcraft and astrology but rather a form of faith in Jesus Christ. Since Italy has about the weakest currency in the whole world, I can't really see that they have the wealth to rule the earth.

Another candidate for "mystery Babylon" could be a rebuilt Babylon. We know that the ancient city of Babylon is being rebuilt right now. In ancient Babylon, a dictator ruled most of that area of the world, and they had a religion involving demons, sorcery, and witchcraft. If this old system and religion were to be reinstituted, this could be the city described in Revelation 17 and 18. This is a likely candidate in my mind, particularly with the wealth centering around that area of the world.

Another possibility would be some other city on the earth, such as San Francisco, New York, Tokyo, London, or even Washington, D.C. If I had to pick one from that list of cities, I would probably choose London. Most of our present–day witchcraft and demonology came to the United States from London. The Rothschild family is supposedly the head of the Illuminati, which is a Luciferian type of organization. Their people regard the Rothschilds as "gods." Many of the characteristics describing Babylon seem to fit London better than most of these other cities.

There is another possible candidate that might surprise you. That is Jerusalem. Let's look at some scriptures that could give support to this idea. But first, remember that the Jews are only one tribe—the tribe of Judah—which is only 8 percent of physical Israel. When they came out of the Babylonian captivity, they brought many non–Israelites with them, because of intermarriage. We don't really know how many of the people who reside in the Palestinian area today are of the pure physical lineage of Abraham. For a moment erase from your mind the teaching that these are "God's people" and that Jerusalem is going to be full of Jewish evangelists after the church is raptured. Let's wipe the slate clean and go back to see what the word of God has to say.

I might say initially that it is interesting that the Jews (the tribe of Judah) are the only tribe that is left intact at all. Christ came from the lineage of David, as prophesied in the Old Testament, and He is called the Lion of the tribe of Judah (Revelation 5:5). It is very possible that for the Antichrist to be accepted as the Messiah, he would have to come from the tribe of Judah which is the only tribe left semi–intact. This is not an anti–Semitic statement on my part at all; I love the Jews. It is simply an observation that he would need to come from the tribe of Judah in order to be accepted as the Messiah. The Antichrist (the dictator beast) will need to be accepted by the "physical" Jews. If he came from, or was based in, Jerusalem, this could enhance his acceptance.

To get some background on Jerusalem and how God looks at her now, let's read the following from Isaiah 1:

> 1 The vision of Isaiah the son of Amoz, concerning Judah and Jerusalem which he saw during the reigns of Uzziah, Jotham, Ahaz, *and* Hezekiah, kings of Judah. . . .

> 4 Alas, sinful nation,
> People weighted down with iniquity,
> Offspring of evildoers,
> Sons who act corruptly!
> They have abandoned the LORD,
> They have despised the Holy One of Israel,
> They have turned away from Him. . . .

> 21 How the faithful city has become a harlot,
> She *who* was full of justice!
> Righteousness once lodged in her,
> But now murderers. . . .

> 24 Therefore the Lord GOD of hosts,
> The Mighty One of Israel declares,
> "Ah, I will be relieved of My adversaries,
> And avenge Myself on My foes.

> 25 "I will also turn My hand against you,
> And will smelt away your dross as with lye,
> And will remove all your alloy.

26 "Then I will restore your judges as at the first,
    And your counselors as at the beginning;
    After that you will be called the city of righteousness,
    A faithful city."

In verse 21, God calls the city which has turned away from him a harlot. Now let's turn to Ezekiel 16:

2 "Son of man, make known to Jerusalem her abominations, . . .

15 "But you trusted in your beauty and played the harlot because of your fame, and you poured out your harlotries on every passer-by who might be *willing*.

16 "And you took some of your clothes, made for yourself high places of various colors, and played the harlot on them, which should never come about nor happen.

17 "You also took your beautiful jewels *made* of My gold and of My silver, which I had given you, and made for yourself male images that you might play the harlot with them. . . ."

43 "Because you have not remembered the days of your youth but have enraged Me by all these things, behold, I in turn will bring your conduct down on your own head, "declares the Lord God, "So that you will not commit the lewdness on top of all your *other* abominations. . . ."

Throughout this chapter Jerusalem is called a harlot, and we see in verse 17 that her harlotry involved riches (commerce). She was immoral for purposes of gain. Let's also look at Jeremiah 2:

2 "Go and proclaim in the ears of Jerusalem, saying, 'Thus says the LORD,

    "I remember concerning you the devotion of your youth,
    The love of your betrothals,
    Your following after Me in the wilderness,
    Through a land not sown. . . ."'"

20 "For long ago I broke your yoke
    And tore off your bonds;
    But you said, 'I will not serve!
    For on every high hill
    And under every green tree
    You have lain down as a harlot. . . ."

Again, God is talking to Jerusalem. He does not call her an adulteress but a harlot; He is saying that Jerusalem has left Him for financial and commercial gain. Interestingly, an avid pursuit of financial and commercial gain is a characteristic of many of the Jewish people. I am not trying to generalize or to put down; I am simply stating an observation.

Let's now look at Matthew 23, where Christ is talking to the people of Jerusalem:

> 34 "Therefore, behold, I am sending you prophets and wise men and scribes; some of them you will kill and crucify, and some of them you will scourge in your synagogues, and persecute from city to city,
>
> 35 that upon you may fall *the guilt* of all the righteous blood shed on earth, from the blood of righteous Abel to the blood of Zechariah, the son of Berechiah, whom you murdered between the temple and the altar.
>
> 36 Truly I say to you, all these things shall come upon this generation.
>
> 37 "O Jerusalem, Jerusalem, who kills the prophets and stones those who are sent to her! How often I wanted to gather your children together, the way a hen gathers her chicks under her wings, and you were unwilling. . . ."

Christ is telling Jerusalem that all of the blood of the righteous people is being laid at her feet. So from scripture, we can see that Jerusalem is a harlot and has shed the blood of the saints. She has left God for financial gain; she has rejected God and His Son.

Many people think that the "Jews" have a good religion. But we know that they have an *invalid* religion because they have rejected Christ. Earlier we talked about the synagogues of Satan. The synagogues of the Jewish people are no longer the synagogues of God because they have rejected Him and His Son. God considers them harlots. Those synagogues are now the synagogues of Satan. So Jerusalem would be a possible candidate for being Babylon, if mystery Babylon is an actual city.

Is Babylon a Country or a System?

We have considered a number of modern cities which could conceivably become the Babylon of Revelation 17 and 18. However, it may be that mystery Babylon is a country rather than a city. If this is the case, probably the two best candidates today would be the U.S. and Russia. They each have a great deal of wealth and massive shipping commerce. Russia has killed multitudes of Christians, so this characteristic might apply to her. Considering the way she is taking giant bites out of the globe, Russia has one of the best chances of ruling the whole earth. I would not discount Russia as being the great harlot. We know that whoever rules the earth first is probably going to be the harlot that we have been discussing.

Babylon also could be a system. Many people say (which I don't quite agree with) that the harlot in Revelation 17 is a religious system, and the harlot in Revelation 18 is a political system. I see little foundation for that concept. Throughout, Babylon is a single commercial and political entity, not two separate systems.

Since Babylon appears to be the financial system of the world, some Christians are warning others that we should "come out of her." They feel that Christians should move to the wilderness and barter, never buying or selling anything. These people fail to take into account that Christ was involved in the world economic system of His day. You will recall that He took a gold coin out of the fish's mouth and told His disciples to give it to Caesar for taxes. Also, His disciples carried a purse of money from which they bought various things. They were consistently making financial transactions. Therefore, I don't believe that the Bible teaches not to make any financial purchases.

Some people feel that the Babylonian religious system of Revelation is actually the major church denominations of today. They postulate that God is saying to "come out" of the "Babylonish system." I don't see how they arrive at this. The religion of Babylon is witchcraft, demons, astrology, Satan worship, and so on. No matter how lukewarm or unresponsive a major denomination is, their religion is not the occult. Hopefully their religion is lifting up Jesus Christ as the Son of God and the *only* way to heaven. As long as they lift Him up, it is difficult to label them "Babylon." Some of them may not be hearing what God is saying—they may have plugged up ears—but wherein Christ is preached, we should all rejoice (Philippians 1:18).

When I hear someone say, "Come out of the denominations, the 'Babylonish religious system,' " my reaction is: "Whoa!" We need to be very cautious about judging, criticizing and labeling other people. It is easy to get drawn into mud-slinging of this type. It may be that God is leading someone out of a major denomination because he does not feel the leaders are sensitive to what the Holy Spirit is doing, but that has nothing to do with a "Babylonish system." The religion of Babylon is purely anti–Jesus; those involved in it want to rely on things other than God to control their future and to guide them.

COME OUT OF BABYLON

I think it is extremely important that we realize what it is that God is telling us to "come out" of. Let's net down the characteristics of this entity, whether it be a system, a city, or a country. We want to come out of anything that deals with *witchcraft* or the *occult*, PERIOD. That means anything, from casually reading the astrology page in the newspaper or buying a book on astrology to getting involved in any way in the occult.

God is a jealous God, and He wants your decisions influenced only by Himself and the Holy Spirit. If you happen to read in the astrology page that today is not a good day for making decisions, so you don't make any, you are allowing astrology to guide you rather than the Spirit of God. He tells us to have nothing to do with astrology.

Bill Gothard tells a story about a grandmother, a mother, and a little girl having a cup of tea. A tea leaf reader came by. They thought it would be cute to have the little girl's tea leaves read. The reader told her that she would marry a man in uniform and have three girls. This really stuck in that little girl's mind. She would not date anybody that did not wear a uniform. She finally did marry someone in a uniform and had two girls. She then had a third child, and it was a boy. In her mind, the child *should* have been a girl, so she totally rejected him. The child was so demon possessed that if he was brought near a church, he would scream at the top of his lungs. The incident with the tea leaves was guiding the girl's future, not the Lord.

We are also to "come out" of anything that gives financial gain in return for not following God's laws or God's direction. What if someone pays you $25 cash for doing something, and six months later it is income tax time; do you put that $25 down? Possibly not. Why? "Well, nobody will ever know about it." Why not put it down? "Well, I'm in the 50 percent tax bracket, and I would have to pay $12 tax on it." If you do not report it, you are breaking God's law that says to obey the law of the land. You are breaking God's law that says you shall not lie or bear false witness. You are stealing from the government. For a measly $12, you are breaking a law that says you shall not steal. You are part of Babylon when you do that sort of thing. Anytime I am willing to break God's laws for financial gain, I am living in Babylon. Revelation 18:4 says to come out of her, lest you be punished with the punishment that she is going to get.

Babylon was eager to get the luxurious things of life. I am not saying that God is going to lead us all to live in poverty in a little shack, but He does say not to love the world (1 John 2: 15). If I love luxurious things, then I become a part of the Babylonian system.

Let's read the following passage from James:

1 What is the source of quarrels and conflicts among you? Is not the source your pleasures that wage war in your members?

2 You lust and do not have; *so* you commit murder. And you are envious and cannot obtain; *so* you fight and quarrel. You do not have because you do not ask.

3 You ask and do not receive, because you ask with wrong motives, so that you may spend *it* on your pleasures.

4 You adulteresses, do you not know that friendship with the world is hostility toward God? Therefore whoever wishes to be a friend of the world makes himself an enemy of God.

5 Or do you think that the Scripture speaks to no purpose: "He jealously desires the Spirit which He has made to dwell in us"?

6 But He gives a greater grace. Therefore *it* says, "GOD IS OPPOSED TO THE PROUD, BUT GIVES GRACE TO THE HUMBLE."

7 Submit therefore to God. Resist the devil and he will flee from you.

8 Draw near to God and He will draw near to you. Cleanse your hands, you sinners; and purify your hearts, you double-minded.

9 Be miserable and mourn and weep; let your laughter be turned into mourning, and your joy to gloom.

10 Humble yourselves in the presence of the Lord, and He will exalt you.

—James 4

The harlot exalts herself. When we exalt ourselves, we are being like the harlot, and we are being a part of the Babylonian system. If we love the things of the world, we become a part of that system. We have a strong admonition to "come out of" loving luxuries. If all of a sudden we get a check for $2000, what's our first thought? Probably, "What can *I* do with this for me?" We should ask the Lord what *He* wants us to do with it. Most Christians today don't operate that way. We should come out of Babylon now, even before she is manifested in physical reality.

If you had asked me five years ago what I thought of mystery Babylon, I would have said something different than what I have just shared. Five years from now I might have a deeper or even different revelation from God. But for now, this is my best thinking. I think that at some point in time, probably out of Jerusalem, an Antichrist will arise and will receive power and authority from the ten wealthiest men in the world, who will pledge to back him to the hilt. They will form an unholy union, and the occult will give them power. They will have a world government and will rule the world. But at some point in time, Babylon (perhaps a city, a country or a system) will get in their way, and these powerful men will decide to destroy Babylon. God will use them as His tools to execute His judgments on Babylon and on all who do not "come out of her."

As events unfold, I may totally change my mind on the physical outworking of this. But on the spiritual side, I think that the Bible solidly warns us to avoid anything, or any activity, that has the characteristics attributed to Babylon.

12

THE RETURN OF CHRIST
AND THE MILLENNIUM
(Revelation 19 & 20)

We have now looked at six of the seven snapshots or mini-movies that occur at various times during the Tribulation. There are seven seals, seven bowls of wrath, seven trumpets, and seven snapshots in all.

SNAPSHOT 7
—THE WEDDING FEAST AND ARMAGEDDON

The seventh snapshot covers the actual battle of Armageddon. This is found in Revelation 19; let's read the first six verses.

1 After these things I heard, as it were, a loud voice of a great multitude in heaven, saying
"Hallelujah! Salvation and glory and power belong to God;
2 BECAUSE HIS JUDGMENTS ARE TRUE AND RIGHTEOUS: for He has judged the great harlot who was corrupting the earth with her immorality, and HE HAS AVENGED THE BLOOD OF HIS BOND-SERVANTS ON HER."
3 And a second time they said, "Hallelujah! HER SMOKE RISES UP FOREVER AND EVER."
4 And the twenty-four elders and the four living creatures fell down and worshiped God who sits on the throne saying, "Amen. Hellelujah!"

5 And a voice came from the throne, saying, "Give praise to our God, all of His bond-servants, you who fear Him, the small and the great."

6 And I heard, as it were, the voice of a great multitude and as the sound of many waters and as the sound of mighty peals of thunder, saying,

"Hallelujah! For the Lord our God, the Almighty, reigns. . . ."

—Revelation 19

This ties in somewhat with the sixth snapshot of the fall of Babylon, the great harlot. The saints rejoiced because Babylon had fallen. Now we see those in heaven rejoicing because Babylon has fallen. At first it appears to be the angelic hosts who are rejoicing, but then, in verse 5, a voice comes from the throne showing us otherwise. This isn't God's voice; probably it is one of the four creatures admonishing Christians to praise. Then a great multitude rejoices.

Let's read the next three verses:

7 "Let's rejoice and be glad and give the glory to Him, for the marriage of the Lamb has come and His bride has made herself ready."

8 And it was given to her to clothe herself in fine linen, bright *and* clean; for the fine linen is the righteous acts of the saints.

9 And he said to me, "Write, 'Blessed are those who are invited to the marriage supper of the Lamb.'" And he said to me, "These are true words of God."

—Revelation 19

In verse 9 we have another beatitude that is registered in strong terms. The angel promises an important blessing for all who are invited to the marriage supper of the Lamb. Let's examine a few passages of scripture which deal with this event, beginning in Matthew:

1 And Jesus answered and spoke to them again in parables, saying,

2 "The kingdom of heaven may be compared to a king, who gave a wedding feast for his son.

3 "And he sent out his slaves to call those who had been invited to the wedding feast, and they were unwilling to come.

4 "Again he sent out other slaves saying, 'Tell those who have been invited, "Behold, I have prepared my dinner; my oxen and my fattened livestock are *all* butchered and everything is ready; come to the wedding feast."'

5 "But they paid no attention and went their way, one to his own farm, another to his business,

6 and the rest seized his slaves and mistreated them and killed them.

7 "But the king was enraged and sent his armies, and destroyed those murderers, and set their city on fire.

8 "Then he said to his slaves, 'The wedding is ready, but those who were invited were not worthy.

9 'Go therefore to the main highways, and as many as you find *there*, invite to the wedding feast.'

10 "And those slaves went out into the streets, and gathered together all they found, both evil and good; and the wedding hall was filled with dinner guests.

11 "But when the king came in to look over the dinner guests, he saw there a man not dressed in wedding clothes,

12 and he said to him, 'Friend, how did you come in here without wedding clothes?' And he was speechless.

13 "Then the king said to the servants, 'Bind him hand and foot, and cast him into the outer darkness; in that place there shall be weeping and gnashing of teeth.'

14 "For many are called, but few are chosen."

—Matthew 22

The king here represents God the Father. The son is Jesus Christ. The nation of Israel is no doubt included among those who reject the invitation to the wedding feast. You can possibly see the fall of Babylon in verse 7; note that the king sent out his armies to destroy the murderers.

This is what the coming of Christ is going to be like. Immediately after the Rapture and the battle of Armageddon, the first big event will be the wedding feast. We will see how this all fits together when we get back to Revelation.

Luke 14:15–24 is a similar parable to the one we have just read. The parable of the ten virgins in Matthew 25:1–13 is also similar. It draws a parallel between Christ and the bridegroom.

Now let's look at John 3:

> 26   And they came to John and said to him, "Rabbi, He who was with you beyond the Jordan, to whom you have borne witness, behold, He is baptizing, and all are coming to Him.
>
> 27   John answered and said, "A man can receive nothing, unless it has been given him from heaven.
>
> 28   "You yourselves bear me witness, that I said, 'I am not the Christ,' but, 'I have been sent before Him.'
>
> 29   "He who has the bride is the bridegroom; but the friend of the bridegroom, who stands and hears him, rejoices greatly because of the bridegroom's voice. And so this joy of mine has been made full.
>
> 30   "He must increase, but I must decrease. . . ."

What John is saying is that Christ is the bridegroom, and John is a friend of the bridegroom. John's joy was to hear the voice of the bridegroom, as a friend.

Does the bridegroom have other friends? Let's look at Mark 2:

> 18   And John's disciples and the Pharisees were fasting; and they came and said to Him, "Why do John's disciples and the disciples of the Pharisees fast, but Your disciples do not fast?"
>
> 19   And Jesus said to them, "While the bridegroom is with them, the attendants of the bridegroom do not fast, do they? So long as they have the bridegroom with them, they cannot fast.
>
> 20   "But the days will come when the bridegroom is taken away from them and then they will fast in that day. . . ."
>
> —Mark 2

Jesus says that His disciples are friends of the bridegroom and that they do not fast as long as He is with them. Thus, the disciples were classified as friends of the bridegroom.

So in these parables and illustrations, we see that people are invited to the marriage feast, which represents the kingdom of heaven. The disciples and John the Baptist were friends of the bridegroom who were participating in this wedding feast. Now let's look at Genesis 29, but I should forewarn you that this may be a jolt for some of you:

> 21   Then Jacob said to Laban, "Give *me* my wife, for my time is completed, that I may go in to her."
>
> 22   And Laban gathered all the men of the place, and made a feast.

23 Now it came about in the evening that he took his daughter Leah, and brought her to him; and *Jacob* went in to her.

24 Laban also gave his maid Zilpah to his daughter Leah as a maid.

25 So it came about in the morning that, behold, it was Leah! And he said to Laban, "What is this you have done to me? Was it not for Rachel that I served with you? Why then have you deceived me?"

—Genesis 29

In the Jewish tradition, the bride was never at the wedding feast. The friends came together and had a wedding feast, probably all day long or even lasting several days. At the end of the feast, they brought in the bride, and the bride and the bridegroom went out together. If Leah had been there throughout the feast, Jacob surely would have known that she was not Rachel.

In Revelation, we are admonished and encouraged to be part of the wedding feast. Most people have been taught that all of the Christians are the bride. Yet the bride is not at the wedding feast. We might ask ourselves: are we—as the body of Christ—part of the groom? Or are we, as Christians, simply guests (friends) at the wedding feast? It just might be possible that as part of Christ's body, we are indeed a part of the bridegroom and not the bride. (You might want to dig into this and find a solid scriptural basis for what you believe.)

Returning to Revelation 19, I praise God that we are encouraged to be at the wedding feast. We can attend only with God's invitation. We have to wear a wedding garment—that is, the robe of the righteousness of Christ, and non–Christians will not be permitted to attend. I believe Christians who are a part of the wedding feast will experience a glorious, joyous time. There will be some wonderful things at the wedding feast which you won't want to miss. *Blessed are those who are invited to the marriage supper of the Lamb!* But you have to know Him personally to receive an invitation.

In verse 10 of Revelation 19 we read this:

10 And I fell at his feet to worship him. And he said to me, "Do not do that; I am a fellow servant of yours and your brethren who

hold the testimony of Jesus; worship God. For the testimony of Jesus is the spirit of prophecy."

The church at Colossae and some of the other New Testament churches had a problem with some members worshiping angels. It was a serious enough problem that it was necessary for Paul to forbid the practice (Colossians 2:18). Here John falls down to worship this angel, and the angel tells him not to, for he says that he is a servant of John and of John's brothers. Hebrews 1 supports this:

13 But to which of the angels has He ever said,
    "SIT AT MY RIGHT HAND,
    UNTIL I MAKE THINE ENEMIES
    A FOOTSTOOL FOR THY FEET"?
14 Are they not all ministering spirits, sent out to render service for the sake of those who will inherit salvation?

According to this passage, the angels are our servants— "ministering spirits, sent out to render service" for the saints. Many Christians aren't sufficiently aware of this provision of God. 2 Kings 6:14-20 records that a great army surrounded Elisha and his servant. Elisha prayed that his servant's eyes would be opened to see the thousands and thousands of the Lord's army that surrounded them. These were servants sent to help Elisha, but Elisha's servant wasn't aware of their presence.

I don't think we can give orders to angels, but we should think of them as servants to us. I think that possibly they may serve us throughout eternity, yet today we think of them in a much different light. So it is not surprising here that the angel has to tell John not to worship him. In places such as Costa Rica where servants are an accepted and integral part of the society, it would be an insult to a servant to be asked to sit at the same table with his master to have dinner; they have an understood and accepted role in life. I think that the angel was insulted that John would try to worship him.

THE RETURN OF CHRIST

Still a part of this seventh snapshot, the exciting return of Christ, in power, is recorded in the remainder of Revelation 19:

11   And I saw heaven opened; and behold, a white horse, and He who sat upon it *is* called Faithful and True; and in righteousness He judges and wages war.

12   And His eyes *are* a flame of fire, and upon His head *are* many diadems; and He has a name written *upon Him* which no one knows except Himself.

13   And *He is* clothed with a robe dipped in blood; and His name is called The Word of God.

14   And the armies which are in heaven, clothed in fine linen, white *and* clean, were following Him on white horses.

15   And from His mouth comes a sharp sword, so that with it He may smite the nations; and He will rule them with a rod of iron; and He treads the wine press of the fierce wrath of God, the Almighty.

16   And on His robe and on His thigh He has a name written, "KING OF KINGS, AND LORD OF LORDS."

17   And I saw an angel standing in the sun; and he cried out with a loud voice, saying to all the birds which fly in midheaven, "Come, assemble for the great supper of God;

18   in order that you may eat the flesh of kings and the flesh of commanders and the flesh of mighty men and the flesh of horses and of those who sit on them and flesh of all men, both free men and slaves, and small and great."

19   And I saw the beast and the kings of the earth and their armies, assembled to make war against Him who sat upon the horse, and against His army.

20   And the beast was seized, and with him the false prophet who performed the signs in his presence, by which he deceived those who had received the mark of the beast and those who worshiped his image; these two were thrown alive into the lake of fire which burns with brimstone.

21   And the rest were killed with the sword which came from the mouth of Him who sat upon the horse, and all the birds were filled with their flesh.

–Revelation 19

Here we see some of the details of the battle of Armageddon. We have encountered the battle of Armageddon twice before in Revelation (Chapters 11 and 16).

In sharp contrast to the feast of the Lamb, which we saw earlier, here we see another feast. At this feast the birds eat the flesh of the people that Christ kills in the battle of Armageddon.

Matthew 24 and Luke 17 record what Christ shared with His disciples concerning the day that the Son of Man will be revealed. He said that two women will be grinding, and one will be taken and the other left; two men will be in the field, and one will be taken and the other left. In Luke, Christ gives an indication as to where these people will be taken:

> 34 "I tell you, on that night there will be two men in one bed; one will be taken, and the other will be left.
> 35 "There will be two women grinding at the same place; one will be taken, and the other will be left.
> 36 ["Two men will be in the field; one will be taken and the other will be left."]
> 37 And answering they said to Him, "Where, Lord?" And He said to them, "Where the body *is*, there also will the vultures be gathered."
>
> —Luke 17

This says that the ones "taken" will be taken to a place where the corpse is, or where vultures gather. So here in Revelation 19, in a sense, we have that scene described again. These people, who war against Christ, will be taken out, and the birds (vultures) will eat their flesh.

We also see in this passage in Revelation 19 that Christ's robe is red with blood. This could represent His own sacrificial blood, or it could be from the blood of the enemy. Those in the army of Christ, of which I think we will be a part, have white robes. They haven't even been involved in the battle. The only person who does any offensive fighting is Jesus, and He uses only the words of His mouth.

Praise God for His power and His glory! He is going to be the King of all kings and the Lord of all lords!

In verse 18, we see that all of the kings and mighty men, as well as all those who accepted the mark of the beast and worshiped him, are going to die, and their flesh will be eaten by the birds.

In verse 20, the dictator beast and the prophet beast are put into the lake of fire. Satan is not thrown in at this time but is chained or bound, as we will see in Revelation 20. This completes the seventh snapshot.

At this point in time, because of the earth upheavals, the earth has physically been plowed up, and all of the evil men have been eliminated. The earth is now ready for the thousand years of Christ's reign. Let's hurry on to read about it . . .

THE MILLENNIAL REIGN OF CHRIST ON THIS EARTH

Now that we have finished the seven snapshots, the chronology is resumed in Revelation 20:

1 And I saw an angel coming down from heaven, having the key of the abyss and a great chain in his hand.

2 And he laid hold of the dragon, the serpent of old, who is the devil and Satan, and bound him for a thousand years,

3 and threw him into the abyss, and shut *it* and sealed *it* over him, so that he should not deceive the nations any longer, until the thousand years were completed; after these things he must be released for a short time.

4 And I saw thrones, and they sat upon them, and judgment was given to them. And I *saw* the souls of those who had been beheaded because of the testimony of Jesus and because of the word of God, and those who had not worshiped the beast or his image, and had not received the mark upon their forehead and upon their hand; and they came to life and reigned with Christ for a thousand years.

5 The rest of the dead did not come to life until the thousand years were completed. This is the first resurrection.

6 Blessed and holy is the one who has a part in the first resurrection; over these the second death has no power, but they will be priests of God and of Christ and will reign with Him for a thousand years.

7 And when the thousand years are completed, Satan will be released from his prison,

8 and will come out to deceive the nations which are in the four corners of the earth, Gog and Magog, to gather them together for the war; the number of them is like the sand of the seashore.

9 And they came up on the broad plain of the earth and surrounded the camp of the saints and the beloved city, and fire came down from heaven and devoured them.

10 And the devil who deceived them was thrown into the lake of fire and brimstone, where the beast and the false prophet are also; and they will be tormented day and night forever and ever.

Satan is bound and is placed in a deep pit called an *abyss,* which is sealed for a thousand years. For one thousand years Satan and his demons will be absent from the face of the earth. At the end of that time, he will be let out. As we see in verse 10, he will eventually wind up in the lake of fire with the dictator beast and the prophet beast.

There are three basic interpretations concerning the one–thousand–year period, commonly called the millennium. They are premillennial, postmillennial and amillennial. (Corrie ten Boom says that it is a "pre–post–er–ous" question!) The post-millennialists say that Christ is going to return at the end of the millennium and that we are going to "bring in the kingdom" prior to His return. This view maintains that the earth is going to get better and better by the efforts of Christians. More Christians are going to witness, more people will come to know the Lord, and so forth. Eventually, as we work our way up by our bootstraps, we will achieve a heaven on earth. We will reign a thousand years, and then Christ will return.

The amillennialists say that there isn't going to be a thousand–year reign, but at some point Christ will take the Christians off of the earth and will wipe out the non–Christians. The premillennialists say that Christ is going to return prior to the millennium and will then reign with His saints here on earth.

With recent world wars and corruption, the postmillennialists are becoming less and less popular with their theory that man is going to get better and better. Considering our degenerating morals, I would have a hard time accepting postmillennialism. I believe the Bible teaches the premillennialist view: that Christ is going to return prior to the thousand years, and we will reign with Him. Verse 4 of Revelation 20 says that those who had not received the mark of the beast came to life and reigned with Christ for a thousand years. I think it is pretty clear, but I do want to leave room for any Christian to believe otherwise.

Verses 4, 5 and 6 are basically all that we know about the millennium from the New Testament . . . just three verses. Most of what we know about the millennium is found in the Old Testament. This is where some difficulties arise. Frequently, the Old Testament prophecies had dual meanings—one which applied to the people at that time and also a long–range meaning which applied to Christ or to Christians. With some of these prophecies, it is hard to know if we are correct in applying them to the millennium. The rule of thumb that I use is that if an Old Testament prophecy appears to have never yet been fulfilled, and it appears to be something that would fit in the millennium, then we are reasonably safe in applying it to the millennium.

THE MILLENNIUM IN THE OLD TESTAMENT

Repeatedly, the Old Testament refers to the "day of the Lord." Let's read a verse from Psalm 90 *(King James Version)*:

4 For a thousand years in thy sight *are but* as yesterday when it is past, and *as* a watch in the night.

It is interesting that it does not say that ten million years is like a day, but rather it says specifically that one thousand years is like a day. If we apply this to the millennium, it is easy to see how the "day of the Lord" could conceivably be a thousand–year period. We find frequently when scriptures in the Old Testament refer to the day of the Lord, they are also referring to the millennium. This is further substantiated by 2 Peter 3:8 which says that ". . . with the Lord one day is as a thousand years and a thousand years as one day."

Let's look at two or three things which we know are going to happen in the millennium, starting with Isaiah:

6 And the wolf will dwell with the lamb,
And the leopard will lie down with the kid,
And the calf and the young lion and the fatling together;
And a little boy will lead them.
7 Also the cow and the bear will graze;
Their young will lie down together;
And the lion will eat straw like the ox.

8 And the nursing child will play by the hole of the cobra,
   And the weaned child will put his hand on the viper's den.
9 They will not hurt or destroy in all My holy mountain,
   For the earth will be full of the knowledge of the LORD
   As the waters cover the sea.

10 Then it will come about in that day
    That the nations will resort to the root of Jesse,
    Who will stand as a signal for the peoples;
    And His resting place will be glorious.

—Isaiah 11

We have not yet seen this fulfilled. It is interesting to note that it never says that the lion and the lamb will lie down together. It says that the wolf will dwell with the lamb, and the leopard will lie down with the kid. The calf and the young lion are also grouped together. Lions and bears will eat grass, so there will not be any killing of animals or human beings for food. It is very possible that we too will be natural vegetarians at that point in time. We see that nature will be restored to its garden of Eden state, and there will be perfect peace and harmony.

Let's now look at Ezekiel 36:

33 ". . . 'Thus says the Lord GOD, "On the day that I cleanse you from all your iniquities, I will cause the cities to be inhabited, and the waste places will be rebuilt.

34 "And the desolate land will be cultivated instead of being a desolation in the sight of everyone who passed by.

35 "And they will say, 'This desolate land has become like the garden of Eden; and the waste, desolate, and ruined cities are fortified *and* inhabited.'

36 "Then the nations that are left round about you will know that I, the LORD, have rebuilt the ruined places and planted that which was desolate; I, the LORD, have spoken and will do it." . . .'"

This describes the earth becoming like the garden of Eden again. Isaiah 2:4 says that people will beat their swords into plowshares and their spears into pruning hooks, and they will study war no more. This again would apply to the millennium. Let's read a verse from Zechariah 14:

9 And the LORD will be king over all the earth; in that day the LORD will be the *only one*, and His name the *only one*.

During the millennium, Christ will be King over the entire earth, and no other person or thing will receive worship.

There is a one world government coming, and Jesus is going to be the head of it. There will be an unsuccessful attempt at such a government with the dictator beast as its head, but it won't last long. Christ's reign, however, will last for a thousand years.

The following passage talks about the physical bodies that we will have when we see Jesus.

> 20 For our citizenship is in heaven, from which also we eagerly wait for a Savior, the Lord Jesus Christ;
>
> 21 who will transform the body of our humble state into conformity with the body of His glory, by the exertion of the power that He has even to subject all things to Himself.
>
> —Philippians 3

Our humble bodies will be transformed to be like His body. His resurrected body could pass through solid doors. Gravity didn't affect it. He could go from point A to point B faster than any known means of transportation. Time and space were irrelevant to Christ's resurrected body. Our body will not have any blemishes, and we will use 100 percent of our new brain. It is going to be very beautiful.

Let's look at 1 Corinthians 15:

> 35 But someone will say, "How are the dead raised? And with what kind of body do they come?"
>
> 36 You Fool! That which you sow does not come to life unless it dies;
>
> 37 and that which you sow, you do not sow the body which is to be, but a bare grain, perhaps of wheat or of something else.
>
> 38 But God gives it body just as He wished, and to each of the seeds a body of its own.
>
> 39 All flesh is not the same flesh, but there is *one flesh* of men, and another flesh of beasts, and another flesh of bird, and another of fish.
>
> 40 There are also heavenly bodies and earthly bodies, but the glory of the heavenly is one, and the *glory* of the earthly is another.
>
> 41 There is one glory of the sun and another glory of the moon, and another glory of the stars; for star differs from star in glory.

> 42 So also is the resurrection of the dead. It is sown a perishable *body*, it is raised an imperishable *body;*
>
> 43 it is sown in dishonor, it is raised in glory; it is sown in weakness, it is raised in power;
>
> 44 it is sown a natural body, it is raised a spiritual body. If there is a natural body, there is also a spiritual *body*.

The Bible tells us that we will have a glorious body in which to rule and reign with Christ!

THE FIRST RESURRECTION

We may have something of a problem understanding the biblical first resurrection. Looking again at verse 4 of Revelation 20, we ask, "Who is part of the first resurrection?" Some people would say, based on Revelation 20:4-5, that the only ones who come to life at the first resurrection and reign with Christ for a thousand years are those who have been beheaded during the Tribulation. I do not think that this is the case; I feel that at least the overcomers and likely all of the Christians will be involved in the first resurrection.

In the Greek, there is much less punctuation and capitalization than we have in English. The *King James Version* has verse 4 of Revelation 20 as one sentence. The *New American Standard* transforms it into two sentences, which I think is an error. I feel there should be a semicolon rather than a period between these two thoughts:

> 4 And I saw thrones, and they sat upon them, and judgment was given to them. [;] And I *saw* the souls of those who had been beheaded because of the testimony of Jesus and because of the word of God, and those who had not worshiped the beast or his image, and had not received the mark upon their forehead and upon their hand; and they came to life and reigned with Christ for a thousand years.
>
> 5 The rest of the dead did not come to life until the thousand years were completed. This is the first resurrection.
>
> —Revelation 20

I think that this passage refers to several groups of people. One group is those sitting upon thrones judging, another group is those who have been beheaded, and a third group is those who have not worshiped the beast. I believe that this first resurrection is talking about all three groups coming back to life and reigning with Christ.

Now the question is, who are the ones sitting on the thrones to whom judgment is given? Let's look back at Revelation 5:

> 9 And they sang a new song, saying,
>
> "Worthy art Thou to take the book, and to break its seals; for Thou wast slain, and didst purchase for God with Thy blood *men* from every tribe and tongue and people and nation.
>
> 10 "And Thou hast made them *to be* a kingdom and priests to our God; and they will reign upon the earth."

Here we see that all Christians are going to reign upon the earth. Let's also consider the following:

> 21 ". . . 'He who overcomes, I will grant to him to sit down with Me on My throne, as I also overcame and sat down with My Father on His throne. . . .'"
>
> —Revelation 3
>
> 26 ". . . 'And he who overcomes, and he who keeps My deeds until the end, TO HIM I WILL GIVE AUTHORITY OVER THE NATIONS;
>
> 27 AND HE SHALL RULE THEM WITH A ROD OF IRON, AS THE VESSELS OF THE POTTER ARE BROKEN TO PIECES, as I also have received *authority* from My Father; . . .'"
>
> —Revelation 2

So the overcomers will be sitting down with Christ on the throne and ruling and reigning over the nations. We just saw that all Christians will reign with Christ. In order to do that, they would need to participate in this first resurrection in Revelation 20:4. Those sitting on the thrones in judgment could be all of the Christians and, at least, the overcomers. Following this group listed in verse 4 of Revelation 20, I think that God singles out in love, for special attention, those who were beheaded for His sake during the Tribulation. However, there would be no reason for the Lord to bring those beheaded during the Tribulation back to life and not to give the martyrs of earlier centuries the same kind of treatment. I am also confident that this will be a glorious day for those who endured the Tribulation, even though they were not beheaded, as the third group listed is those who had not received the mark of the beast and worshiped his image.

Who are we going to be reigning over? I don't think that all non–Christians will have accepted the mark of the beast *and* worshiped him, nor do I think that everyone alive on the earth will have been killed at the battle of Armageddon. I think there will be some non–Christians remaining on the earth after the Rapture and battle of Armageddon, and we will be ruling and reigning over these people.

The resurrected Christians won't die because their bodies will be imperishable. The people remaining alive on the earth will probably have a longer life span than today because the environment is going to be pure. They will be having children and their children will have children, and so forth. After a thousand years, there will be a multitude of people, none of whom would ever really have had a chance to accept or reject the Lord because they would never have been tempted. (Satan will be bound during this time.) So at the end of the one thousand years, they will be given a chance to accept the Lord or reject Him. During the millennium they would have been following Jesus out of default, in a sense. They will have a chance, of their own volition, to say yes or no.

We saw earlier that Satan will be bound during this thousand–year period (Revelation 20:2–3). At the end of the millennium, Revelation 20:7–8 tells us that he will be released. He will come out and deceive a great number of people and gather them together for war. This time it doesn't appear that Christ will personally be involved in the war. Let's review what happens:

> 9 And they came up on the broad plain of the earth and surrounded the camp of the saints and the beloved city, and fire came down from heaven and devoured them.
>
> 10 And the devil who deceived them was thrown into the lake of fire and brimstone, where the beast and the false prophet are also, and they will be tormented day and night forever and ever.
>
> —Revelation 20

It says that fire comes down from heaven and devours them. We see that as part of this judgment the devil, the beast and the false prophet will all be thrown into the lake of fire.

THE GREAT WHITE THRONE JUDGMENT

After the thousand years is completed, and Satan has been cast into the lake of fire, the earth will be destroyed. Then God will judge all of the people who have ever lived. This is described in the remainder of Revelation 20:

> 11 And I saw a great white throne and Him who sat upon it, from whose presence earth and heaven fled away, and no place was found for them.
>
> 12 And I saw the dead, the great and the small, standing before the throne, and books were opened; and another book was opened, which is *the book* of life; and the dead were judged from the things which were written in the books, according to their deeds.
>
> 13 And the sea gave up the dead which were in it, and death and Hades gave up the dead which were in them; and they were judged, every one *of them* according to their deeds.
>
> 14 And death and Hades were thrown into the lake of fire. This is the second death, the lake of fire.
>
> 15 And if anyone's name was not found written in the book of life, he was thrown into the lake of fire.

Verse 11 says that the existing heaven and earth flee away. They will no longer exist. Some of the details concerning this destruction are found in 2 Peter 3:

> 10 But the day of the Lord will come like a thief, in which the heavens will pass away with a roar and the elements will be destroyed with intense heat, and the earth and its works will be burned up.
>
> 11 Since all these things are to be destroyed in this way, what sort of people ought you to be in holy conduct and godliness,
>
> 12 looking for and hastening the coming of the day of God, on account of which the heavens will be destroyed by burning, and the elements will melt with intense heat!
>
> 13 But according to His promise we are looking for new heavens and a new earth, in which righteousness dwells.

God has promised He will never again destroy the earth by water, but here we see that He will destroy it by fire. There will be an end to this physical earth, but it will be *after* the millennium. So planet earth will exist for at least one thousand more years. The "end of the world" is not near, but many, including myself, feel that the "end of this *age*" is near.

The great white throne judgment occurs sometime between the destruction of the old heaven and earth and the creation of the new heaven and earth. At this judgment, two books are opened: the book of life and the book of deeds (Revelation 20: 12–20).

It is interesting that all of the dead will be judged according to their deeds. Even those bodies which have disintegrated in the sea will be reassembled and brought back for judgment. When we Christians stand before God, He will see us as perfect because Christ's blood has washed away all of our sin! Because of Him, our names are written in the Lamb's book of life! Thank you, Lord!

Revelation 20:14 tells us that death and Hades will be thrown into the lake of fire. Already, the dictator beast, the prophet beast, and Satan are in the lake of fire. We see in verse 15 that anyone whose name is not found in the book of life is thrown into the lake of fire also. We escape the lake of fire, not because of what we have done (our deeds), but rather because our names are written in the book of life. Our names are written there only because we have received Jesus Christ as our Savior by faith. (If you are not absolutely sure that your name *is*, right now, in the book of life, please be sure to read Appendix B.)

It is possible that Christians will also stand before the great white throne of judgment. We may not, but I believe that we will. If we do, when God opens the book of deeds, under my name He will see all of the good deeds that Christ did. If He were looking in the book of deeds under the name of Jesus Christ, He would see all the bad deeds that I have done. All of my bad deeds have been placed in Christ's account, and all of His righteousness was put in my account when I received Him as Savior and Master. If we do stand before God, we will be wrapped in the robe of the righteousness of Jesus, and God will see us as perfect.

However, the Christians do not get off quite that easily. We must stand before the judgment seat of Christ. Let's see what 2 Corinthians 5 has to say on this:

10 For we must all appear before the judgment seat of Christ, that each one may be recompensed for his deeds in the body according to what he has done, whether good or bad.

This is addressed to Christians. So we surmise that the basic judgment of Christians is going to be before the judgment seat of Christ, not at the great white throne judgment. We are going to receive recompense according to what we have done, whether it be good or bad.

Let's look further:

11 For no man can lay a foundation other than the one which is laid, which is Jesus Christ.

12 Now if any man builds upon the foundation with gold, silver, precious stones, wood, hay, straw,

13 each man's work will become evident; for the day will show it, because it is *to be* revealed with fire; and the fire itself will test the quality of each man's work.

14 If any man's work which he has built upon it remains, he shall receive a reward.

15 If any man's work is burned up, he shall suffer loss; but he himself shall be saved, yet so as through fire.

16 Do you not know that you are a temple of God, and *that* the Spirit of God dwells in you?

17 If any man destroys the temple of God, God will destroy him, for the temple of God is holy, and that is what you are.

—1 Corinthians 3

This passage is talking about *Christians* standing before the judgment seat of Christ. Our works—whatever we have built with our lives upon the foundation of Jesus Christ—will be tested with fire.

Revelation 21:4 says that God will "wipe away every tear from their eyes." Does this refer to the tears of non–Christians? No. They will have been cast into the lake of fire and will be weeping and wailing forever. It is possible that this refers to the tears that we will shed when standing before the judgment seat of Christ. This may be saying that God will wipe away the memories of the times when we have failed Christ in our lives. God could have *decreed* our tears away, but He *wipes* them away instead. He will touch, lovingly and gently, each of our cheeks and *wipe* away each tear, and we will never cry again. That is beautiful!

It is possible that we will not go before the judgment throne of God, but if we do, we will stand in a perfected state. We will have experienced the judgment seat of Christ, where fire will have removed all impurities. There is a strong admonition in this to live seeking and hungering after God, and following Him, so that when we come before the judgment seat of Christ, we will be rewarded, rather than suffer loss. Those aren't my terms; those are the terms that the Bible uses. I don't know their full meanings. However, we do know that we want to build well as we build our lives on the foundation of Christ.

13

THE NEW HEAVEN
AND THE NEW EARTH
(Revelation 21 & 22)

Now we are going to enjoy looking at the climax of Revelation. As we shall see when we read Revelation 21, there will be a new heaven and a new earth because the present heaven and earth will have been destroyed. These last two chapters of Revelation describe in detail what the new earth—our eternal home—will be like. They also deal with the new Jerusalem (the heavenly Jerusalem), which will be a part of this new earth.

First, we should realize that nothing in either of the last two chapters of Revelation is going to significantly affect our daily lives or our relationship to the Lord. It really makes no difference *where* we will spend eternity. It doesn't make any difference whether it's on a cloud or a floating paradise that God has created, or on His new earth. The important thing is that we will be with our Lord forever, and He will be our light and our love!

Similarly, it really does not matter exactly what the new Jerusalem is. The main thing to understand and appreciate is that this will be a place that God and Christ have prepared, in which we will live for eternity.

In spite of the fact that these things do not affect us in a practical way now, for some reason God has devoted the last two chapters of the Bible to them. He must want us to under-

274

stand where we will be for eternity so that we can look forward to being there with Him. Now let's see how the Scriptures begin to describe this place in the first eight verses of Revelation 21:

1 And I saw a new heaven and a new earth; for the first heaven and the first earth passed away, and there is no longer *any* sea.

2 And I saw the holy city, new Jerusalem, coming down out of heaven from God, made ready as a bride adorned for her husband.

3 And I heard a loud voice from the throne, saying, "Behold, the tabernacle of God is among men, and He shall dwell among them,

4 and He shall wipe away every tear from their eyes; and there shall no longer be *any* death; there shall no longer be *any* mourning, or crying, or pain; the first things have passed away."

5 And He who sits on the throne said, "Behold, I am making all things new." And He said, "Write, for these words are faithful and true."

6 And He said to me, "It is done. I am the Alpha and the Omega, the beginning and the end. I will give to the one who thirsts from the spring of the water of life without cost.

7 "He who overcomes shall inherit these things, and I will be his God and he will be My son.

8 "But for the cowardly and unbelieving and abominable and murderers and immoral persons and sorcerers and idolaters and all liars, their part *will be* in the lake that burns with fire and brimstone, which is the second death."

We have briefly touched on some of these things before. In 2 Peter 3:10–12, we read that the earth and heavens will melt with intense heat. That is talking about the current heaven and the current earth. It is interesting that before our atomic age we would not have had any concept as to how this could be done. Now we know that it could easily be done through atomic warfare. After the existing heaven and earth are destroyed, God will create a new heaven and a new earth. We don't have any idea how big this new earth will be. It could be as big as our entire universe, or even smaller than the present earth. We are told in verse 1 that on this new earth there will no longer be any sea. It will be all "land," probably a giant garden.

Verse 2 talks about the new Jerusalem which is the bride. For the present, we will skip this, as we will discuss it later. Verse 3 says that the tabernacle of God is among men and that

He "shall dwell among them" and they "shall be His people." A tabernacle is literally a tent, which in a larger sense means a dwelling place. God's dwelling place was, at one time, on Mount Sinai, where Moses received the Ten Commandments. Then, at a later time, the Hebrew people built a tabernacle and God chose to dwell in it within the holy of holies. Then, under Solomon's reign, a temple was built, and God chose to move into the holy of holies there. At the death of Christ, the curtain of the holy of holies was split, and that sacred place was, in one sense, vacated by God. For the first time people could go inside, but God no longer dwelt there. Because of Christ's death, God now dwells inside Christians.

God's tabernacle (dwelling place) is now *within us,* but on the new earth He is going to be *among us* in a complete way. His being *among us* means we will know His love and care in a new and exciting way.

Verse 4 says that God will wipe away every tear from our eyes. He could have *decreed* that all tears be done away with, but He did not. Occasionally, when my wife, Jeani, cries, I take my thumb and wipe away her tears. There is somehow a caring and a tenderness expressed when I personally wipe away her tears. God won't just *order* our tears away; He will personally wipe away the tears of each individual because He cares for us and loves us that much. This is such a beautiful picture of what our relationship with God is going to be like. His dwelling place will be among us in the complete sense. Anything negative— crying, pain, and death—will have passed away.

In verse 5 we hear the voice of God. He has spoken only three times before in the book of Revelation (in Chapters 1:8, 16:1, and 16:17). Here He says: "Behold, I am making all things new." When He says *"all things new,"* I don't think we have any concept of what that means. I'm really looking forward to that time! He goes on to say: "Write, for these words are faithful and true." He reemphasizes that what He is saying is true.

In verse 6, God says that He is the Alpha and the Omega, the beginning and the end. He does not say, "I am the first and the last." That belongs to Christ (we will discuss this later in this chapter). He is the A to Z, the beginning and the end. God had no beginning and has no end, like a circle has no beginning and no end. Also in verse 6, He says that He will give to those who are on the new earth the water of life without cost. Praise You, Father!

Verse 7 says that only the overcomers will inherit these things. I didn't say this. The Bible says that these things are reserved for the overcomers. (This is why I so strongly encourage Christians to endeavor to become overcomers.) The overcomers will inherit the things stated in verses 1–6:

1. The new heaven and earth
2. The new Jerusalem
3. God dwelling among them (in the new Jerusalem)
4. Tears being wiped away by God
5. The spring of the water of life

God will be their God, and they shall be His sons. I would like to underscore the words *His sons.* We concentrate so much on our relationship to Christ that often we don't think about our relationship to God the Father. Evidently this is going to be rectified at this time. The overcomers are going to become His sons. In John we read this:

> 12 But as many as received Him, to them He gave the right to become children of God, *even* to those who believe in His name,
>
> 13 who were born not of blood, nor of the will of the flesh, nor of the will of man, but of God.
>
> —John 1

This does not say that Christ instantly makes all who receive Him into sons of God, but He gives us the *right* to *become* sons of God. I think this is part of the "all things made new" that is yet ahead of us. When that occurs, we are going to be God's sons in a fuller and more complete way than we could ever imagine.

Then in verse 8 the glory of the overcomers is contrasted with the fate of the non–Christians (the cowardly, unbelieving, murderers, immoral persons, liars, and so forth). The non–Christians will be thrown into the lake of fire instead of inheriting the new earth and spending eternity with the Lord. "The cowardly" is an interesting phrase. It might be that being cowardly could even apply to Christians. I believe Christ was talking about Christians in Mark when He said this:

> 38 "For whoever is ashamed of Me and My words in this adulterous and sinful generation, the Son of Man will also be ashamed of him when He comes in the glory of His Father with the holy angels."
>
> —Mark 8

Christ is saying that if we are ashamed of Him, He will be ashamed of us. Being ashamed of Christ would be an act of cowardice on our part. There is a verse that I memorized a long time ago which has been such a beautiful help to me in this area:

> 17 If the LORD had not been my help,
> My soul would soon have dwelt in *the abode of* silence.
>
> —Psalm 94

Often, when I feel that I should say something for the Lord, but I feel ashamed or afraid (cowardly), I think of this verse. Unless the Lord is my help, I am going to dwell in silence. But mentioning this verse to the Lord gives me the boldness to speak out.

I think there will be times during the Tribulation when we will be tempted to deny the Lord rather than to stand up for Him. At that point we will have to ask God to be our help. He certainly will answer that prayer. Praise God!

THE BRIDE FROM HEAVEN

We are now going to examine the next portion of Revelation 21. This passage talks about the exciting new Jerusalem:

> 9 And one of the seven angels who had the seven bowls full of the seven last plagues, came and spoke with me, saying, "Come here, I shall show you the bride, the wife of the Lamb."
>
> 10 And he carried me away in the Spirit to a great and high mountain, and showed me that holy city, Jerusalem, coming down out of heaven from God,
>
> 11 having the glory of God. Her brilliance was like a very costly stone, as a stone of crystal–clear jasper.

12   It had a great and high wall, with twelve gates, and at the gates twelve angels; and names *were* written on them, which are *those* of the twelve tribes of the sons of Israel.

13   *There were* three gates on the east and three gates on the north and three gates on the south and three gates on the west.

14   And the wall of the city had twelve foundation stones, and on them *were* the twelve names of the twelve apostles of the Lamb.

15   And the one who spoke with me had a gold measuring rod to measure the city, and its gates and its wall.

16   And the city is laid out as a square, and its length is as great as the width; and he measured the city with the rod, fifteen hundred miles; its length and width and height are equal.

17   And he measured its wall, seventy-two yards, *according to* human measurements, which are *also* angelic *measurements.*

18   And the material of the wall was jasper; and the city was pure gold, like clear glass.

19   The foundation stones of the city wall were adorned with every kind of precious stone. The first foundation stone was jasper; the second, sapphire; the third, chalcedony; the fourth, emerald;

20   the fifth, sardonyx; the sixth, sardius; the seventh, chrysolite; the eighth beryl; the ninth, topaz; the tenth, chrysoprase; the eleventh, jacinth; the twelfth, amethyst.

21   And the twelve gates were twelve pearls; each one of the gates was a single pearl. And the street of the city was pure gold, like transparent glass.

One of the seven angels in verse 9 is beckoning John to come see the bride. In verse 10 we see that the bride is the new Jerusalem. At first it might seem a bit confusing that the bride is equated to a city, the heavenly Jerusalem. Most of us have always been taught that the church is the bride of Christ. Examining the bride of Christ to determine who or what she is is something that we should do at this point.

WHO IS THE BRIDE OF CHRIST?

The traditional view is that the church—all those who have received Jesus Christ as their Savior—is the bride of Christ. Probably 99 percent of all Christians today would hold that view. Since the Bible clearly says that the new Jerusalem is the bride of Christ, in order to hold this position we would have to equate Christians to the new Jerusalem. Some people would have a difficult time equating a city to people.

On the other hand, it is not as difficult as it might seem. For example, when the Bible says that Sodom and Gomorrah were wicked, is it talking about the stones and the timbers that composed the buildings, houses and walls of these cities? I doubt it very seriously; those inanimate objects are amoral, neither good nor bad. When the Bible says that Sodom and Gomorrah were wicked, even though literally it is talking about two cities, in reality it is talking about the inhabitants of those cities.

Similarly, when Christ lamented over Jerusalem and said that He would have enjoyed gathering together her children as a mother hen gathers her chicks under her wings, was He addressing the stones that composed the walls and the buildings of Jerusalem? Was he crying over those stones and timbers? No. Obviously He was crying out to the *inhabitants* of Jerusalem; He wanted to nurture and comfort those precious people, but they were unwilling to receive Him as Lord and Savior. Here again, even though Christ was addressing the city of Jerusalem, He was really referring to the inhabitants.

Following this line of reasoning, if the new Jerusalem is the bride of Christ, and if Christians are the inhabitants of that city, Revelation 21 could legitimately be referring to the believers— the inhabitants of the new Jerusalem—as the bride of Christ.

There are two scriptures that imply that Christians might be the bride of Christ. The first one is found in Ephesians 5:

28 So husbands ought also to love their own wives as their own bodies. He who loves his own wife loves himself;

29 for no one ever hated his own flesh, but nourishes and cherishes it, just as Christ also *does* the church,

30 because we are members of His body.

31 FOR THIS CAUSE A MAN SHALL LEAVE HIS FATHER AND MOTHER, AND SHALL CLEAVE TO HIS WIFE; AND THE TWO SHALL BECOME ONE FLESH.

32 This mystery is great; but I am speaking with reference to Christ and the church.

Many interpret this as referring to Christ and the church in a husband and wife relationship. There are other things that it could imply, but one implication is that the church is the bride of Christ.

The other scripture is found in 2 Corinthians 11:

> **2 For I am jealous for you with a godly jealousy; for I betrothed you to one husband, that to Christ I might present you *as* a pure virgin.**

The common interpretation of this is that Paul is saying that he betrothed us to a husband, and that husband is Christ.

At times in the Scriptures it seems that the heavenly Jerusalem is a *place* that the Christians will enjoy forever. At other times, when the Bible refers to the new Jerusalem, particularly when it talks about it being the bride, it is referring to the inhabitants. According to the Scriptures, the inhabitants are restricted to those whose names are written in the Lamb's book of life. But remember, Revelation 21:7 said that the new Jerusalem is to be inherited by the overcomers. Perhaps they are the only inhabitants, and the rest of the Christians can only visit the new Jerusalem. But since the traditional view held by almost all Christians is that all Christians are the bride of Christ, this is the one that we will use in this chapter in dealing with the new Jerusalem.

THE NEW JERUSALEM

We *know* from Revelation 21:9–10 that the new Jerusalem is the bride of Christ. Let's now look at this incredible city in detail. Verse 16 of Revelation 21 tells us that the city is laid out as a square, 1500 miles on a side. It is as high as it is wide and long. If you compared the city to the size of the United States, you would find that it would cover the eastern half of the country, from Texas to Florida, up to New York, over to Chicago, and back to Texas. That would be the perimeter around the base of the city. It would also be that high, which is way above our atmosphere.

Another interesting consideration is that the *New American Standard Bible* translates the 1500 miles as 12,000 *stadia*.

How many edges are there to a cube? . . . 12. Twelve times 12,000 is what? . . . 144,000! Do you see the connection? It will be the *perfect* size. Isn't that beautiful!

Let's review verse 17 of Revelation 21:

> **17 And he measured its wall, seventy-two yards, *according to* human measurements, which are *also* angelic measurements.**

We don't know if the 72 yards is a height or a width measurement of the wall. However, 72 yards is 144 cubits! In the Old Testament we see "spiritual" numbers like 7 and 12. Yet when you get into God's eternal scene, everything seems to be coming out to 144. Going on in this chapter, we read:

> **18 And the material of the wall was jasper; and the city was pure gold, like clear glass.**

—Revelation 21

The easiest way to think of the building material of the city would be to visualize a diamond-like substance. What the Lord showed me is that it is like a diamond except that the glory of the Lord will permeate it. If you hold a diamond up to a red light, it looks red. Since the city is pure gold and the building material is "clear glass," the golden glory of the Lord will permeate it and cause it to take on a golden glow.

Now, we will examine verses 10–14 and 19–21 together. According to these verses, the city has 12 gates, 3 on each side. On each gate is written the names of the 12 tribes of Israel. The gates are actually 12 pearls, each one a giant, single, beautiful pearl. Cultured pearls are grown by placing a grain of sand or the chip from a clam inside an oyster. This inflames the oyster, and it begins to coat the substance repeatedly, producing a pearl. Symbolically, a pearl is something that was ugly and bad (an irritant to the oyster), coated with something that is beautiful and pure. In a sense, that is what Christ did for us with His blood. God couldn't have picked a more appropriate substance for the gates—the only way to enter the city. We can enter the city only because Christ has covered our sins with His blood. Wow!

Another significant thing about these beautiful gates is that on them are written the names of the 12 tribes of Israel.

Among other things, this shows us that those from the Old Testament who were counted righteous because of their faith and obedience will be a part of this city.

Just as we know the Old Testament saints will be included so also will the New Testament saints. Verse 14 of Revelation 21 says that the wall of the new Jerusalem has 12 foundation stones, and on them are written the names of the 12 apostles of Christ. Just as the 12 sons of Jacob represent the Old Testament saints, here the 12 apostles represent the New Testament saints.

We are told that the material of the wall is jasper (verse 18), and we are given some information concerning the foundation stones. An interesting comparison can be drawn between the stones that make up the foundation and the stones of the high priest's breastplate described in Exodus 28. Just as the breastplate was adorned with 12 precious stones, so will the wall of the holy city have 12 foundation stones. Four of these foundation stones—the sapphire, the emerald, the beryl and the amethyst—were also a part of the high priest's breastplate. Perhaps this is symbolic of the continuity that exists between the Old and New Testaments, showing that God's plan is consistent and that His Spirit is behind all these developments.

THE LIGHT OF THE NEW JERUSALEM

In the new Jerusalem (the bride) there will be no temple and no light source (such as the sun and the moon). The remainder of Revelation 21 and the first five verses of Revelation 22 tell us why:

22 And I saw no temple in it, for the Lord God, the Almighty, and the Lamb, are its temple.

23 And the city has no need of the sun or of the moon to shine upon it, for the glory of God has illumined it, and its lamp *is* the Lamb.

24 And the nations shall walk by its light, and the kings of the earth shall bring their glory into it.

25 And in the daytime (for there shall be no night there) its gates shall never be closed;

26 and they shall bring the glory and the honor of the nations into it;

27 and nothing unclean and no one who practices abomination and lying, shall ever come into it, but only those whose names are written in the Lamb's book of life.

—Revelation 21

1 And he showed me a river of the water of life, clear as crystal, coming from the throne of God and of the Lamb,

2 in the middle of its street. And on either side of the river was the tree of life, bearing twelve *kinds of* fruit, yielding its fruit every month; and the leaves of the tree were for the healing of the nations.

3 And there shall no longer be any curse; and the throne of God and of the Lamb shall be in it, and His bond-servants shall serve Him;

4 and they shall see His face, and His name *shall be* on their foreheads.

5 And there shall no longer be *any* night; and they shall not have need of the light of a lamp nor the light of the sun, because the Lord God shall illumine them; and they shall reign forever and ever.

—Revelation 22

Praise the Lord! There will be no need for a temple in the new Jerusalem, for the Lord God and Jesus, the Lamb, will be its temple. There will be no need for external light because the glory of God and the glory of the Lamb will be the light that permeates it. This light will never go out, and there will never again be any night. Isn't that fantastic!

Verses 24 and 27 of Revelation 21 are particularly significant. There are "nations" that live on the new earth and walk by the light of the new Jerusalem and "kings of the earth" who evidently come into the new Jerusalem but do not dwell in it. Verse 27 tells us that these people are Christians because no one can come into the new Jerusalem unless his name is written in the Lamb's book of life.

As we will see when we discuss the first five verses of Revelation 22, God's bond-servants (overcomers) actually dwell in the new Jerusalem and reign with God and Christ over these eternal Christian nations.

The first two verses of Revelation 22 talk about a river of life coming from the throne of God and of the Lamb. This river is located in the middle of a street in the new Jerusalem. The word *street* is singular; this may mean that there is only one street running around the periphery of the wall, spiraling inward and culminating at the throne of God and of Christ. Or, it may mean that there is one main street running through the city. On each side of the river, in the middle of this golden boulevard, is the tree of life.

When was the last time we read about the tree of life? . . . In the garden of Eden. We see that it will be made available to us here in the new Jerusalem. It will have 12 kinds of fruit, one for every month, and the leaves will be "for the healing of the nations." I wondered about that, and what the Lord showed me is that we are going to be eating delicious fruit during eternity; the leaves, in a sense, will also be good to eat, to keep all spiritual impurities and ills out of the city. It will be a way of continual purification before the Lord.

Verse 3 of Revelation 22 says that His bond–servants are going to serve the Lamb in the city. Verse 4 makes a beautiful promise, telling us that we *"shall see his face"!* Back in Exodus 33 (verse 29), we are told that no man can see the face of God. In 1 Corinthians 13 we read about seeing through a glass darkly (as translated from the Greek). But in the new Jerusalem, God's bond–servants shall see Him face to face!

Looking at verse 4, we can see that God's bond–servants are the overcomers, for it says, "His name shall be on their foreheads," and back in Revelation 3 we read this:

> 12   ". . . 'He who overcomes, I will make him a pillar in the temple of My God, and he will not go out from it anymore; and I will write upon him the name of My God, and the name of the city of My God, the new Jerusalem, which comes down out of heaven from My God and My new name. . . .'"

From this verse we can see that God will write His name, as well as the names of Christ and the new Jerusalem, on the overcomers. Also, they will be made pillars in the temple of God, and they will not go out from it any more. (Back in Revelation 21:22 we see that the Lord God Almighty and the Lamb are the temple of the new Jerusalem.) Thus, we can equate the bond–servants and the overcomers.

The exciting thing is that if we are willing to be God's bond-servants and overcomers, we are assured of dwelling in the new Jerusalem, serving our Lord face to face and ruling with Him over the Christian nations on the new earth.

Verse 5, in a sense, summarizes the new Jerusalem. There won't be any night, there won't be any need of light, for the Lord will illumine His bond-servants, and they will reign forever. It looks as if the overcomers (bond-servants) will reign over the kings of the earth and the nations mentioned in Revelation 21:24. This means that the overcomers will be reigning forever with Him, not just for the duration of the millennium.

I'm looking forward to spending billions of years on the new earth and in the new Jerusalem, enjoying the glory, the light and the delights of the Father and of the Lamb. We will praise, honor and worship them through all eternity!

JOHN AND THE ANGEL

Returning to verses 6-9 of Revelation 22, we find the angel talking to John:

6 And he said to me, "These words are faithful and true"; and the Lord, the God of the spirits of the prophets, sent His angel to show to His bond-servants the things which must shortly take place.

7 "And behold, I am coming quickly. Blessed is he who heeds the words of the prophecy of this book."

8 And I, John, am the one who heard and saw these things. And when I heard and saw, I fell down to worship at the feet of the angel who showed me these things.

9 And he said to me, "Do not do that; I am a fellow servant of yours and of your brethren the prophets and of those who heed the words of this book; worship God."

Verse 7 is repeating the beatitude that we began with in Revelation 1:3. A blessing is pronounced upon those who *heed* the words of this prophecy. However, in this case it does not include "he who reads." If you have gotten this far, you have already *read*. Now, we find repeated the admonition to *heed* the words of the book of Revelation. (This will be the subject of Chapter 14 of this book.)

In verses 8–9 the angel is saying that he is a fellow servant of John's to God. However (as we saw in Chapter 12), Hebrews 1:14 tells us that angels are ministering servants sent out to render service for the saints. In 1 Corinthians 6 we read this:

> 3 Do you not know that we shall judge angels? How much more, matters of this life?

Here we see that we will act as judges over the angels. What the Lord showed me through this is that we should view the angels as God sees them, rather than attempting to worship them, as John did. Most Christians would never dream of "worshiping" an angel. However, there are some who would lift angels up and give them a very prominent place; others would yearn to have an encounter with an angel. I believe that these are counterfeit forms of worship. We should seek to lift up only Jesus and to have an encounter with *Him*.

There will be times during the Tribulation when angels will be involved with us in spiritual warfare on our behalf, but in the end they will be our servants, and we will actually judge them. It is important that we not overemphasize the role of angels, nor underemphasize their function. Some Christians today are mistakenly *seeking* to have face-to-face encounters with angels. While God may send an angel to you in just such a way, you certainly should not seek that. We should not be concentrating on these servant beings, but rather we should be focusing on the King.

Let's read the next portion of Revelation 22, where Christ begins talking to John in verse 10:

> 10 And he said to me, "Do not seal up the words of the prophecy of this book, for the time is near.
>
> 11 "Let the one who does wrong, still do wrong; and let the one who is filthy, still be filthy; and let the one who is righteous, still practice righteousness; and let the one who is holy, still keep himself holy."
>
> 12 "Behold, I am coming quickly, and My reward *is* with Me, to render to every man according to what he has done.
>
> 13 "I am the Alpha and the Omega, the first and the last, the beginning and the end."

14 Blessed are those who wash their robes, that they may have the right to the tree of life, and may enter by the gates into the city.

15 Outside are the dogs and the sorcerers and the immoral persons and the murderers and the idolaters, and everyone who loves and practices lying.

16 "I, Jesus, have sent My angel to testify to you these things for the churches. I am the root and the offspring of David, the bright morning star."

17 And the Spirit and the bride say, "Come." And let the one who is thirsty come; let the one who wishes take the water of life without cost.

John is told in verse 10 not to seal up the words of the prophecy of this book. In other words, he isn't to keep them to himself. You have probably heard the expression: "He is so heavenly minded that he is no earthly good." Today I think it is probably the opposite. Most people are so earthly minded that they are no heavenly good. In fact, even in most modern-day presentations of the gospel, the emphasis seems to be primarily on the "here and now." We tend to say, "Accept Christ, and have an abundant life and a right relationship with God." We generally leave out much of what is contained in the book of Revelation, and many of us turn up our noses at "old-fashioned" preachers who say to repent and turn to Christ, or spend eternity in hell (actually they mean the lake of fire).

If you look at the total message of the book of Revelation, it emphasizes that the non–Christians are going to have a horrible time on the earth when they experience the outpouring of God's wrath, and they will spend eternity in the lake of fire. Christians will be protected through most of the Tribulation and will spend eternity on a brand new earth with the Lord. This is what I think Christ is saying when He tells John not to seal up the words of this prophecy. Most people who witness for Christ feel that they must not "scare" people into becoming Christians. So they ignore or water down the consequences of not accepting Christ. Yet the Lord is saying that He wants people to be aware of the eternal consequences of rejecting Him. I think that the church today has been negligent in alerting non-Christians to these facts. True, we don't want to *scare* people into making decisions for Christ, but they do need to be aware of the potential consequences of not accepting Him. For the non–Christian, rejecting Christ will not only result in tragedy in the years ahead during the Tribulation, but will also result in everlasting separation from God in the lake of fire.

In verse 13 of Revelation 22, Christ says that He is the Alpha and the Omega, the beginning and the end. He also says that He is the *first* and the *last,* which is an ancient military expression. If a king were about to seize a city, he would send a messenger in with the message to "surrender or die." The messenger would say that he was the first messenger they were going to receive *and* the last one. He was really saying that he was the *only* one. In addition to being the Alpha and the Omega, the beginning and the end, Christ is saying that He is the first and the last messenger, the only true messenger from God and our only Savior. There will not be any others.

In verse 14 is another beatitude, "Blessed are those who wash their robes . . . ." Those who "wash their robes" will have the right to enter the city and to eat of the tree of life. The Lord is asking us to wash ourselves and to become clean and pure so that we can inherit the things that He has prepared for us.

CONCLUSION OF REVELATION

Now let's examine the last four verses in the Bible:

18   I testify to everyone who hears the words of the prophecy of this book: if anyone adds to them, God shall add to him the plagues which are written in this book;

19   and if anyone takes away from the words of the book of this prophecy, God shall take away his part from the tree of life and from the holy city, which are written in this book.

20   He who testifies to these things says, "Yes, I am coming quickly." Amen. Come, Lord Jesus.

21   The grace of the Lord Jesus be with all.

—Revelation 22

I have struggled over what comments to make in this book because I do not want to add anything or take anything away from the prophecy in Revelation. There are dire consequences for anyone who does. But as clearly as possible, I have tried to help you to understand what the book of Revelation is saying. In areas where the meanings are unclear to me, I have tried to qualify my statements, labeling personal opinions. Before the Lord, I have tried my best to help you to understand what is in this book and how it relates to the rest of the Scriptures, and how it *can* affect your life. When some of these things happen, you will know they are part of God's plan. There is peace in knowing that we will have God's protection and His mark on our foreheads *(if* we are His bond–slaves). If we have His seal of protection, many of the plagues will pass over us.

In verse 20 Christ says that He is coming quickly, and John says "Amen" to that and prays that the Lord Jesus will return quickly. I would certainly join John in that prayer, and say, "Even so, come, Lord Jesus."

The book of Revelation and the Bible end with an incredibly significant prayer (verse 21). John is praying that everyone will experience the grace of the Lord Jesus. God's mercy cancels and forgives the death penalty on our lives because of our sins. God's *grace* goes beyond the mercy of forgiveness, giving us the *right* to be *joint heirs with Christ* and to inherit all of the riches of the new heaven and the new earth. Praise God for His *grace* and for the wonderful things that He has in store for those who know Him, love Him, and obey Him through His Son, Jesus Christ.

Thank you, Lord, for your grace, and may it abide upon every reader of this book.

14

HOW TO "HEED"
THIS REVELATION

At the very beginning of the book of Revelation, we had a blessing (beatitude) pronounced on those who read, hear, *and* *heed* the things written in the book of Revelation:

> 3 Blessed is he who reads and those who hear the words of the prophecy, and heed the things which are written in it; for the time is near.
>
> —Revelation 1

Then, at the end of the book of Revelation, we again have a blessing (beatitude) for those who *heed* the words of this prophecy. Evidently God thought it so important that we *heed* the things in the book of Revelation, that He repeated this beatitude; it appears once at the beginning of the book and once at the end:

> 7 "And behold, I am coming quickly. Blessed is he who heeds the words of the prophecy of this book."
>
> —Revelation 22

Satan would like to convince us that we cannot understand the book of Revelation, and he will do anything that he can to prevent us from examining its message. God, realizing this, promised blessings to those who read it, understand it, and then actually *heed* the things found in this book of prophecy. We obviously must understand what we are reading before we can heed it.

Since this command from God to heed the things found in the book of Revelation is so strong, we thought it would be well to have a concluding chapter in this book that summarizes the things we have discussed that we could actually heed in our daily lives. The remainder of this chapter will be in somewhat of an outline form. We will take chapters of the book of Revelation and point out verse numbers in the chapter that contain things that perhaps we should be heeding.

We have left space at the bottom of each page, so that you can write down additional things that God tells you to heed. You could also use this space to record what specifically you think God wants you to do, based on the general things that we suggest. For example, maybe God will really speak to someone about heeding verse 6 of Revelation 1, where it says that we *are priests*. God may then tell that person specifically to set aside a time daily to offer up a sacrifice of praise. He could write this specific instruction of God on the bottom of the page.

There is much to heed in Revelation. Let us now look at just some of the things God may be wanting you and me to do.

THINGS TO HEED FROM REVELATION 1

Verse 1: This revelation is to be shown to God's bond-servants; we could well pray and seek to be a bond–slave of God the Father.

Verse 3: We can heed the beatitude that commands us to read and heed the things written in the book of Revelation.

Verse 5: We can learn to utilize the full implication that we *have* already *been released* from our sins, not just forgiven. We can remind ourselves of how much Christ loves us.

Verse 6: This verse says that we are priests of God. We should be about performing our duties as priests.

Verse 10: We can seek to be "in the Spirit on the Lord's day."

Verse 17: When we're afraid, we can imagine Christ's right hand upon us and Him telling us not to be afraid (as He did to John).

Verse 18: We can live recognizing that *Christ* has the keys to death and hell, which means that we won't die until *He* is ready for us to do so.

THINGS TO HEED FROM REVELATION 2

Verse 2:   We can recognize that Christ cannot endure evil men, and that we should put to the test those who claim to be apostles to see whether or not they are false.

Verse 4:   We can be sure that we never leave our first love.

Verse 5:   When we fall, we can repent and do the deeds that we did at first.

Verse 7:   We can seek to be an overcomer so that we can eat of the tree of life in the Paradise of God.

Verse 9:   We can remind ourselves that Christ is aware of any tribulation or poverty that we might experience.

Verse 10:   We do not have to be afraid, regardless of what we are about to suffer, because Christ told us not to be afraid. He also told us, in this verse, to be faithful unto death, and He would give us the crown of life. Praise God!

Verse 11:   We are again admonished to be an overcomer, so that we will not be hurt by the second death.

Verse 14:   We are not to commit acts of immorality.

Verse 17:   Again we are admonished to be an overcomer. If we are, Christ will give us some of the hidden manna and a white stone with a new name written on it.

Verse 20:   We should not tolerate teachers and prophets who are immoral.

Verses 26-28:   We are admonished to be an overcomer, and if we are, Christ will give us authority over the nations and He will give us the morning star.

THINGS TO HEED FROM REVELATION 3

Verse 2: We are admonished to wake up and strengthen the weak things that were about to die, because our deeds have not yet been completed.

Verse 4: We are encouraged not to soil our garments. If we don't we will walk with Him in white.

Verse 5: We are again admonished to be an overcomer. If we are, we will be clothed in white garments and our name will not be erased from the book of life, and Christ will confess us before His Father.

Verse 8: We are encouraged to keep Christ's word and not to deny His name.

Verse 12: We are again encouraged to be an overcomer, and if we become one, He will make us a pillar in His temple and we will never go out from it anymore, and He will write on us His new name, the name of God and the name of the city of God, the new Jerusalem.

Verse 16: We are encouraged not to be lukewarm. The Christians who are lukewarm, Christ will vomit out of His mouth.

Verse 19: Christ says those that He loves, He will reprove and discipline, and we should be zealous to repent when He disciplines us. When He is disciplining us, we should remind ourselves that it is *because He loves us* so much.

Verse 20: Each Christian is encouraged to open wide the door of his life, so that Christ can come in and have a feast with him.

Verse 21: Christ once more tells us to be an overcomer; and if we do, we will be able to sit down with Him on His throne.

THINGS TO HEED FROM REVELATION 4

Verse 2: John was shown things while He was "in the Spirit." We should learn to walk in the Spirit so that God can reveal rich and deeper things to us.

Verse 5: As we consider the lightning, thunder and power emanating from the throne of God, we should live aware of His incredible power and be fully convinced that nothing is too hard for Him to handle.

Verses 10-11: We should sing in the Spirit with the elders that God is worthy to receive glory and honor and power, and live our lives accordingly.

THINGS TO HEED FROM REVELATION 5

Verses 4-7: We should realize our unworthiness, and that only Christ is worthy. He is the only One in the whole universe worthy to take the scroll and to open the seals.

Verse 9: We could join with those in heaven in singing a new song, because Christ has purchased us with His blood!

Verse 13: We should realize that eventually *every created thing* in heaven and on earth and under the earth and on the sea, and all things in them, are going to be blessing and praising Christ the Lamb.

THINGS TO HEED FROM REVELATION 6

Verse 1: We should be aware that God and Christ (not Satan) are in control of the Tribulation. No event occurs until God says that it is time for it to happen.

Verses 3-4: We should realize that there is a world war coming, but that it will only occur when Christ breaks the seal designating that it is time for it to begin. We can ask God if we should make any preparation for it.

Verses 5-6: A famine of major proportions is coming, and we can ask God what, if anything, He would like us to do to prepare for it and to prepare to help the hungry.

Verses 7-8: There will be an incredible number of deaths because of famine, pestilence and animals. We should be asking the Lord to guide us as to how to deal with this situation, and to comfort those who will have loved ones that will have died.

Verses 9-11: There will be persecution of Christians and martyrdom. We can begin to pray that God would give us the strength to "love not our life," but to be willing to lay it down for our Savior.

Verses 12-17: There are major earth upheavals coming, such that the sun will become black (probably from volcanic ash in the air). These earth upheavals will be of such a magnitude that the rulers, leaders and great men will flee to the caves and the rocks of the mountains and will desire to die. Here again, we can ask the Lord if there is anything that we should do spiritually or physically to prepare for that day.

THINGS TO HEED FROM REVELATION 7

Verse 3:   At one point God will stop the Tribulation until He seals His bond-servants on their foreheads. If we are here at that time, we definitely want to be sealed, because there is protection from some of the plagues in Revelation for those who have God's seal. But, remember, only God's bond-servants (bond-slaves) will be sealed. We could reread Deuteronomy 15 to see what being a bond-slave entails, and then yield all of our rights and possessions totally to God, to be sure that we are His bond-slave.

Verses 13-14:   We are told that there will be Christians who will come out of the great Tribulation. It says that they have washed their robes in the blood of the Lamb and have made them white. We can be encouraged by this to go to Christ continually for cleansing of our sins by His precious blood.

Verses 16-17:   We can rejoice that someday we will never again hunger or thirst, because Christ will be our shepherd and will guide us to the springs of the water of life!

THINGS TO HEED FROM REVELATION 8

Verse 4: We are told in this verse that the incense that went up to God was the prayers of the saints. We must realize that our prayers are a sweet fragrance to God, and we should look forward to a time of prayer with Him.

Verse 7: One of the plagues in Egypt that is coming upon the earth again is hail mixed with fire and blood. We can ask God if there is anything that He wants us to do to prepare for this. If He says, "Nothing," then do nothing, with real peace.

Verse 8: A great fiery mountain is going to be thrown into the sea. This could be a heavenly body, such as a comet, or the result of a nuclear explosion. When it happens, we need not be afraid, because it will occur at the command of the Lord.

THINGS TO HEED FROM REVELATION 9

Verses 3-6: There are locusts coming that will sting men like scorpions; they will hurt only the men who do not have the seal of God on their foreheads. Since we will have the seal of God on our foreheads, we will not be tormented by this plague, and we should both try to comfort those who will be tormented and to share the Gospel with them. God may want to begin to prepare us now for this ministry.

Verses 13-16: The river Euphrates is going to be involved during the Tribulation, and there is an army of 200 million that is going to be released to kill one-third of mankind. Again, we should be aware of this so that when it happens we will not be afraid, and will know that God is in control of the Tribulation and all of the events in it.

THINGS TO HEED FROM REVELATION 11

Verses 3-5: The Lord is going to give authority to His two witnesses (I believe this is two companies, not two individuals) and supernatural power to command fire to come down and devour their enemies. We need to live holy and righteous so that God can entrust us with this type of power, if He so chooses.

Verse 6: God also is going to give to His witnesses the power to shut up the sky so that it will not rain, to turn waters into blood, and to smite the earth with any type of plague. God wants us to be pure and holy, and to move only when He speaks, so He can give us this kind of power.

Verse 7: Eventually, the dictator beast (controlled by Satan) will make war with the two witnesses and will kill them. However, we should not be afraid because . . .

Verses 11-12: The two witnesses will be raised up and will go to heaven. Praise God! Death cannot hold us because Christ has conquered death!

Verses 17-18: We know when the seventh trumpet sounds Christ will begin to reign. The dead will be judged, and we who are Christ's bond-servants are going to receive a reward. For this we can rejoice!

THINGS TO HEED FROM REVELATION 12

Verses 10-11:   We will overcome Satan because of:
1. The blood of the Lamb
2. The word of our testimony
3. We do not love our life even unto death

When we get into spiritual warfare, we should use these three weapons that the Lord has said will overcome Satan.

Verse 6 and Verses 13-16: The woman (the church) someday is going to flee into the wilderness. However, it will be to a place that God will have already prepared, and He will furnish the transportation and the food once she flees. It is possible that the overcomers will remain behind to fight Satan. But whether we will be part of the woman that flees to the wilderness or the overcomers that remain to fight, we should trust God for our strength and our protection.

THINGS TO HEED FROM REVELATION 13

Verse 7:   The dictator beast is going to be making war with the saints and, at this point, he is going to overcome them. We should rejoice if God counts us worthy to die for Him.

Verse 8:   All those on the earth will worship the dictator beast, except those whose names are written in the Lamb's book of life. We can rejoice that our name is written there, and therefore we will not be worshiping the Antichrist.

Verses 16-17:   We can rejoice that we don't have to worry about taking the mark of the beast on our foreheads, because God's seal will already be there, *if* we are God's bond-servants. However, since we will not have the mark of the beast, we will not be able to buy or sell. We can ask God if there is anything physically or spiritually that we should do in order to prepare for the time when we will not be able to buy or sell. We should also have a heart for evangelism to help our loved ones and friends become Christians, so that they too will not take on the mark of the beast.

THINGS TO HEED FROM REVELATION 14

Verse 11: Whoever receives the mark of the beast, the smoke of their torment will go up forever and ever. We should make our non–Christian friends aware of this, so that they can have the opportunity to receive Christ and to avoid the mark of the beast.

Verse 12: Christians are encouraged to persevere, to keep the commandments of God, and keep their faith in Jesus. We should daily pray that we might do these things.

Verse 13: We are told that we are going to be blessed (happy) if we die in the Lord. The Spirit will give us rest from our labors, and our good deeds and our martyrdom will follow us. This is an encouragement to be willing to die for Christ.

Verses 16 and 19: There are going to be two harvests. First will be the harvest of the righteous to be brought into God's barns, and then the harvest of the unrighteous, who will experience the full wrath of God. We can praise God that we will not experience His wrath, but will experience His gracious provision instead!

THINGS TO HEED FROM REVELATION 16

Verse 2:   When the first angel pours his bowl of wrath out upon the earth, it will cause malignant sores upon the men who have the mark of the beast and who worship his image. (Again, those who have the seal of God on their forehead will be spared from this plague.) This should give us motivation to be certain that we are bond–slaves of God.

Verse 4:   The rivers and springs of waters are going to become blood. Since fresh water will be undrinkable, there may be something that the Lord wants you to do in preparation for this time. If He tells you to do something, do it. If not, don't worry about it.

Verse 12:   We know that the Euphrates will dry up, and the kings of the east will come across it. When this occurs, it will be a milestone telling us that Armageddon is about to happen. When you see this occur, rejoice, for the coming of Christ will be near.

Verses 20–21:   There are going to be earth upheavals of the magnitude that every island and every mountain will not be found. Also, in this final plague we see hailstones weighing 100 pounds. Because God has forewarned us that these times are coming, they need hold no fear for us.

THINGS TO HEED FROM REVELATION 17 AND 18

In these chapters we see Babylon, the harlot, which is an economic system with the occult as its religion. She rules over the kings of the earth. We are encouraged to "come out of her" so that we do not participate in her sins and receive her plagues. We can pray and ask the Lord to make us aware of what the Babylonian system is, and to give us the strength and the discernment to come out of her. Once she is destroyed, we are to participate in the rejoicing over God's destruction of her.

THINGS TO HEED FROM REVELATION 19

Verse 8:   We want to be clothed in white linen, clean and bright, which is the righteous acts of the saints. We should be praying and seeking to do righteous acts to provide these garments.

Verse 9:   We know that we will be blessed if we are invited to the marriage supper of the Lamb. Thus, we want to pray that we will be ready and have oil in our lamps, so that we can come in and share in the marriage feast.

Verses 13–14:   When Christ returns, He will have a red robe because it has been dipped in blood, and we will follow Him dressed in linen, clean and white. Again, we want to practice righteousness, so that we can be properly dressed, as part of His army.

THINGS TO HEED FROM REVELATION 20

Verse 4:   We want to be in the overcomer category so that we can come to life and reign with Christ for a thousand years. Pray and seek to become an overcoming soldier of Christ.

Verse 15:   At the great white throne judgment, anyone whose name is not found written in the book of life will be thrown into the lake of fire. We want to be absolutely sure that our name is written in the book of life; this occurs when we receive Christ as our Savior, Lord and Master, and obey Him.

THINGS TO HEED FROM REVELATION 21

Verses 1-2 and Verses 7-8: We are told that the over-comers are going to inherit the new Jerusalem and the new earth. Again we need to pray and seek to be an overcomer, to the glory of Christ.

Verse 4: We can praise God that someday He will wipe away every tear from our eyes and that there will no longer be any more death, or crying, or pain. Hallelujah! That should be an encouragement to us now when we experience hurts and dis-couragements and the death of loved ones.

Verses 9-10: When we read about the bride, the new Jeru-salem, coming down from heaven, we know that this is an in-credible gift from God. We can praise Him that right now He is preparing a place for us!

Verses 23-26: There will be no sun or moon in the new universe that God is going to create, but the Father and the Lamb will be the light of it! We can begin to thank God even now for all that He has in store for us and we can rejoice that we will be bringing our glory and honor into the city to give to God.

Verse 27: Only those whose names are written in the Lamb's book of life can ever enter the city. We can praise God if we know that our names are written in the Lamb's book of life. Again, if we are not certain, we can get our hearts right with God and receive His Son, Jesus, as our Lord *and Master,* that we might have this assurance.

THINGS TO HEED FROM REVELATION 22

Verse 7: Once more we are admonished to heed the words of this prophecy, the book of Revelation.

Verse 9: We are admonished to worship God.

Verse 10: We are told not to seal up the words of this prophecy. We are to share it. Perhaps we can teach through the book of Revelation in our church or Bible study groups, or even give someone a copy of this book. Possibly, as we witness, we should include the consequences of not receiving Christ.

Verse 14: We are encouraged to wash our robes, that we might have a right to the tree of life and to enter into the gates of the city.

Verse 17: All of those who are thirsty can take the water of life without cost. We can praise God for that, and help lead others to the Living Water, Jesus.

THERE IS MUCH TO HEED IN THE
BOOK OF REVELATION

There are many other things that one could *heed* in the book of Revelation, other than these contained in this brief outline. We know that if you pray about it, God will show you exactly what you should be doing (heeding) out of this wonderful book.

My real prayer and desire in writing this book is to help remove from people's hearts some of the stigma, mystery and fear of the book of Revelation. If nothing else, if people can simply read it for themselves, the Spirit of God can make it real and alive to them and can bless them for reading it. Hopefully, this book has helped to do this for you and has helped make the book of Revelation understandable.

But, like with anything else of God, it is not enough simply to understand; it must become part of our lives, or it does us no good at all. Therefore, God has told us, in very strong terms that we should also *heed* the book of Revelation, as well as understand it. Hopefully, we have helped you to see many things in the book of Revelation that can be heeded, and actually should be heeded, in our daily lives. Please pray for me, as I pray for all of those who will read this book, that we all might bring glory to Christ and to God the Father through our words and our lives.

APPENDIX A

DETAILED OUTLINE
AND INDEX

APPENDIX B

HOW TO BECOME
A CHRISTIAN

If you are reading this I am assuming that you are not sure that you have received Jesus Christ as your personal Savior. Not only is it possible to know this for sure, but God *wants* you to know. This is what 1 John 5:11–13 has to say:

> 11 And the witness is this, that God has given us eternal life, and this life is in His Son.
>
> 12 He who has the Son has the life; he who does not have the Son does not have the life.
>
> 13 These things I have written to you who believe in the name of the Son of God, in order that you may know that you have eternal life.

These things are written to us who believe in the name of the Son of God, so that we can *know* that we have eternal life. It is not a "guess so," or "hope so" or "maybe so" situation. It is so that we can *know* for certain that we have eternal life. If you do not have this confidence, please read on.

In order to get to the point of knowing that we have eternal life, we need to first go back and review some basic principles. First, it is important to note that all things that God created (the stars, trees, animals, and so on) are doing exactly what they were created to do, except man. Isaiah 43 indicates why God created us:

7 ". . . Everyone who is called by My name,
And whom I have created for My glory,
Whom I have formed even whom I have made."

Here it says that humans were created to glorify God. I am sure that neither you nor I have glorified God all of our lives in everything that we have done. This gives us our first clue as to what "sin" is. We find more about it in Romans 3:

23 . . . for all have sinned and fall short of the glory of God . . .

This says that we have all sinned and that we all fall short of the purpose for which we were created—that of glorifying God. I have an even simpler definition of sin. I believe that sin is "living independent of God." A young person out of high school can choose which college to attend. If he makes this decision apart from God, it is "sin." This was the basic problem in the garden of Eden. Satan tempted Eve to eat the fruit of the tree of "the knowledge of good and evil." He said that if she would do this, she would know good from evil and would be wise like God. This would mean that she could make her own decisions and would not have to rely on God's wisdom and guidance. Since you and I fit in the category of living independent of God and not glorifying Him in everything we do, we need to look at what the results of this sin are.

First let me ask you what "wages" are. After thinking about it, because you probably receive wages from your job, you will probably come up with a definition something like "wages are what you get paid for what you do." That is a good answer. Now let's see what the Bible has to say concerning this, in Romans 6:

23 For the wages of sin is death, but the free gift of God is eternal life in Christ Jesus our Lord.

Here we see that the wages of sin is death—spiritual, eternal death. Death is what we get paid for the sin that we do. Yet this passage also gives us the other side of the coin: that is, that through Jesus Christ we can freely have eternal life, instead of eternal death. Isn't that wonderful?!

But let's return for a moment to this death penalty that the people without Christ have hanging over their heads, because of the sin that they live in. In the Old Testament God made a rule: "The soul who sins will die" (Ezekiel 18:4). If we were able to live a perfect, sinless life, we could make it to heaven on our own. If we live anything less than a perfect life, according to God's rule, we will not make it to heaven, but instead will be sentenced to death. All through the Bible we find no one living a good enough life to make it to heaven.

This brings us to the place where Jesus Christ fits into this whole picture. His place was beautifully illustrated to me when I was considering receiving Christ as my Savior, by a story about a judge in a small town.

In this small town, the newspapermen were against the judge and wanted to get him out of office. A case was coming up before the judge, concerning a vagrant—a drunken bum—who happened to have been a fraternity brother of the judge when they were at college. The newspapermen thought that this was their chance. If the judge let the vagrant off easy, the headlines would read, "Judge Shows Favoritism to Old Fraternity Brother." If the judge gave the vagrant the maximum penalty, the headlines would read, "Hardhearted Judge Shows No Mercy to Old Fraternity Brother." Either way they had him. The judge heard the case and gave the vagrant the maximum penalty of thirty days or $300 fine.

The judge then stood up, took off his robe, laid it down on his chair, walked down in front of the bench and put his arm around the shoulders of his old fraternity brother. He told him that as judge, in order to uphold the law, he had to give him the maximum penalty, because he was guilty. But because he cared about him, he wanted to pay the fine for him. So the judge took out his wallet and handed his old fraternity brother $300.

For God to be "just," He has to uphold the law that says "the soul who sins will die." On the other hand, because He loves us He wants to pay that death penalty for us. I cannot pay the death penalty for you because I have a death penalty of my own that I have to worry about, since I, too, have sinned. If I were sinless, I could die in your place. I guess God could have sent down millions of sinless beings to die for us. But what

God chose to do was to send down *one* Person, who was equal in value, in God's eyes, to all of the people who will ever live, and yet who would remain sinless. Jesus Christ died physically and spiritually in order to pay the death penalty for you and me. The blood of Christ washes away all of our sins, and with it the death penalty that resulted from our sin.

The judge's old fraternity brother could have taken the $300 and said thank you, or he could have told the judge to keep his money and that he would do it on his own. Similarly, each person can thank God for allowing Christ to die in his place and receive Christ as his own Savior, or he can tell God to keep His payment and that he will make it on his own. What you do with that question determines where you will spend eternity.

Referring to Christ, John 1:12 says:

> **12   But as many as received Him, to them He gave the right to become children of God, *even* to those who believe in His name . . .**

John 3:16 says:

> **16   "For God so loved the world, that He gave His only begotten Son, that whoever believes in Him should not perish but have eternal life. . . ."**

Here we see that if we believe in Christ we won't perish, but we will have everlasting life and the right to become children of God. Right now you can tell God that you believe in Christ as the Son of God, that you are sorry for your sins and that you want to turn from them. You can tell Him that you want to accept Christ's payment for your sins, and yield your life to be controlled by Christ and the Holy Spirit. (You must accept Christ as your Savior *and your MASTER.)*

If you pray such a prayer, Christ will come and dwell within your heart and you will *know for sure* that you have *eternal life.*

If you have any questions about what you have just read, I would encourage you to go to someone that you know, who really knows Jesus Christ as his Savior, and ask him for help and guidance. After you receive Christ, I would encourage you to become part of a group of believers in Christ who study the

Scriptures together, worship God together and have a real love relationship with each other. This group (body of believers) can help nurture you and build you up in your new faith in Jesus Christ.

If you have received Christ as a result of reading these pages, I would love to hear from you. My address is at the end of this book.

Welcome to the family of God.

Jim McKeever

APPENDIX C

MEET THE AUTHOR

Jim McKeever

Jim McKeever is an international consulting economist, lecturer, author, world traveler, and Bible teacher. His financial consultations are utilized by scores of individuals from all over the world who seek his advice on investment strategy and international affairs. He has spoken at monetary, gold and tax haven conferences in London, Zurich, Bermuda, Amsterdam, and Hong Kong, as well as all over the North American continent and Latin America.

As an economist and futurist, he has shared the platform with such men as Ronald Reagan, Gerald Ford, William Simon, William Buckley, Harry Browne, Harry Schultz, Philip Crane, Alan Greenspan, heads of foreign governments and many other outstanding thinkers. As a money manager, he manages millions of dollars for his clients.

Mr. McKeever is the editor and major contributing writer of *McKeever's Individual Strategy Letter (MISL).* He was formerly editor of *Inflation Survival Letter.* For five years after completing his academic work, Mr. McKeever was with a consulting firm which specialized in financial investments in petroleum. Those who were following his counsel back in 1954 invested heavily in oil.

For more than ten years he was with IBM, where he held several key management positions. During those years, when IBM was just moving into transistorized computers, he helped that company become what it is today. With IBM, he consulted with top executives of many major corporations in America, helping them solve financial, control and information problems. He has received many awards from IBM, including the "Key Man Award" and the "Outstanding Contribution Award." He is widely known in the computer field for his books and articles on management, management control and information sciences.

After leaving IBM, Mr. McKeever founded and was president of his own consulting firm. In addition to directing the activities of more than 100 employees, he personally gave consultation to the chief executives of client organizations. Some of the men who sought his counsel were Dr. Bill Bright, Nicky Cruz, Dr. Ted Engstrom, Dr. Lloyd Hubbard, Josh McDowell, and Dr. Stanley Mooneyham.

In 1972, Mr. McKeever sold his interest in this consulting firm and resigned as president in order to devote his "business" time to writing, speaking and consulting.

In addition to this outstanding business background, Mr. McKeever is an ordained minister. He has been a Baptist evangelist, pastor of Catalina Bible Church for three and a half years (while still with IBM) and a frequent speaker at Christian conferences. He has the gift of teaching and an in–depth knowledge of the Bible.

Mr. McKeever has been a regular guest on Pat Robertson's "700 Club" and on other Christian television programs. He is in demand as a speaker at major Full Gospel Businessmen's (FGBMFI) meetings. In speaking at Christian rallies, fairs and conventions, he has shared the program with the following: Josh McDowell, Dr. Bill Bright, Terry Bradshaw, Dr. Walter Martin, Phil Keaggy, Leon Patillo, Paul Little, Dr. Ted Engstrom, Dr. Carlton Booth, Bob Turnbull, Andre Kole, Dr. Ralph Byron, and many other outstanding men of God.

Mr. McKeever is president of Ministries of Vision, which is a nonprofit organization established under the leading of the Holy Spirit to minister to the body of Christ by the traveling ministry of many anointed men of God, through books, cassettes, seminars, conferences, and the newsletter, *End–Times News Digest*. The various ministries of Ministries of Vision are supported by the gifts of those who are interested.

APPENDIX D

CONTACT THE AUTHOR

The following pages give information on other books and services by the author. If you are interested in these or in any of the teaching cassettes, we have included a coupon that you can mail in.

If you would like to contact Jim McKeever, see the last page in this book.

CHRISTIANS WILL GO THROUGH THE TRIBULATION
—And how to prepare for it
by Jim McKeever

This book could affect every major decision that you make!

Most Christians have only heard about a pre-Tribulation Rapture, and probably believe in it because they have not heard a viable alternative presented intelligently. This book is solidly based on the word of God and shows clearly why Christians will go through all, or at least part, of the Tribulation.

If a Christian believes that we are indeed going through the Tribulation, the next question is, how near is it? If the Tribulation is thousands of years away, there is no need to prepare for it. On the other hand, if we are living in the end times, preparation to go through the Tribulation is essential.

This book goes on to discuss both physical and spiritual preparation for the Tribulation. It gives practical, "how to" suggestions for preparation.

PRAY ABOUT ORDERING THIS VITAL BOOK

In times past God did not remove His people from trials, but allowed them to go through them victoriously (Daniel in the lion's den, the three Hebrews in the fiery furnace, the children of Israel in the Egyptian plagues). It is possible that you will go through the Tribulation. The Holy Spirit can use this book to help you understand and prepare.

- -

Omega Publications   BO—401
P.O. Box 4130, Medford, OR 97501

I am enclosing the amount shown below for _____ copies of *CHRISTIANS WILL GO THROUGH THE TRIBULATION—And how to prepare for it:*

_____ Copies of hardback at $10.95 each =	$_____
_____ Copies of softback at $ 5.95 each =	$_____
Please add $.50 postage and handling per book.	$_____
TOTAL	$_____

Name _____

Address _____

City _____ State _____ Zip _____

End-Time News Digest

The *End-Time News Digest* is a newsletter published by Ministries of Vision, of which Brother McKeever is president, and is printed and distributed by Omega Publications.

The *End-Time News Digest* not only reports the news that is important to Christians, much of which they may have missed in our controlled media, but also gives an analysis of it from the perspective of a Spirit-filled Christian. In addition it suggests actions and alternatives that would be appropriate for a Christian to take.

The *End-Time News Digest* also has a physical preparation section which deals with various aspects of a self-supporting life-style. The spiritual preparation section deals with issues of importance to both the individual Christian and the body of believers.

All of the contributing writers to this newsletter are Spirit-filled Christians. Brother McKeever is the editor and major contributing writer. God gives him insights that will help you, open your eyes to new things and lift you up spiritually.

- -

BO—401

Ministries of Vision
P.O. Box 4130
Medford, OR 97501

Please send me information about receiving your newsletter, *End-Time News Digest.*

Name _____

Address _____

City, State _____ Zip _____

CLOSE ENCOUNTERS OF THE HIGHEST KIND
by Jim McKeever

This is another book by Jim McKeever. Every believer will want to read this book and give copies to his non-Christian friends. After getting their attention with UFO's, this book introduces them to the spiritual world and encounters with God in the Old Testament. It then shows them step by step how they, today, can have an encounter with God by receiving Jesus Christ as Savior and Master.

You owe it to your non-Christian friends and relatives to provide them with a copy of this exciting book. (It would make an excellent Christmas gift.) They will not be able to put it down and yet, at the same time, they will have a clear presentation of the Gospel of Jesus Christ.

CONTENTS OF THE BOOK

Please read the titles of the exciting chapters and you will see why both believers and unbelievers will be interested:

Chapter Titles

1. Man's Desire for Close Encounters
2. Close Encounters with Terrestrial Beings
3. Close Encounters of the First Kind—Sightings of UFO's
4. Close Encounters of the Second Kind—Evidence of UFO's
5. Close Encounters with Extraterrestrial Beings
6. Close Encounters with the Spirit World
7. Close Encounters with Satan
8. Close Encounters with God
9. How You Can Experience a Miracle
10. How You Can Have Supernatural Power
11. The Close Encounter of the Highest Kind
12. There are Close Encounters in Your Future

Chapter 9, "How You Can Experience a Miracle," discusses the miracle of the new birth, and how one can experience it. In Chapter 10, "How You Can Have Supernatural Power," the author discusses the filling by the Holy Spirit and the power that comes from this to live an abundant life today.

If you want to know what the "Close Encounter of the Highest Kind" is, which is discussed in Chapter 11, you will have to read the book to find out.

THE SEVEN KINDS OF CLOSE ENCOUNTERS

CE 1 – Sighting
CE 2 – Evidence
CE 3 – Contact
CE 4 – Communication
CE 5 – Commitment
CE 6 – Transformation
CE 7 – Union

The author then discusses these seven levels of close encounters in their relationship between two human beings, between a human and extraterrestrial beings (if they exist), spiritual beings, Satan and finally, God through His Son, Jesus Christ.

There is much about UFO's and the demonic world in this book that Christians *need to know*.

Omega Publications   BO–401
P.O. Box 4130, Medford, OR 97501

Please send me information on Jim McKeever's book CLOSE ENCOUNTERS OF THE HIGHEST KIND.

Name _____

Address _____

City _____ State _____ Zip _____

CASSETTES BY JIM McKEEVER

TEACHING CASSETTES ($4 contribution per tape)

Quantity   Contribution

_____ _____ *The Overcomers*
_____ _____ *Spiritual Warfare* (2 tapes)
_____ _____ *The Two Greatest Lessons that God Has Taught Me*
_____ _____ *Becoming an Overcomer* (Album containing 4 tapes listed above — $16)
_____ _____ *A Christian and His Money*
_____ _____ *New Covenant vs. Old Covenant—Who Is Israel?*

THE REVELATION SERIES

_____ _____ The entire *Revelation Series*, plus *The Overcomers* and *Spiritual Warfare* ($49 contribution for these 16 tapes in cassette album). Includes the following:

#1 *An Encounter With Jesus* (Revelation 1)

#2 *The Letters to the Churches* (Revelation 2 & 3)

#3 *The Climax of the Bible* (Revelation 4 & 5)

#4 *The Rapture and the Tribulation*

#5 *The Seven Seals and an Interlude* (Revelation 6 & 7)

#6 *The First Six Trumpets* (Revelation 8 & 9)

#7 *The Little Scroll, the Two Witnesses and the Seventh Trumpet* (Revelation 10 & 11)

#8 *The Woman, the Man Child and the First Beast* (Revelation 12 & 13:1-10)

#9 *The Second Beast and the 144,000* (Revelation 13: 11-18 & 14)

#10 *The Seven Angels and the Seven Bowls of Wrath* (Revelation 15 & 16)

#11 *Mystery Babylon* (Revelation 17 & 18)

#12 *The Return of Christ and the Millennium* (Revelation 19 & 20)

#13 *The New Heaven and the New Earth* (Revelation 21 & 22)

_____ _____ TOTAL ENCLOSED FOR TEACHING CASSETTES
_____ _____ Additional Gift for Ministries of Vision

- -

Ministries of Vision   BO—401
P.O. Box 4130, Medford, OR 97501

Please ship me the tapes indicated above:

Name _____

Address _____

City _____ State _____ Zip _____

THE ALMIGHTY
AND THE
DOLLAR

This is the title of a one-day seminar sponsored by Ministries of Vision that Mr. McKeever and some of his Christian associates conduct for churches and Christian organizations. In it are discussed such vital topics for the Christian as:

* Stewardship of your assets as well as your income.
* How to protect your investments from inflation.
* Estate planning and making a will.
* Insurance.
* Family budgeting and banking.
* Investments in stocks and bonds.
* Gold and silver investments.
* Real estate investments.
* Personal investment strategy.
* Physical preparation for troubled times.
* Planning and goal setting for Christian families.
* Developing a plan of action to achieve these goals.
* A Christian's attitude toward all of this.

This seminar can be of personal benefit to many members of the body of Christ, and can collectively benefit the local body of believers. Since a limited number of these seminars can be conducted each year, please give prayerful consideration to it before requesting one.

Jim McKeever   BO—401
Ministries of Vision
P. O. Box 4130
Medford, OR 97501

Please send me information about conducting the seminar "THE ALMIGHTY and the DOLLAR" for my church or Christian organization.

Name _____

Address _____

City, State _____ Zip _____

Organization _____

344

ONLY ONE WORD
by Jim McKeever

BOOKLET

"If you picked up a hitchhiker and led him to Christ, and in parting company you only had time to give him one piece of advice to encourage a good start in his Christian life . . . what would that one word be?"

This booklet by Jim McKeever answers this vital question. Read what Bob Munger (producer of such movies as "Born Again") has to say about it:

"Only One Word was one of the most helpful insights I have ever gotten from Christian literature in 25 years as a Christian. This article is must reading for every Christian leader in the world."

_ _

BO–401

Ministries of Vision
P.O. Box 4130
Medford, OR 97501

Please send me:

_____	Copies of *Only One Word* (for a contribution of $1 each)	$_____
	Additional gift for Ministries of Vision	$_____
	Please add $.25 postage and handling per booklet.	$_____
	Total Contribution	$_____

Name _____

Address _____

City _____ State _____ Zip_____

WHY WERE YOU CREATED?
by Jim McKeever

BOOKLET

Everything in nature does what it was created to do. The birds fly south in the winter and back north in the spring. The plants and trees drop their leaves in the fall and put out new leaves in the spring. The planets rotate about the sun and the sun, as part of this galaxy, rotates in a giant pinwheel fashion. Everything that was created, no matter how small or how large, does what it was created to do, except one—man. Man is the only one that does not do what he was created to do.

Do you even know why you were created? How can you possibly be doing what you were created to do, unless you know *why* you were created? This is one of the most critical questions a Christian can ask himself.

This booklet by Jim McKeever will help you discover the Bible's answer to this question. Order your copy now!

- -

BO—401

Ministries of Vision
P.O. Box 4130
Medford, OR 97501

Please send me:

_____ Copies of *Why Were You Created?* $_____
(for a contribution of $1 each)
Additional gift for Ministries of Vision $_____
Please add $.25 postage and handling
per booklet. $_____

                        Total Contribution $_____

Name _____

Address _____

City _____ State _____ Zip _____

McKEEVER'S INDIVIDUAL STRATEGY LETTER

McKeever's MISL is an action-oriented newsletter with "how to do it" information. It is produced 20 times per year and contains a main article by Mr. McKeever. His articles in times past have dealt with Swiss banks, commodities, tax havens, solar energy, other physical survival topics, new investment opportunities and many more critical topics which are very helpful to Christians during these rapidly changing times.

In each issue there is a section on gold and silver, another on the stock market, a model portfolio, and a summary of significant items from other financial newsletters.

In addition, Mr. McKeever gives his recommandations in key investment areas.

Above all, it is written from a Christian perspective, which should be of vital concern to Christians.

Many consider it to be the top newsletter in its field. It is the only "one stop" newsletter that covers all areas of investments and preparations for coming terrible times. It has a finger on the pulse of world events to alert you to appropriate actions when anything significant occurs in the world economic system.

- -

BO–401

Omega Publications
P.O. Box 4130
Medford, OR 97501

Please send me information about subscribing to McKeever's MISL.

Name _____

Address _____

City, State _____ Zip _____

PAUSE NOW AND THINK OF WHO YOU KNOW THAT WOULD ENJOY AND BENEFIT FROM THIS BOOK, *NOW YOU CAN UNDERSTAND THE BOOK OF REVELATION*.

NOW READ THE NEXT PAGE . . .

NOW YOU CAN UNDERSTAND THE BOOK OF REVELATION

by Jim McKeever

Now that you have read this thought-provoking book, why not send copies to your loved ones, so that it might be a blessing to them too?

If you would like to give away some copies, we could mail them directly to your friends, with a card saying that the book is a gift from you, or we could send them all to you to distribute personally.

- -

Omega Publications   BO-401
P.O. Box 4130
Medford, OR 97501

I am enclosing the amount shown below for additional copies of *NOW YOU CAN UNDERSTAND THE BOOK OF REVELATION:*

( )_____ Copies of hardback at $10.95 each = $_____

( )_____ Copies of softback at $ 5.95 each = $_____

Please add $.50 per book for postage and handling. $_____

Send these copies to: TOTAL $_____

My Name _____

My Address _____

City, State_____ Zip _____

Gift to: _____

Address _____

City, State_____ Zip _____

Gift to: _____

Address _____

City, State_____ Zip _____

Gift to: _____

Address _____

City, State_____ Zip _____

Gift to: _____

Address _____

City, State_____ Zip _____

TO THE AUTHOR

The various services and materials available from Mr. McKeever are shown in summary form on the reverse side. Please indicate your area of interest, *remove this page and mail it to him*.

Mr. McKeever would appreciate hearing any personal thoughts from you. If you wish to comment, write your remarks below on this reply form.

Comments:

Attach
Here

Place
Stamp
Here

TO:

JIM McKEEVER
P.O. Box 4130
MEDFORD, OR 97501

- - - - - - - - - - - - - - - Fold Here - - - - - - - - - - - - - - -

BO—401

NAME _____ PHONE _____

ADDRESS _____

CITY _____ STATE_____ ZIP _____

Dear Jim,

I am enclosing a check (payable to Omega Publications) for:

☐ $_____ for____ hardback copies of *Now You Can Understand the Book of Revelation* at $10.95 each.

☐ $_____ for____ softback copies of *Now You Can Understand the Book of Revelation* at $5.95 each.

☐ $_____ for____ softback copies of *Christians Will Go Through the Tribulation—And how to prepare for it* at $5.95 each.

$_____ TOTAL ENCLOSED

Please send me information on:

☐ Cassettes and other books by you.

☐ Your financial and survival newsletter, *McKeever's Strategy Letter (MISL)*.

☐ Your Christian newsletter, *End-Times News Digest (END)*.

☐ Your speaking at our church or Christian conference.

☐ Please read the comments on the other side.